Karl Shaw has worked as a journali
in marketing. His books include *I   . The
Alarming History of European Royalty*; *5 People Who
Died During Sex: and 100 Other Terribly Tasteless Lists*;
*Curing Hiccups With Small Fires: A Delightful Miscellany
of Great British Eccentrics*; and *10 Ways to Recycle a
Corpse.*

Also by Karl Shaw

The Mammoth Book of Losers
The Mammoth Book of Tastless and Outrageous Lists
The Mammoth Book of Oddballs and Eccentrics
The Giant Bathroom Reader

MAD, BAD AND DANGEROUS TO KNOW

The Extraordinary Exploits of the
British and European Aristocracy

KARL SHAW

ROBINSON

ROBINSON

First published in Great Britain in 2017 by Robinson

A CIP catalogue record for this book
is available from the British Library

ISBN: 978-1-47213-669-5

Typeset by Hewer Text UK Ltd, Edinburgh
Printed and bound in Great Britain by CPI Group (UK) Ltd, Croydon CR0 4YY

Papers used by Robinson are from well-managed
forests and other responsible sources

MIX
Paper from
responsible sources
FSC® C104740

Robinson
An imprint of
Little, Brown Book Group
Carmelite House
50 Victoria Embankment
London EC4Y 0DZ

An Hachette UK Company
www.hachette.co.uk

www.littlebrown.co.uk

Contents

'A degenerate nobleman is like a turnip. There is nothing good of him but that which is underground.'

Anon.

MAD, BAD &
DANGEROUS
TO KNOW

THE
EXTRAORDINARY
EXPLOITS OF
THE BRITISH &
EUROPEAN
ARISTOCRACY

Introduction

It used to be very simple being an aristocrat.

To begin with, you were born into a family whose genetic health had been seriously impaired down the centuries by its habit of marrying first cousins. You would probably have an annoying surname whose pronunciation bears no relation to the spelling – Cholmondeley (Chumley), Featherstonehaugh (Fanshaw), Fotheringay (Funjee), Marjoribanks (Marshbanks) and so on. You would be ignored by your emotionally dysfunctional parents until you were old enough to carry a shotgun, having been packed off to a public school at the age of eight so they could spend more quality time with their dogs. You would have grown up to be socially inept, hopeless around girls (or boys, if you were a girl) and probably unable to tie your own shoelaces without the help of a servant. Then you would marry well, preferably into yet another aristocratic family you were already related to, or one of less impressive pedigree but vast wealth.

When you eventually inherited your grand, hereditary title you would preside over an impressive agricultural estate, which would provide you with a massive income to fund your work-free lifestyle. Meanwhile you would find ways of coping with superhuman levels of boredom. You might sit in parliament, or add to the family's art collection, or join a club, where high-stakes gambling would allow you to show off both your extraordinary wealth and your even more extraordinary nonchalance as you lost it. Meanwhile, your calendar would be divided between your country mansion, where winter was spent killing wild animals, and the London pad, where your unmarried daughters were matched with eligible bachelors they were already related to, etc. etc. Then you'd die, whereupon respectful servants and tenants would mourn you and you could expect, as a mark of eternal gratitude, a carved tomb in the family mausoleum.

That was then. It's rather different for the aristocracy now. They are still with us, against considerable odds, having survived the perils of inbreeding, agricultural decline, estate taxes and world war. Some of them are still fabulously rich. Others are pretty ordinary people with regular jobs who just happen to have inherited a grand-sounding title from a distant ancestor.

How did they get here in the first place? Their original

titles were handed out by grateful monarchs as rewards for support in battle. Later, they were awarded for good work in politics or public service. Others were due to someone's sterling efforts in the sack. King Charles II may have been the first British sovereign ever to use a condom, but there are dozens of dukes, earls and barons today who can trace their good fortune directly back to the king's failure to wear one. He had no legitimate heirs but fathered at least seventeen bastards and was happy to recognise many of them by giving them titles. For example, the current Duke of Buccleuch, one of Europe's largest private landowners, acquired his title via royal mistress Lucy Walter, who died of syphilis aged twenty-eight. Some ennoblements came about, as the late Earl of Onslow put it, 'simply because someone's forebear got tight with the Prince Regent'. The Prince's younger brother William IV, as Duke of Clarence, rewarded his mistress, the actress Mrs Jordan, who bore him ten illegitimate children, by giving the eldest, George, the title Earl of Munster. The ungrateful son was so annoyed by the thought that he really should have been Prince of Wales that he shot himself in 1842. Nobody ever said it was easy being a bastard: ask William I.

The lion's share of this book is given over to the British aristocracy. With all due respect to those interested in, for example, the Transylvanian nobility there is a good reason for this.* Since the late 1700s, the British aristocracy has been overwhelmingly the most exclusive, richest and powerful elite in Europe. Why did this happen in Britain and not Germany? Or Italy? Or Spain? It was largely thanks to the ruthlessly clinical rule of primogeniture,

* There's better news for fans of this genre in Chapter 10.

which means that the eldest son won the jackpot, inheriting both the land and the title. This was really tough on his younger brothers and sisters, who only got token handouts (or in some cases, nothing at all), but it ensured that the estate and the money remained intact. In Europe, on the other hand, the noble estates were repeatedly divided up among all the family on the death of the owner, which led to lots of small, less wealthy estates and a massive number of relatively worthless titles.* So, relatively speaking, European aristocrats really are two a penny; or as the 18th-century Irish writer Oliver Goldsmith put it, 'I have known a German prince with more titles than subjects and a Spanish nobleman with more names than shirts.' Which, I hope most people would agree, makes them slightly less interesting in terms of their wealth and power than their British counterparts.

So, what have the aristocracy ever done for us? Apart from the Derby, safari parks, Earl Grey tea, the Queensberry Rules, cardigans, the Elgin marbles, polo, fair play, pig sticking, association football, stiff upper lips, rugby, wellies, cricket and sadism? And sandwiches, let's not forget those.

To be fair, the aristocracy has also supplied some great characters in fiction, such as the upper-class twit Bertie Wooster whose skills are restricted to stealing policemen's helmets. There's Nancy Mitford's Uncle Matthew, who would 'hunt' his children with a pack of bloodhounds, and Jilly Cooper's Chessie France-Lynch, who liked to backstroke topless just to shock the servants. And of course there's also the sentimental *Downton Abbey* world of the

---

* The French aristocracy also followed the rule of primogeniture until the Revolution abolished it.

upper class in their country estates where happy, kindly aristocrats are lovingly and gratifyingly served by well-fed, contented domestic servants.

Fiction has never quite done justice to the real deal. There's no literary equivalent of Victor, 6th Marquess of Bristol, who was given to taking potshots at his houseguests from the upstairs windows of his home and once fired into the ceiling of a London pub. Or Sherman Stonor, 6th Baron Camoys, who once rebuked Harrods' pet department because they didn't stock baby elephants when he wanted one for his wife's birthday. Or the 5th Earl of Hardwicke, whose only claim to fame, apart from losing his entire family fortune on the horses, is that he invented a preparation that gave his top hat extra shine. Or the 4th Lord Oranmore and Browne, who raised pigs in his drawing room in the hopeful expectation that livestock reared in posh surroundings would fetch a better price on the market. Or for that matter William Eden, 7th Baronet of West Auckland in the County of Durham, who insisted on having a wall of the Cavendish hotel in Piccadilly knocked down so that he could enjoy his own private entrance. And let's not forget Angus Montagu, 12th Duke of Manchester, who once served time in the US for fraud but was let off by an English judge on the grounds that if intelligence were to be ranked on a scale up to 10, the duke would struggle to reach 1.

This book is about how some of the more colourful characters in the upper classes marked time between cradle and grave: the mad gamblers; the absurd duellists; members of clubs with silly rules; braying, tweed-clad grotesques; inbred, constipated upper-crust duffers; and, just occasionally, clever men and women who did something really useful with their time and their money.

For want of a better way of organising things I have arranged them by theme – hellraisers, gamblers, duellists, eccentrics, adulterers and so on. The Sutherlands get a chapter all of their own, partly because they were the wealthiest of all the European aristocracy and partly because, where I grew up, at one time they owned more or less everything as far as the eye could see, including a magnificent country palace, Trentham Hall, which they could apparently afford to maintain, fully staffed, despite hardly ever going near it; then, when it became an inconvenience, they offered it to the local council, who turned it down because it cost too much to run, so the Sutherlands simply had it bulldozed (because they could). The 13th Earl of Eglinton also gets his own chapter because he has a strong claim on the title Upper-Class Twit of the Nineteenth Century.

Finally, a few words of explanation about what for most people is an unfamiliar and frankly baffling subject: aristocratic status and titles (if you have a maze in your garden, you can skip this bit).

The five ranks of the British peerage are, in descending order of importance, duke, marquess, earl, viscount and baron.* In Western Europe, the equivalent of a British earl is a count. Dukes are one rung down from royalty in the social pecking order and are the most rare. At the time of writing, of over 800 hereditary titles in Britain today,

---

* In 1611 James I introduced the baronetcy, which was basically offered for sale as a fundraiser for the monarchy and a replacement for the grossly devalued knighthood. This could be purchased at the knockdown price of £100 each.

there are just 24 dukedoms.* They are much more likely to become extinct than be created; the last non-royal dukedom was created for the Duke of Fife by Queen Victoria in 1900 and it's very unlikely there will ever be another one. Because of complex inheritance laws there are also a few grey areas. For example, a peer's eldest son would have a courtesy title of Lord so-and-so. For example, the eldest son of the Earl of Bedford was known as Lord Tavistock, although technically he remained a commoner until his father died and he succeeded to his title in his own right. A peer can also hold several titles at the same time. This is because it could take a family several generations to reach the top of the aristocratic hierarchy by a gradual accumulation of wealth, land and status. For example, the 1st Duke of Ancaster and Kesteven was also the 4th Earl of Lindsey and the 17th Baron Willoughby de Eresby. The original barony was a Norman title and his family had steadily moved up the ranks to a dukedom.

* Not counting six royal dukes (seven including the Queen) – that is, those with titles granted to members of the monarch's family.

1

Dirty, Rotten, Rich Scoundrels

'I like the sound of breaking glass'.

That is the motto of the Bullingdon Club, a top-secret drinking society drawing its membership from Oxford's super-rich. In order to join, it is alleged, club members would often have to burn a £50 note in front of a beggar.* Once enrolled they were enticed to a life of hard-core drinking and ritualised chequebook vandalism. The club

---

* Not to be confused with Oxford's Piers Gaveston Society, some of whose members like to insert their members into dead livestock. Allegedly.

was once banned from entering a fifteen-mile radius of Oxford after all 550 windows of Christ Church were smashed in one night. At one Bullingdon party, the club invited a string band to play, then proceeded to destroy all of the instruments, including a Stradivarius. At another club event, plates, glasses and bottles of wine were smashed into the walls of a pub leaving a trail of debris that was compared by eyewitnesses to a scene from the Blitz. Their motto was particularly true of one member who, at a restaurant in Berkshire, took it upon himself to eat his wine glass rather than his Michelin-starred meal. Recent Bullingdon members have gone on to hold some of the most powerful and influential offices in the country.

The 'Bullers' are pale imitators of a tradition of upper-class yobbery that has existed for centuries. Their spiritual forefathers were called rakes, a shortened version of *rake-hell*, a term first used by playwrights of the late sixteenth century to describe 'an aristocratic man of dissolute and promiscuous habits'. In his 1755 *Dictionary*, Samuel Johnson defined a rake as 'a loose, disorderly, vicious, wild, gay, thoughtless fellow addicted to pleasure'.

The gold standard of English rakery was set at the Restoration court of King Charles II by a group of decadent upper-crust delinquents known as the 'merry gang', who tore around London on a reckless *Clockwork Orange*-like spree of bad behaviour ranging from loutish pranks to the genuinely criminal. One of the gang's leading lights was Sir Charles Sedley, chiefly known for a notorious stunt at the appropriately named Cock Tavern in Bow Street when he and several cronies stood naked on the balcony, pretended to sodomise each other, then hurled bottles of urine at the crowd below. Sedley ended this piece of street theatre by ordering a glass of wine, 'washed his prick in it', drank it and then called for another with which he drank the king's health.

Sedley once hired a gang of thugs to viciously beat up an actor called Edward 'Ned' Kynaston because the thespian bore a resemblance to him (clearly, being a ringer for someone else was a serious affront to the Restoration code of gentlemanly honour). Even Samuel Pepys, who knew a thing or two about bad behaviour, was appalled by the merry gang's antics.

Like the Bullingdon clubbers, the merry gang's acts of criminality went largely unpunished. In 1662, another high-profile member of the gang, Charles Sackville, 6th Earl of Dorset, and several drunken noble cronies, robbed and murdered a tanner named Hoppy. In defence they claimed they had mistaken him for a highwayman and the case was dropped. On another occasion Sackville got into a fight at Epsom, which resulted in the death of a night watchman; again, no charges were brought.

When it came to Restoration bad-boy behaviour, John Wilmot, 2nd Earl of Rochester, took the biscuit, or rather the whole barrel of biscuits. He was a wit, poet and play-wright, duellist, philanderer and suicidally heavy drinker, not necessarily in that order. He first appeared at court in 1665 as a precocious eighteen-year-old, having returned from his Grand Tour with a souvenir – his first dose of the pox. He was described as 'one of the handsomest people in England'. Well-mannered, witty, with immense personal charm, Rochester was hugely popular with both women and men, especially the king, who saw him as a surrogate son of sorts, due to the unstinting support of the 1st Earl, Henry Wilmot, for the exiled royal court, and also for

Rochester's own valiant service in the Second Anglo-Dutch War.

It wasn't easy to shock the hard-living bunch of revellers at the court of King Charles II, but Rochester gave it his very best shot. First and foremost on his mind was sex. In his spare time he wrote eye-popping pornographic poems and plays, including the obscene Restoration closet drama *Sodom*, first published in 1684. Subtle it was not; the play's characters included Bolloxinion, King of Sodom; his queen, Cuntigratia; Buggeranthos, general of the army; and a trio of maids of honour called Fuckadilla, Cunticulla and Clytoris. He even wrote an obscene poem mocking the king himself.

For all his celebrated charm and wit, there was a dark, deeply unpleasant side to Rochester as a brutal and quite cynical exploiter of women. He once seduced a miser's pretty young wife, persuaded her to steal her husband's money, then when he'd had enough of her, passed her on to one of his friends. The husband, who had lost his money and his wife, hanged himself, much to Rochester's amusement. When he wasn't debauching the young women of court, he was downing ridiculous amounts of any alcoholic beverage at hand (he once admitted being continually drunk for five years) or fighting duels.

King Charles turned a blind eye to the young earl's excesses because of his entertainment value, but Rochester couldn't help pushing his luck. Impatient of slow negotiations for the hand in marriage of the wealthy fifteen-year-old heiress Elizabeth Malet, whom Rochester hoped would solve his mounting debt problem, he had her abducted. The furious king clapped him in the Tower for three weeks to cool his heels. It was a pattern often repeated; time and time again the cocksure Rochester would overstep the mark and Charles would banish him from court like a naughty child, then when the dust had settled he would be forgiven and permitted to return.

The last straw came in 1675. Charles had a priceless glass astronomical instrument erected in his palace gardens, his pride and joy. A sensible courtier might have admired it from a distance and steered well clear. Neither sensible nor sober, Rochester smashed it to bits. He was banned from court permanently and Charles stopped his allowances. From then on it was all downhill. His innards pickled by alcoholism, his body raddled with multiple varieties of venereal disease, his nose eaten away by syphilis, he died blind, incontinent and in agony aged thirty-three.

SNOBBERY WITH VIOLENCE

Being a member of the aristocracy in the seventeenth century was a licence to get away with acts of extreme bad behaviour, violence or actual murder. In 1664 a nobleman from Sheffield was let off after beating a man, putting a bridle in his mouth and riding him for half an hour. In 1681 the Earl of Eglinton walked away scot-free after killing a man called Maddox in an alehouse in Doncaster because the victim had made an offhand remark about the Scottish peerage. In 1684 a night watchman, John Sparks, was found murdered in London after accidentally bumping into an unidentified nobleman in a dark alley. There were dozens more stories of aristocratic violence, including the well-born 'Mohocks' who were supposed to have attacked prostitutes on the streets for fun in London in the early 1700s. Historians have been unable to find any evidence that the Mohocks were ever more than a popular myth, but the fact that so many people were prepared to believe in them shows how ingrained the idea was that the well-connected could behave as badly as they wished and still bribe their way out of any scrape. Well, almost any scrape.

The Shirleys were an ancient and noble English family who counted among their number a couple of famous warriors, including Sir Ralph Shirley, who was one of Henry V's commanders at Agincourt, and his great-grandson, another Sir Ralph, who fought bravely at the Battle of Stoke in 1487. The 7th Baronet Shirley, raised to the peerage as Earl Ferrers in 1711, was said to have fathered fifty-four children, half of them legitimately. However, it is for a record held by his psychopathic grandson that the Shirleys are chiefly remembered.

Laurence Shirley, 4th Earl Ferrers, inherited his title from his insane uncle in 1745 and with it estates in Leicestershire, Derbyshire and Northamptonshire. He was a heavy drinker with an uncontrollable temper. In 1752 he married Mary, the younger daughter of William Meredith, but she left him after he kicked her unconscious in front of the servants. Mary obtained a legal separation on grounds of cruelty, an extremely rare ruling at the time. Ferrers also stabbed one of his servants in the chest with a knife, hit him over the head with a candlestick, then kicked him in his groin so hard that the man was unable to control his bladder for several years afterwards – all because of a delivery of bad oysters. In January 1760 his temper got the better of him again and he shot dead through the chest a manservant called Johnson. An eyewitness to the crime noted that after shooting Johnson, Ferrers 'remained querulous about the performance of his pistol'.

Ferrers was confident that his status would protect him from prosecution and was astonished to find himself arrested. Tried for murder by his peers in Westminster Hall, he conducted his own defence, pleading insanity. He did such a good job that the court adjudged him sane. On 5 May 1760, dressed in his wedding suit, Ferrers was hanged, as opposed to decapitated, a privilege normally reserved for the peerage. He had petitioned the king to be beheaded, as befitting a man of his rank, but George II rejected his appeal, fearing that if he was afforded any special treatment it would reinforce the widespread (and entirely justified) view that the justice system in England had one law for the poor and another more lenient version for the rich.

The hanging of a nobleman attracted even bigger crowds than usual and a special new gallows was constructed at Tyburn for the occasion. Ferrers asked to be dispatched with a silk rope – another belated nod to his noble status – but he had to suffer the indignity of hemp, thus becoming the first and last member of the English aristocracy to be hanged as a common criminal. The hanging was botched and he took several minutes to die, during which an unseemly squabble broke out between the assistant hangman, to whom Ferrers had given five guineas to finish him off quickly, and the hangman, who thought the money should be his.

TOASTING CATS AND DEFLOWERING MAIDENS

Clubs were an essential aspect of the eighteenth-century nobleman's lifestyle.* For the truly hard-core rake,

* Ned Ward's bestselling *Secret History of Clubs*, published in

however, the gentlemen's clubs of St James's were much too civilised. In the early 1700s several exclusive gatherings for well-heeled reprobates sprang up in Britain and Ireland, later dubbed by the ever-hysterical Victorians as 'hellfire clubs'.

Probably the first organisation to bear the name Hellfire Club* was founded in 1719 by the 1st Duke of Wharton, a complicated character described by one biographer as 'two men: one, a man of letters, and two, a drunkard, a rioter, an infidel and a rake'. Wharton's debauchery was the stuff of legend. Throughout his life he accumulated vast debts and squandered entire fortunes, one of which came from selling his title back to King George I. He lost around 600 times the average London income in the South Sea Bubble stock market crash of 1720. It was said that he was only sober for one month of his life and that was what killed him.

Wharton was an atheist and liked to ridicule religion by presiding over mock-Christian gatherings with 'satanic' trappings in a room over a London pub. Members indulged in daring blasphemies such as playing cards on Sunday, reading Lucretius and eating pigeon pie. After just two years Wharton's club was outlawed by an act of parliament

---

1709, listed several actual organisations, like the Whig Kit-Cat Club, along with some he might have made up, such as the Farting Club and the Beggar's Benison club in Anstruther, whose members allegedly met for drink and mutual masturbation.

* This is contested. In 1682, Philip Wharton's father, 'Honest Tom' Wharton, is said to have attended a meeting of a hellfire club convened by a mysterious Mr Bray. They got drunk, deflowered maidens and desecrated a church.

– probably the only club in world history to have been so. To have worried the establishment that much in such a short time was quite an achievement.

The 'hellfire' label was subsequently revived several times as a designation for upper-class debauchery. Another hellfire club was founded in Ireland in 1735 by Richard Parsons, 1st Earl of Rosse, a hedonistic character whose drink-fuelled lifestyle constantly courted public outrage: he supposedly once stripped naked to receive the eminent Samuel Madden, clergyman and Dublin Society improver. Club members, known as 'bucks', met in the Eagle Tavern in Dublin where they drank whiskey and gave themselves to 'eccentricity and violence', including the odd satanic cat burning. One evening a member was caught cheating at cards. A 'court' was convened and the verdict was that the guilty member should be hurled through the window of the third-floor gaming room: he died in the fall, impaled on the railings below. One of the club's leading lights was Colonel 'Handsome Jack' Hayes St Leger, a disastrous gambler who was said to be so obsessed with Mary, the Duchess of Rutland, that he used to drink the dirty water she had bathed in.

One of the more sinister members of the club was the 4th Lord Santry, once accused of murdering a sick sedan chairman for a prank. Because of his aristocratic connections, Santry was never charged with any crime in that instance, but in 1738 he did stand trial for the murder of Laughlin Murphy, a club porter he had stabbed in a drunken rage. He was found guilty, pardoned and forced into exile in England, where he lived out his days plagued by depression and crippled by gout, abandoned by his former friends.

Another infamous 'buck' was the wealthy landowner Richard Chappell Whaley, known as 'Burn Chapell' after his Sunday morning habit of riding around the countryside setting fire to Catholic churches. During one typical evening of drunkenness a footman accidentally spilled some drink on Whaley's coat. He reacted by pouring brandy over the footman and setting him alight. The man fled downstairs clutching at a tapestry hanging by the hall door, trying to douse the flames. Within minutes the whole house was ablaze. Many people died in the fire but Whaley survived by leaping out of a window.

The apple didn't fall far from the tree. Whaley's son, Thomas 'Buck' Whaley, inherited a large fortune at the age of sixteen then won, and lost, an even greater fortune in bizarre wagers. He took £25,000 from the Duke of Leinster by riding to Jerusalem and back within a year – no mean feat in 1789 – and, for a bet of £12,000, rode a horse in a death-defying leap from the drawing room on the second floor of his house over a carriage parked outside the door and onto the street thirty-odd feet below. He won his wager, surviving with a broken leg, but killed the horse. Whaley was once said to have set a mantrap, which caught a farmer's daughter: according to legend, he had her killed and smoked 'like a side of pork' and served to his friends.

The flamboyant Whaley died at the age of thirty-four, either from alcoholism or a chill, or he was stabbed in a jealous rage by a woman, depending on whom you believe, following a masochistic squandering of his personal fortune estimated at £400,000 in his lifetime. With his demise the Dublin Hellfire Club closed its doors for the last time.

The most famous hellfire club, allegedly out-debauching all others, was founded by Sir Francis Dashwood, 15th

Baron le Despencer, in 1749. Like many 'facts' about this most secret society, the truth is hidden from view. The club's real name was the Order of the Friars of St Francis of Wycombe and it started out as a collective of young aristocrats who had visited Italy on the Grand Tour. Horace Walpole, 4th Earl of Orford and author, said the nominal qualification for membership was to have been to Italy, but the real one was 'being drunk for most of the time during their stay there'.

The club's original forty members met on the first Sunday of every month at the Bedford Head Tavern in Covent Garden, London, or at the nearby George and Vulture. They had a rule that their members had to have their portrait painted in oils by the resident artist George Knapton. Most of them chose to do so wearing fancy dress. The most famous portrait in the series shows the club's founder Dashwood, dressed as a Franciscan monk while leering at the pudenda of the Medici Venus.

Dashwood was born in 1708 into a family of turkey merchants who had raised themselves into the ranks of the aristocracy by a combination of political cleverness and strategic marriage. His mother died when he was two years old and he was soon packed off to Eton where, at sixteen, on hearing of his father's death, he locked himself in a cellar for a week to get drunk. In 1726, the fledging rake left England for his Grand Tour of the Continent. During his travels abroad he picked up an interest in Turkish erotica and allegedly seduced the Empress Anne of Russia while impersonating King Charles XII of Sweden – quite a feat, considering that Charles was already long dead at the time. Dashwood's next prank caused considerably more uproar. In 1740 he went to Rome for the conclave that would elect the new pope. On Good Friday it was the custom for penitents to flagellate themselves in the Sistine Chapel. Fortified by large amounts of wine, Dashwood tested the faith of the pious locals himself by thrashing them with his horsewhip.

Dashwood's new club started out modestly enough, as a forum for some silly dressing-up, binge drinking and rowdy behaviour combined with the odd bit of vandalism that caused some heated comment in the press. In time, however, the members decided to look for somewhere more private, away from the prying eyes of the public. Dashwood acquired a tumbledown thirteenth-century abbey at Medmenham, a few miles from West Wycombe, a site that could be easily accessed from London by sailing up the Thames on a barge. He rebuilt the abbey and had a motto from Rabelais, reading '*fay ce que voudras*' ('Do what thou wilt'), carved over the door. The club was partly an excuse for Dashwood to act out his sexual and religious fantasies. In his quieter moments, in between serving as Postmaster General, he was co-author of a revised version of the *Book of Common Prayer*, but, somewhere along the way, he became an avowed atheist with a fixed contempt for religion. As for Dashwood's sex drive, Walpole said he had 'the staying power of a stallion and the impetuosity of a bull'.

He spent a fortune on turning his new property into a garden of earthly delights. He commissioned a landscape artist to produce pornographic topiary shrubberies including hedges sculpted into giant erect penises. There were also loveseats, in the literal sense, scattered around the gardens so that aroused couples could act on their impulses while taking a stroll. The grounds around the abbey were honeycombed with caves, lavishly furnished with couches of silk and velvet, and the walls were festooned with pornographic tapestries and oil paintings.

What exactly went on in the abbey's grounds is mostly speculation because all of the club's original documents were destroyed or disappeared (during Queen Victoria's reign the minute book kept by the club's steward was burned, supposedly because it was considered too obscene for publication). At the time and since, there were rumours of black masses and sundry wildly blasphemous ceremonies culminating in drunken orgies involving pliant women dressed as nuns and, at least on one occasion, a baboon which had been brought over from India. These orgies were said to have been enjoyed by at least one prime minister, a Chancellor of the Exchequer, a First Lord of the Admiralty and sundry cabinet ministers. The sounds of drunken revelry and general mayhem coming from the caves around the abbey were interpreted as human sacrifices and it was said that animals that had been set alight were seen running from cave entrances. Whether the stories were true or not, the terrified locals kept their distance, leaving the club's members to get on with their vices in peace.

Truth be told, it is unlikely that Dashwood's Hellfire Club completely lived up to its wild reputation. Some early accounts about the goings-on were written by his political enemies, so the activities attributed to him are at best exaggerated. His club fizzled out some time in the early 1760s, although according to local legend it went literally underground, as the nearby caves were still being used for 'strange rites' for years afterwards. None of this seems to have done Dashwood's career much harm, because he was appointed Chancellor of the Exchequer in June 1762, despite confessing that he had such a poor head for figures that he struggled to add up his bar bill.

Upper crust

In eighteenth-century England, a reputation for being one of the most notorious debauchees in the country was no bar to a serious political career. One of the most high-profile members of the Hellfire Club was Dashwood's good friend John Montagu, 4th Earl of Sandwich, immortalised by the meal of that name. In popular legend the idea came to him during a marathon session at the gaming table when he ordered his servants to fetch him some roast beef stuck between two pieces of bread*: someone shouted, 'I'll have the same as Sandwich', and a convenience snack was born. It seems rather harsh on a man who had such a long career in public service (First Lord of the Admiralty on three occasions between 1748 and 1782, Postmaster General 1768–71) that he is only remembered for discovering the delights of hand-held comestibles, but there you go.

In his day Sandwich was better known for his sexual appetites. In appearance he was quite odd. A tall, ungainly figure who was said to walk around as though he didn't have total control over his limbs, he had a long, thin face,

---

* The Earl of Sandwich (or more accurately the cook) deserves some credit for helping sandwiches gain popularity, but variations of it had been around for centuries. Farm labourers in France had been eating meat between sliced bread long before it had a name and the earliest form of a sandwich has been traced back to the time of King Herod, circa 110 BC.

described as 'that of a man who had been half-hanged and cut down by mistake'. His character references weren't very flattering either. Horace Walpole, who knew him at Eton, said there was 'a darkness, a design and cunning in his character which stamp him as a very unamiable young man'. Another contemporary said he was 'mischievous as a monkey and lecherous as a goat'. In fact, he seems to have been universally disliked, by men, anyway. Women didn't appear to have found his half-hanged look too much of a problem. Among his private papers are letters from dozens of female admirers who found him irresistible. He kept numerous mistresses, many at his place of work, so he didn't have to waste time leaving his desk (his lordship was very much into convenience). His habit of taking home prostitutes probably contributed to the break-up of his marriage to Dorothy Fane, the daughter of an Irish peer, in 1740. She suffered from mental illness and was declared insane in 1767. In the meantime he hooked up with seven-teen-year-old milliner's daughter Martha Ray, twenty-five years his junior, having allegedly seduced her with spiked champagne. From 1759 onwards she lived as his full-time mistress.* Despite the age difference and their informal status theirs was a comfortable arrangement. Martha bore Sandwich at least five (and possibly as many as nine) children and they appeared everywhere in public as a couple.

---

* The earl's famous sally to the dramatist and actor Samuel Foote, that he would meet his end either by the pox or by the hangman's noose, brought Foote's lightning reply: 'That depends, my lord, on whether I embrace your mistress or your principles.' The quip is often misattributed to John Wilkes, but the mistress in question was indisputably Martha Ray.

The earl, meanwhile, sponsored her education and subsequent successful career as a soprano on the London stage.

Their story did not have a happy ending. Around 1775 Martha Ray met a young army lieutenant called James Hackman. Although she was almost twice his age, Hackman became infatuated with her. Whether or not Martha had feelings for him is not clear; certainly many people at the time suspected that they became lovers. Hackman sold his commission in the 68th Foot Regiment and joined the Church, hoping that his new, more respectable status would impress Martha and woo her away from Sandwich. However, when he proposed marriage, she replied with a curt message requesting that he should pester her no more. On 7 April 1779 the jilted Hackman shot her dead at point-blank range with a pistol on the steps of the Covent Garden Theatre, then turned a second weapon on himself in an apparent suicide attempt. It either misfired or he lost his nerve and failed to pull the trigger; in any event according to several astonished eyewitnesses he then proceeded to beat himself around the head with the pistol butt.

Hackman's trial, barely a week after the shocking murder, was a sensation. The whole of London was riveted by details of the 'girl meets boy, boy shoots girl' romantic tragedy involving a high-profile government minister, a vicar and an actress. Hackman pleaded not guilty due to temporary insanity, claiming that he had only intended to kill himself. His plight attracted a great deal of sympathy but it wasn't enough to get him off the hook and, before the week was out, he was dangling from a Tyburn noose before a huge crowd. His last words, reported by the diarist James Boswell, were 'Dear, dear Miss Ray.'

The man who gave his name to the sandwich died of a digestive disorder in 1792.

YOU SCREAMED, M'LORD?

Beating up the night watchman and stealing doorknockers were among the more wholesome pastimes enjoyed by the young noblemen of the eighteenth century. The true rake was also a compulsive brothel-botherer and, if he lived in London, he wasn't stuck for choice.

By the middle of the century prostitution was the single most important industry in the capital of the strongest economy in the world and worth an estimated ten million pounds a year – at least one billion pounds today. Luxury brothels in and around Mayfair attracted wealthy businessmen from the city, politicians from the nearby parliament and aristocrats from the adjacent gentlemen's clubs of St James's. A visiting Dutchman joked that the money spent in the Mayfair brothels in a single evening would keep the Dutch economy going for six months. There was never a more lucrative time or place in history to be a whore.

The heart of the aristocratic red light district was an alley just off Pall Mall called King's Place, where establishments featuring London's liveliest and most beautiful girls charged prices only the very wealthy could afford. One of the Georgian über-madams, Sarah Prendergast, grew rich on the takings from her most regular customer, William Stanhope 2nd Earl of Harrington, known to the girls of Mayfair as Lord Fumble. The earl appears to have had an astonishingly high sex drive: he was described in *Westminster Magazine* as 'a person of most exceptional immorality'. In addition to the small harem he kept at his mansion, he and his wife, Lady Caroline, visited Sarah Prendergast's brothel in King's Place together up to four times a week.

Like most madams of high-class brothels, Mrs Prendergast kept only a handful of resident girls and sent out for reinforcements when they were needed. When business was slow, for example during the summer when their wealthy clientele went to the country or to a spa, the madams would close shop and follow, taking their choice girls with them. One evening in 1778 the fifty-nine-year-old earl turned down the three resident whores Sarah offered him, so she sent out for a couple of 'fresh country tits' from another establishment, Mrs Butler's. He paid the girls three guineas apiece for 'manual dalliance', which was rather less than they were expecting for their services. When the disappointed ladies returned to Mrs Butler's she demanded her cut of 25 per cent of the takings; the girls refused to pay up, so she hid their clothes. The police were called and both Mrs Butler and her husband were arrested.

Lord Harrington was furious when details of his two girls' four-times-weekly habit were leaked to the press. Mrs Prendergast, desperate not to upset her best customer, bought up all the copies of the paper she could manage and paid the whores five pounds to drop all charges. To cheer up the old earl she threw a grand ball at which 'the finest women in all Europe' would appear *puris naturalibus*. The earl, to show there were no hard feelings, so to speak, chipped in with fifty pounds towards the cost. The ball was a huge success. Mrs Prendergast made a profit of one thousand pounds: in all the excitement Lord Fumble fell down dead a few weeks later.

One of Mrs Prendergast's rivals was the Mayfair-based Irish prostitute Laura Bell, known as 'the Queen of London Whoredom'. She and the visiting Prince Jang Badahur, ruler of Nepal, were participants in what may have been the most expensive one-night stand in history, in 1850, when Ms Bell charged him a quarter-of-a-million pounds for services rendered. The super-rich prince paid up without a murmur. The India Office, learning of the amazing outlay, instead of hurrying him out of the country before he completely ruined himself, as might have been expected, reimbursed him in full in the interests of maintaining good British–Nepalese relations. Ms Bell used the money to retire in luxury to a large house in London's fashionable Grosvenor Square with her new husband, the eccentric Captain Augustus Thistlethwayte, nephew of the Bishop of Norwich. The marriage ended four years later in unusual circumstances. When Thistlethwaytes wanted to summon his valet, instead of the more traditional method of ringing a bell, he fired his revolver through the ceiling. On 9 August 1887 he was found dead in his bedroom after accidentally shooting himself while trying to alert his manservant.

DEGENERATE DOUGLAS

For more than sixty years the biggest single contributor to the financial success of the London sex industry was William Douglas, 4th Duke of Queensberry, known simply as 'Old Q'. His career as a rake was long and unrelenting. In his youth he was famous as a successful gambler. His reputation was sealed after a famous 'chaise match' in 1750, when he bet a thousand guineas that a carriage could carry a passenger nineteen miles in one hour at Newmarket.

This bet was billed as 'the race against time' and many thought it a wildly optimistic undertaking, given the terrible state of the roads and the bulky, cumbersome carriages without springs or tyres, which would surely struggle to do it in twice the time. With typical cunning and ingenuity, Queensberry stretched the definition of 'carriage' to the limit with a purpose-built stripped-down vehicle shell made from lightweight materials pulled by specially trained horses and won the wager with ease. The only blot on his otherwise unstoppable trajectory up the social ladder was that his success at gambling made him so many enemies that he was blackballed for membership of Boodle's and Almack's.

Queensberry also acquired an unrivalled knowledge of the turf and he formed a successful racing partnership with the jockey 'Hellfire Dick' Goodison, so called for his scorching finishes in Queensberry's racing colours of red and black. He had a famous racing rivalry with the young Irishman Richard Barry, 7th Earl of Barrymore – 'Hellgate' to his friends in recognition of his reputation as a hard-core rake. Barry was the eldest of four siblings. His younger brother Henry was born with a permanent limp and was known by all as 'Cripplegate'. Another brother, Augustus, was a prolific gambler known as 'Newgate' – it being the only debtors' prison he had not been inside. Their sister Caroline was known as 'Billingsgate' because she swore like a fishwife.

Not that Hellgate minded his nickname – in fact he wore it with pride. Apart from his wild lifestyle he was also known as a sportsman. He rode his own horses to victory and was passionate about boxing, both as a participant and as a gambler. He bet heavily and was said to have lost £300,000 by the time he was twenty-one. In 1788 the Duke of Bedford bet Barrymore a thousand guineas that he couldn't eat a live cat. The wager attracted a lot of public attention and there were several letters in the press on the subject of cat-eating; one reader claimed he had seen a Yorkshireman eat a live black tomcat to win a bet of two guineas. Barrymore was said to have fancied his chances, having previously dined on kitten, but in the event he got cold feet and wrote to the editor of *The World* claiming that they were mistaken in their report; he had only bet that he could find 'a man who would eat a cat'. Sadly there is no record as to whether or not he ever found a cat-eater to bail him out of the wager.

Facing bankruptcy, Barrymore married, but to everyone's amazement, not for money. In 1792 he eloped with seventeen-year-old Charlotte Goulding, the daughter of a sedan-chair man: like her husband, she too was a bare-knuckle boxer. Hellgate's short and frenetic existence ended suddenly at the age of twenty-four. While driving in his carriage, a loaded gun propped against the side accidentally went off, shooting him in the eye.

Queensberry's gambling career alone would have earned him a footnote in history, but even this was eclipsed by his startlingly dynamic libido. He was a debaucher of girls as young as fifteen, especially dark, Italian-looking ones, many supplied by the London madam Mother Windsor. On his regular visits to brothels he was accompanied by his friend, the society wit George Selwyn, whose tastes were more morbid. He was sexually aroused by public executions, which he occasionally attended in women's clothing. Selwyn was also suspected of having necrophiliac tendencies. His forgiving friends laughed off his lifelong obsession with death and corpses as nothing more than a harmless idiosyncrasy.*

Queensberry was fifty-two when he inherited the dukedom in 1778 and was described at the time as a small, slightly built man with a large, beaky nose. He never married, although his name was linked to several society women, including Lord Pelham's sister Frances. Pelham was appalled at the prospect of Queensberry copping off with his sister and had her suitor thrown out of the house. Queensberry's response was to buy the adjoining property at 17 Arlington Street where he constructed a bow window so that he could spy on her. By the time Pelham died two years later and Frances was free to marry, Queensberry had moved on and was living with his latest squeeze, Marchesa Fagnani, a successful singer and dancer who had married into the Italian aristocracy and whom he shared with her many lovers including Selwyn and Lord Pembroke. It was said that Queensberry paid off her husband's gambling debts in exchange for his wife's sexual favours. He also annoyed Lord Nelson by paying too much attention to his mistress Emma Hamilton. The hero of Trafalgar once wrote to her a testy note: 'As for Old Queensberry, he may put you in his will or scratch you out as he pleases, I care not.'

It is as an incontinent seducer of young women well into his dotage that Queensberry is chiefly remembered. The

---

* When his friend Henry Fox, Lord Holland, was on his death-bed Selwyn called to see him. A servant asked his lordship if Selwyn should be shown in. Holland replied, 'If I'm alive I will be delighted to see him, and I know that if I'm dead he will be delighted to see me.'

elderly roué was a regular fixture on the balcony of his London house, No. 138 Piccadilly, where he spent his days ogling women who passed beneath, occasionally dispatching his runner, a man called Jack Radford, to proposition any pretty victim that took his fancy.

Although he had lost the sight in one eye, his hearing and most of his teeth and was severely arthritic, Old Q was still harassing women into his early eighties. He maintained his sex drive with a strict fitness regime and the help of the former physician to Louis XV, Père Elysée, who, it was rumoured, was paid a bonus every time his lecherous patient could manage an erection. Old Q's death, it was said, was eventually hastened by eating too much fruit. His deathbed was covered with more than seventy love letters, some from women he had never even met. Remarkably, he had managed to avoid venereal disease throughout his life – an exceptional feat for an eighteenth-century rake. He was said to bathe in gallons of milk in the belief that it was good for his libido. J. H. Jesse, writing in 1843, thirty-three years after the duke's death at eighty-six, recalled that in London there was still an almost universal mistrust of milk in case it had been used in one of 'Old Q's' baths.

Queensberry liked to boast that he had more ready cash than any man in the country, so his will was one of the great talking points of the age. In his final year alone he added thirty-five codicils and his estate took years to unravel – so long that many of the beneficiaries, including Emma Hamilton, died without receiving a penny. By the time the final settlement from his will had been made in 1831 it was calculated that £1.5 million pounds had been paid out (about one hundred million pounds today). Although he denied paternity, he left the bulk of his inheritance to the girl he believed was his daughter, Maria, known as Mie-Mie, by the Marchesa Fagnani. Mie-Mie was considered quite a catch because she came with considerable wealth, as 'Old Q' and his perverted friend George Selwyn had both left her fortunes, each in the belief he was her father. Remarkably, she went on to marry a Regency rake who threatened to out-debauch even Queensberry.

When she was twenty-one Mie-Mie eloped with Francis Seymour-Conway, 3rd Marquess of Hertford, known as 'red herrings' on account of the bushy growth of ginger whiskers framing his bald head. Their open marriage was the scandal of the age. At one point he maintained a non-exclusive ménage with a married woman and all three of her daughters. Hertford's valet, Nicholas Suisse, acted as pimp and procurer, supplying him with prostitutes of either sex.

Hertford was said to have paid the nineteen-year-old Tuscan Comtesse de Castiglione, by repute Europe's most beautiful and accomplished courtesan, the sum of one million francs to spend one night with him on the understanding that she indulge his every whim. Afterwards, she was confined to bed for three days and thereafter they gave each other a wide berth, it was said, out of mutual respect. In his final years, Hertford became grossly fat, swollen with gout, infected with venereal disease and unable to speak due to paralysis of the tongue – most likely the effects of a stroke – meanwhile living with a company of prostitutes. One account of his last days has him being driven around London, and then carried every afternoon by two footmen up the steps of a brothel. He died in 1842 aged sixty-five, just days after taking part in an orgy at an inn in Richmond. The diarist Charles Greville wrote: 'There has been, as far as I know, no example of undisguised debauchery exhibited to the world like that of Lord Hertford.' He also left an estate worth two million pounds, much of it in priceless art, the basis of what is now thought to be one of the world's finest private art collections on public display at Hertford House, London.

BYRON'S HERO

According to Dr Samuel Johnson, the most extraordinary event of his day was the mysterious death of Thomas, 2nd Baron Lyttelton of Hagley Hall near Birmingham, in 1779.

Lyttelton was straight from Georgian-rake central casting. He ran up enormous gambling debts, fought duels, debauched women and succumbed to drug and alcohol addiction.

At the age of sixteen Lyttelton was already being linked with various 'unsavoury' women and was packed off on a Grand Tour by his disappointed father with the hope that travel would bring some maturity. It didn't. In 1772, in order to pay his ever-mounting gambling debts, he married Apphia Peach, the wealthy, much older widow of the governor of Calcutta and owner of a fortune of twenty thousand pounds – roughly £1.2 million today. The marriage didn't get off to a good start; as they left the church after the wedding ceremony, Lyttelton strode off to his carriage alone, leaving his new bride behind. When he realised what he'd done he went back to apologise, then compounded his error by addressing her as Mrs Peach. Within three months he deserted her for a barmaid with whom he absconded to

Paris, then spent the next few years touring Europe's brothels. When he returned he got into a brawl over an actress in Vauxhall pleasure gardens, then decamped to the continent again to wait for the scandal to blow over. Soon afterwards his father died (of despair, it was said), elevating Thomas to the peerage.

The responsibility of running a large estate did nothing to slow down his reckless lifestyle and throughout the late 1700s the antics of the 'wicked Lord Lyttelton' continued to entertain readers of the popular London scandal sheets. At one time his name was linked with the actress Mary Robinson, known as Perdita, who achieved celebrity status as a mistress of the Prince of Wales. Lyttelton, it was widely reported, had sex with her inside a closed horse-drawn carriage while Mr Robinson rode behind on horseback.

Although evidently unsuited to political life, he was granted a lucrative sinecure, the ancient post of Chief Justice in Eyre beyond Trent. He was on the verge of being dismissed from his position when he collapsed and died unexpectedly at his home in Surrey aged thirty-five. According to legend, his death was foretold by a bird that flew into his bedroom and warned him that he had three days left to live. The cause of his death wasn't known, but given his long-standing drink and drug addiction, it is probably much less a mystery than was commonly supposed at the time.

Thanks to his notoriety and the apparently strange circumstances of his premature death, Lyttelton remained in the public imagination and in print to achieve legendary status. Sex scandals and aristocratic vice were great news for the publishing industry, especially when they involved a sinner like Lyttelton who had been punished with a dramatic and early death. A book, *Letters of the Late Lord Lyttelton*, became a bestseller, running to six editions. In fact Lyttelton's frank correspondence with his relatives revealed the much-traduced libertine as a highly likeable character with natural charm and a great sense of humour. Whether he deserved it or not, his reputation as a hellraiser had a much greater significance because of the influence he had on a much more legendary rake born nine years after his death: George Gordon Noel, 6th Baron Byron.

THE WICKED LORD #2

There was more than a little madness in Byron's family. Lord George Gordon, a distant ancestor of Byron, organised massive Protestant riots against Catholics in London in 1780, then converted to Judaism after being confined in the Tower of London. Gordon's mother, meanwhile, liked to ride through the streets of Edinburgh on a pig. When her husband died she developed an unrequited passion for King Stanisław of Poland and once invited him to tea, despite never having met him before.

Byron's title and inheritance came to him from his great-uncle William, the 5th Lord Byron, variously known as 'the wicked Lord' and 'the Devil Byron' after his reputation for settling disputes violently. In 1765 he killed his cousin William Chaworth in a so-called 'duel' – more likely a drunken brawl – fought over a difference of opinion on how to hang game correctly. William Byron was convicted of manslaughter and forced to pay a small fine; he celebrated by hanging the sword he used to run through Chaworth's stomach on his bedroom wall. On another occasion he had a disagreement with his coachman and shot him mid-journey. He dragged the man's body into the coach next to his wife and took the reins himself. Eventually Lady Byron fled, leaving her husband to his reclusive life at Newstead Abbey with his mistress, a servant known as Lady Betty. Despite his own somewhat unconventional life, when his son, another William, eloped with his own first cousin Juliana, Lord Byron was horrified. He wanted his son to marry into money to wipe out the family debts and Juliana didn't live up to his financial expectations. When William junior made it clear that he was going to marry his lover in spite of his father's wishes, Byron decided to take revenge by ruining the family completely, leaving his heir with nothing but debt and dereliction. He allowed his stately pile to crumble into disrepair, slaughtered thousands of deer and decimated the local forestry. By the time the disappointed and malevolent 5th Lord Byron died in 1798, the estate was almost worthless.

His vindictive plan backfired, because the son he had come to despise never got to inherit the debt that was due to become his burden. William Byron junior died in 1776 and his son, Lord Byron's grandson, was killed in battle in 1794. The debt was inherited instead by his great nephew, George Gordon, with whom William Byron had no quarrel at all.

The 6th Lord Byron was an only child raised by his mother in Aberdeen. The poet's absentee father, a rake known to his cronies as 'Mad Jack', died in penury in France when his son was only three, a suspected suicide, having abandoned Byron's mother, Catherine, soon after Byron was born. Catherine Byron was a domineering and somewhat hysterical woman who may have passed on to her son the family tendency towards mental instability: one of Byron's most recent biographers makes a case that he probably suffered from an inherited manic-depressive illness.

Byron's sex life got off to a flying start when he was seduced by his teenage nanny, an alcoholic, Calvinist Bible teacher called Mrs Gray, when he was just nine years old. He was ten when he succeeded his great uncle and inherited the vast Gothic pile of Newstead Abbey. It was a mixed blessing; the building was dilapidated and there were no funds for its upkeep, but Byron loved the idea of being a baron. He was already beginning the process of moulding his own bad-boy image.

When Byron was a boy he read about the adventures of the 'wicked Lord Thomas Lyttelton'. It clearly left a mark on him and he seems to have been thrilled by the idea of being an aristocratic rebel (at Cambridge, he responded to a regulation forbidding dogs by keeping a pet bear in his room). In letters to his friends, he liked to sign off as 'the wicked Lord Byron'. In 1835 the editor of Byron's works noted: 'There is here, evidently, a degree of pride in being thought to resemble the wicked Lord Lyttelton.' Indeed, there would be striking similarities between their respective careers. As precocious heirs to a barony, they both ran up huge debts in their youth, slept their way through half the British aristocracy and had disastrously brief marriages, followed by dramatically early deaths.

Byron was a very unlikely candidate for Regency pin-up. He was born with a deformity his contemporaries described as a club-foot, a condition most modern medical experts prefer to view as a dysplasia, a failure of a body part to form properly, which left him with an abnormally small and inward-turning foot and a pronounced limp. When a gentleman is noted for his Byronic looks you would expect him to be dark, handsome and brooding, in a sexy sort of way, but most of the time Byron was quite chubby and pasty-faced. At five-foot eight-inches tall his weight varied from a hefty fourteen-stone six-pounds down to nine-stone eleven-pounds. Byron battled with his weight all his life, piling on the pounds to the point of self-disgust, then methodically starving himself with various fad diets, including one comprising red cabbage washed down with cider or hock. By 1821 he was eating just once a day, taking quantities of vinegar to lessen his appetite and dosing himself with Epsom salts, magnesia and strong laxatives. In between, he boxed and played cricket, wearing several layers of clothing to try to sweat the weight off.

Although short, fat and disabled, his verse made him a nineteenth-century rock star; while women swooned over his dark, smouldering looks, men imitated his moody, brooding silences and even his limp. Females everywhere were anxious to throw themselves at this most famous of writers and he was more than happy to oblige. He was married briefly to an aristocrat's daughter, Anabella Milbanke, but they were separated within the year; according to gossip he continued to sodomise his wife far into the advanced stages of her pregnancy.

The eccentric Lady Caroline Lamb, wife of the politician William Lamb, Lord Melbourne, was one of his easier conquests. The jilted Caroline returned to haunt Byron by spreading a highly damaging rumour that the poet was gay; at the time convicted homosexuals could expect to be publicly hanged and most likely pelted with dead cats. In fact, Byron's attraction to boys had been known since his time at Harrow public school, where he referred to his entourage of adoring younger pupils as his 'Theban band'. He liked sex with boys, or women dressed as boys. One night he smuggled a mistress past the reception desk of a London hotel by dressing her as a boy and passing her off as his younger cousin; there was some confusion among the hotel staff when the boy miscarried in Byron's room. In addition to Byron's estimated five hundred heterosexual conquests (he spent so much on female prostitutes that the owner of a brothel once advised him to slow down a bit) there were homosexual flings with various men including his fellow Harrovian the Earl of Clare, a fifteen-year-old choirboy John Edleston, his fencing master Henry Angelo and the famous pugilist, 'Gentleman' Jackson, not to mention sundry Greek youths.

Byron's appetite for sex scandalised London, but he overstepped the mark with his incestuous relationship with his half-sister Augusta Leigh, which he flaunted in his poem 'The Bride of Abydos'.* He became a social pariah and briefly considered suicide. 'I should, many a good day, have blown my brains out,' he reflected, 'but for the recollection that it would have given pleasure to my mother-in-law.'

In 1816, he left England never to return, leaving in his wake a trail of broken hearts, illegitimate children and

---

* Some historians of the Regency period have hinted that incest was probably rife at the time. Horace Walpole alluded darkly to the subject in one his letters: 'I am glad you are aware of Miss Pitt [Lord Chatham's sister] . . . her very first slip was with her eldest brother, and it is not her fault that she has not made still blacker trips.'

greatly boosted sales.* In Venice, he kept up his reputation for exotic sexual experimentation and his expensive taste in whores, procured for him by his gondolier. Byron kept lists of his lovers and apparently slept with more than 250 women in one year alone. When Percy Bysshe Shelley visited him he found him indulging in sexual practices which 'are not only not named, but I believe seldom ever conceived in England'. Another friend who visited him in Italy in 1818 wrote that Byron 'could not have been more than thirty, but he looked forty. His face had become pale, bloated and sallow. He had grown very fat, his shoulders broad and round, and the knuckles of his hands were lost in fat.'

For all great pin-ups, dying young was unfortunately part of the deal. Bored with his self-imposed exile from England, Byron went off to join the war for Greek independence but became ill with a violent fever. The favoured medical practice of the day, blood-letting, weakened him further. He developed a severe infection caused by unsterilised equipment and died in 1824, leaving his military action and several of his literary works unfinished. Byron requested that his body should not be disturbed after his death, but almost as soon as he had taken his last breath his corpse was hacked open by the attending doctors. Part of his skull and his internal organs were removed for souvenirs, then he was stitched up again so ineptly that friends who saw his body when it was returned to England couldn't recognise him.

* Byron was famously dismissive of fellow Romantic poets. He said John Keats' writing was 'a sort of mental masturbation' and often referred to William Wordsworth as 'Turdsworth'.

TAINTED LOVE

While Byron was making waves in London, another louche literary figure was being laid to rest in France, leaving behind the questionable legacy of lending his name to the 'S' in S&M.

The Marquis de Sade, Paris-born aristocrat and writer Donatien Alphonse François (1740–1814), spent much of his life either locked up in prisons and lunatic asylums, or doing things that would get him put in prisons and lunatic asylums. In popular folklore he is regarded as the wickedest man of the eighteenth century, but he was largely a man of his time. As his biographer, Francine du Plessix Gray, has pointed out, casual cruelty and sexual deviance among the French aristocracy were pretty much the order of the day.

Sade had sexual depravity in his genes. His father, a diplomat, was arrested for picking up boys in the Tuileries Palace gardens in Paris. Another unsuitable role model, his uncle, the very unclerical Abbé de Sade, in whose house he spent many of his early years, slept simultaneously with two women, a mother and daughter.

During this time the young Sade was allowed to have the run of his uncle's vast library of fashionable erotica. One of his father's mistresses, the Princesse de Charolais, had her portrait painted in the habit of a Franciscan nun, not out of piety but as a way of arousing her lovers. Her brother, the Comte de Charolais, was arguably the most depraved of the bunch. He shot peasants (not pheasants) for sport and took pot-shots at workmen repairing roofs in a neighbouring village. The resulting murders were excused by a pardon from the indulgent Louis XV, although the Comte had to beg for it. The Comte once invited Madame de Saint-Sulpice to dinner, got her drunk, inserted a firework into her vagina, lit the blue touch paper and retired. She was badly burned.

In person Sade was small and fat, but nonetheless something of a hit with the eighteenth-century ladies. After a spell in the army, where he gained a reputation for philandering and high-stakes gambling, he was pushed into an arranged marriage with the rather plain daughter of a wealthy bureaucrat. Within three months of the wedding Sade had returned to his bachelor ways, setting up an alternative address where he would take prostitutes. His first major scandal took place in 1768, when he invited a woman back to his chateau, imprisoned her, then physically and sexually abused her until she escaped through a second-floor window.

Most unusually for an age of rigid class distinctions, Sade didn't much like the company of his fellow aristocrats. He never fought a duel and didn't seem to be at all interested in hunting. He much preferred to go whoring with his faithful valet Latour, taking it in turn to be pleasured by one another with prostitutes as spectators. In 1772 Sade and his manservant were sentenced to death for having sex with each other and for poisoning several prostitutes with Spanish Fly, a supposed aphrodisiac designed to put someone in the mood (if by 'in the mood' you mean 'severe abdominal pain'). The guilty parties fled to Italy to avoid prosecution.

Fortunately Sade had a very sympathetic and accommodating wife, who helped organise orgies and haggled with prostitutes on her husband's behalf. Unfortunately, his wife came with baggage – specifically, a mother-in-law who didn't very much approve of her daughter's marriage to the man who invented sadism. Incredibly, his wife continued to stand by him, even when he ran off to Italy with her younger sister, a virginal nun, although this was the last straw for his mother-in-law, who used her influence to have him put away for a long stretch. In 1777, he was placed in the dungeon at Vincennes prison, later moving to the famous Bastille in 1784, where he began to write.

Sade's taste for writing pornography was not unique; writing porn for profit seems to have been a well-beaten path among hard-up members of the French aristocracy. His most infamous work, *The 120 Days of Sodom*, which the author boasted was 'the most impure tale that has ever been written', was completed in just over a month on a continuous roll of paper smuggled into the prison. There isn't room to list all the forms of debauchery he wrote about; suffice to say it was a catalogue of six hundred depraved sexual acts, committed by four libertines who lock themselves in a castle with several dozen victims (including their own daughters).

Sade was locked up with such regularity that, despite two daring prison breaks, he spent almost thirty of his seventy-four years of life behind bars in one location or another. His patient wife stood by him throughout, making sure he was well stocked with essentials, which in her husband's case mostly comprised drugs, sex aids, and huge amounts of cake, on which he grew enormously obese. At one point she even disguised herself as a man to help one of her husband's escapes, presumably so she could watch him in a room full of prostitutes burying his nose between their buttocks to smell their farts.

Miraculously, Sade escaped the guillotine during the French Revolution, only to be arrested again. The authorities decided that his writings were so perverse that they wanted him incarcerated for being mad as well as bad. He spent his final twelve years in the insane asylum at Charenton, near Paris, where he took advantage of the under-age daughter of the asylum's laundress. He died there in 1814 virtually in the arms of his teenage mistress.

'A RAKEHELLY DEMENTED EXISTENCE'

The Regency-era bad boy – certainly madder, badder and more dangerous than Byron, if a lot less famous – was Thomas Pitt, 2nd Lord Camelford.

Pitt's family was a force to be reckoned with. His uncle, William Pitt, was a former prime minister. His cousin, another William, was a prime minister-in-waiting, while various other relatives also held positions of power. Young Thomas Pitt was a wild and unruly boy. He ran away from Charterhouse school when he was fourteen and persuaded his parents to let him join the Royal Navy. In 1789 his father pulled some strings and got him appointed as midshipman on HMS *Guardian*, a sloop taking a load of plants, passengers and convicts to Australia. Somewhere in the Indian Ocean the ship hit a giant iceberg. Most of the crew abandoned ship but a few, including Pitt and the captain, remained on board and eventually managed to bring the crippled *Guardian* back to Capetown. Thomas Pitt returned to Britain a hero, barely fifteen years old. The adventure convinced him that his future lay on the waves. Through his father's influence he was enrolled as a midshipman on an expedition to chart the north-west coast of North America – one of the last major areas that still needed to be explored – led by Captain George Vancouver.

Vancouver was one of the greats of British maritime history but he was also one of the oddest. He served his apprenticeship as a midshipman trainee under Captain James Cook and went on to become the youngest warship captain in the Royal Navy. Vancouver's four-and-a-half-year voyage to the north-west coast was one of the most celebrated expeditions in the annals of exploration, navigating the coast of Pacific America and the Hawaiian Islands, voyaging ten thousand miles while charting over 1,700 miles of coastline. He disproved the existence of the fabled Northwest Passage at the latitudes long suggested and his discoveries influenced the location of several international borders.

There were also some astonishing mistakes. He somehow failed to discover two of the largest and most important rivers on the Pacific coast: the Fraser River and the Columbia River – not an easy thing for anyone to do, let alone a man of Vancouver's experience, considering that they are among the largest rivers in the Pacific Northwest region of North America. As science history author Stephen R. Brown noted, Vancouver's failure to spot these rivers, while at the same time charting hundreds of relatively insignificant features such as inlets and small islands, is hard to fathom and had major implications for the development of the Pacific Northwest.

Vancouver was not an easy man to get along with and was prone to violent fits of rage. According to medical historians, this excitability was probably aggravated by the hyperthyroid condition Graves' disease. Whatever the cause, he was in the habit of handing out thrashings at the drop of a hat. He seems to have been particularly irked by the presence of his young midshipman Thomas Pitt. During one of

Vancouver's periodic volcanic outbursts he had the boy flogged for trying to barter for the sexual favours of a Tahitian girl with a metal barrel hoop. He had him flogged again when he accidentally broke a compass glass, then had him clapped in irons for a fortnight for falling asleep on duty. Finally, the young seaman was sent home in disgrace. The punishments weren't unduly harsh by Vancouver's standards but being flogged as a common seaman was a terrible humiliation for a proud young aristocrat like Thomas Pitt; he would never forgive or forget Captain George Vancouver.

On his way back to England the young seaman found out that his father had been dead for well over a year. No longer midshipman Pitt, he was now the Right Hon. Lord Camelford, Baron of Boconnor. With the title came vast estates in Cornwall and Dorset and an annual income of over twenty thousand pounds.

It doesn't seem to have occurred to George Vancouver that flogging the former prime minister's nephew might be storing up trouble. When the captain finally finished his great survey he returned home to London, where Camelford's friends, including his cousin the then prime minister, William Pitt, lambasted him in the press. Camelford also sent Vancouver an abusive letter challenging him to a duel. When Vancouver declined, Camelford decided to take more direct action. One day, Vancouver and his brother Charles were strolling through London's West End when Camelford appeared from out of the blue and began thrashing them with his cane. They fought back and passers-by pulled the men apart. Eventually Camelford retreated, continuing to shout threats of violence as he left. The incident was famously lampooned in a cartoon by Camelford's friend James Gillray: 'The Caneing in Conduit

Street'. Although Camelford was the aggressor, the cartoon made Vancouver a laughing stock. Already a very sick man, he never fully recovered from the assault. Camelford's powerful allies continued to harass Vancouver in the press until his early death two years later.

The young Lord Camelford was still determined to make his mark in the Royal Navy and, with some more family string-pulling, he received the rank of lieutenant and went to sea again, this time as acting commander of the sloop *Favourite* in the West Indies. His behaviour during his time there was nothing short of demented. One night he was commanding his ship near Grenada when he fired a broadside at what he thought was an enemy fort, but which turned out to be English. Luckily, the English commander fought him off. A few days later Camelford attempted to press some seamen into service. This was perfectly legal because Britain was at war, but when Camelford encountered resistance he stabbed to death a carpenter called Howard, then shot and stabbed to death another man called Thomas. In 1798 he was reported to have killed a Lieutenant Tremlett in a duel in Martinique, then horsewhipped a naval storekeeper who was slow at his job.

Camelford's erratic behaviour finally became impossible to overlook after he shot dead a fellow officer, Charles Peterson, because he refused to obey an order. Camelford was court-martialled, but yet again his family connections saved him and he was acquitted. By now, however, the Commanding Officer of the West Indies Fleet had seen enough. Not wanting any more of his men killed or his forts attacked, he shipped Camelford home to England.

Camelford's naval career ended abruptly. In 1798 he

was arrested at Dover while attempting to sail to France in a wild-looking state, carrying a couple of pistols and a sharpened dagger. He claimed that he wanted to visit Paris as a tourist and take a look around to see if much had changed since the revolution. Britain was at war with France and an act of parliament made it a capital offence for anyone to attempt to travel there without authorisation. The law was very clear on the matter; a man called Langley had recently been hanged for doing just that. A special session of the Privy Council was convened to decide Camelford's fate. The Privy Council, whose membership included several of his close relatives, including the Prime Minister, Pitt, the Foreign Secretary, Lord Grenville and the president of the Council, Lord Chatham, recommended a royal pardon. It came with an added proviso, however, that Camelford should never again be entrusted with a ship, on the grounds that he was insane.

Camelford liked nothing more than a good dust-up, and to be fair he was built for it. He was six-foot two-inches tall, lithe and muscular, a fine swordsman, could shoot with the best (almost) and was extremely handy with his fists. He also went around with a spectacularly aggressive pit bull terrier, a dog that was reputed to have survived 104 fights. His cousin Lady Stanhope recalled the reaction Camelford got whenever he walked into a room: 'It was quite a scene to notice how the men shuffled away and the women stared at him.'

Camelford and Lady Stanhope were besotted with each other and for a while it seemed likely that they would marry. In the end nothing came of it, but it isn't clear what happened to cause the break-up. Perhaps she was warned off by her relatives, concerned that a first-cousin marriage wasn't such a good idea, as Lady Stanhope was also considered by some to be as mad as a hatter.

Camelford was also an important patron of the English prize-fighting scene. One day he invited the famous bare-knuckle pugilist Daniel Mendoza, 'the Fighting Jew', to his house. The nobleman suggested that the two should spar, insisting that Mendoza shouldn't go easy on him. Mendoza obligingly knocked Camelford straight through a glazed door of a bookcase, slicing his lordship's head open. Camelford picked himself up and demanded that they continue the bout armed with sticks, but once again Mendoza saw him coming and dealt Camelford a violent blow over the ear. Battered and bloodied, Camelford suggested they resume the contest with fencing swords, and marched off to fetch some blades. Mendoza sensibly made a bolt for the door as soon as the coast was clear.

Over the next few years there was more wild, violent behaviour. One of Camelford's hobbies was 'boxing the watch' – beating up the patrolmen keeping order on the streets of London. One evening, at the Theatre Royal in Drury Lane, when an elderly man politely asked him to move away from a window he was obstructing, Camelford knocked him down a flight of stairs then beat him so savagely that the old man almost lost the sight in one eye. For this assault he was fined five hundred pounds. The press dubbed him 'the half-mad Lord'.

In 1802 Camelford tried to slip away to France again, successfully this time, with a false name and passport, where, according to his biographer Nikolai Tolstoy, he was planning to assassinate Napoleon with a repeating pistol. Camelford was arrested by the French police who found him acting suspiciously near the Tuileries. He told them that he was a long-standing supporter of the revolution and had come to Paris to offer his support. Fortunately, at the time of his arrest he didn't have his weapon on him, so the French authorities held him for a few months and sent him back to England, dismissing him as 'a tiresome eccentric'. The Foreign Secretary avoided embarrassment by effectively hushing up the incident.

Strangely, despite his supposed attempt to kill Napoleon, which his biographer surmises was an attention-seeking stunt, there may have been a grain of truth in Camelford's claim that he was in fact a republican sympathiser. He had twice recently voted in the House of Lords to make peace with France and had befriended the noted republican sympathiser Horne Tooke, much to the embarrassment of his cousin. In January 1802 he refused to light his house to celebrate the peace with France, so an angry mob smashed his windows. He waded in and fought the mob single-handed until he was eventually bludgeoned into submission and was fined five hundred pounds for his trouble.

In 1804 he picked a fight too far with a friend, Captain Thomas Best, over a prostitute called Fanny Simmonds. She had been Best's mistress, but at the time was sleeping with Camelford. Upset by some alleged remarks that Best had made to her about him at the opera, Camelford challenged his friend to a duel. Best had a reputation as a fine marksman and was arguably the best shot in England, but Camelford refused to back down. Best begged his friend to reconsider, but Camelford replied simply, 'Best, this is child's play, the thing must go on.' Camelford knew the most likely outcome; the night before the duel he inserted a new paragraph in his will exculpating his friend and taking full responsibility for the duel.

On 7 March the two friends met again, twenty paces apart, in a field behind Holland House in west London. Camelford fired first and missed, Best replied and hit Camelford on the right side of the chest below the shoulder, the bullet passing through his lung, lodging in his spine. Best rushed to his fallen friend and held his hand. Camelford told him, 'Best, I am a dead man, you have killed me, but I freely forgive you.' He lingered in agony for three days until the following Saturday evening. Word went around London that the 'half-mad Lord' had died defending the honour of 'a fashionable prostitute'. Camelford was just twenty-nine years old. Lord Rosebery wrote of him later: 'His was a turbulent, rakehelly, demented existence. He revived in his person all the pranks and outrage of the Mohawks. Bull terriers, bludgeons, fighting of all kinds were associated with him; riots of all kinds were as the breath of his nostrils.'

PAINTING THE TOWN RED

Henry de La Poer Beresford, 3rd Marquess of Waterford, was a Victorian hellraiser's hellraiser. The *Oxford Dictionary of National Biography* lists him as 'reprobate and landowner'. Born into one of Ireland's most distinguished aristocratic families, he got his title and his pile at the disastrously young age of seventeen while still at Eton, where he showed his civic spirit by stealing the head master's whipping block.* When not taking part in various

---

* He had often felt the rod of the fearsome Dr Keate, the great flogging headmaster who once birched eighty boys in a single day and was said to be more familiar with his pupil's backsides than their faces.

orgies of drunken exhibitionism and random pugilistic encounters, Waterford made wild bets and got involved in destructive practical jokes. When the law took note and hauled him before the magistrate, he simply dipped into his inheritance, paid off the fine, then went out and did it all over again.

He spent a large part of his inherited fortune paying for the damage he caused. In his gentleman's club, Crockford's, he put his fist through a valuable French clock. He shot out the eyes of his family portraits with a pistol for target practice. He and friends made sport of stealing brass doorknockers in the West End or amused themselves by tossing eggs at people from their carriage.

One day, on a whim, Waterford started a riot in Haymarket in London by serving free gin in half-pint mugs to passers-by. He was once charged with dangerous driving after running his horse and carriage at breakneck speed through a crowded street. When summoned to appear before Marlborough Street magistrates, Waterford arrived at court mounted on his horse and demanded they both be let in; he said that his horse was a star witness for the defence because 'only he knows how fast he was going'. The judge, who knew a nutcase when he saw one, elected to wash his hands of the case and acquitted him.

In one of Waterford's most infamous pranks he wrote to the Greenwich Railway Company in London, offering to give them ten thousand pounds if they would arrange for him to see an actual train crash. He specified that both engines had to be driven towards each other at top speed. The GRC politely declined.

On another occasion Waterford hired eight cabs and a troupe of musicians to sit on the cab roofs, playing while they were driven round the streets at high speed. He took the reins of the leading cab and drove so recklessly he almost got himself killed. He once rode his horse into the Kilkenny Club House in Ireland, guided it upstairs, jumped the dining-room table and then returned to the street. One night in Irvine in Scotland, on the eve of the infamous Eglinton Tournament (see Chapter 12), he charged around the town on horseback wearing a full suit of fluted-steel German armour.

The only useful thing to come of Waterford's otherwise pointless existence was his alleged contribution to the wealth of English idiom. The origin of the phrase 'paint the town red' is said to date from 1837, the year Waterford and a group of cronies ran amok in the Leicestershire town of Melton Mowbray and daubed red paint over the town's tollbooth and several buildings. When members of the local constabulary arrived to restore order, Waterford's rowdies chucked red paint over them as well. The following day the marquess was fined a hundred pounds for assault.*

The marquess's generally loutish temperament also made him one of the candidates put forward by early speculators as to the identity of Springheeled Jack, an entity reported in the popular press throughout the mid-Victorian period in England, as responsible for a number of random

---

* This origin of the phrase 'paint the town red' is hotly contested, although not by Melton Mowbray's local tourism office. The earliest known reference in print dates back to Rudyard Kipling nearly fifty years after the alleged event that inspired it and places the use of the phrase in the American Wild West when intoxicated cowboys fired their guns into the air, allegedly threatening to 'paint the town red' with blood if anyone tried to stop them.

attacks on strangers throughout London, although you have to assume that Waterford's death in 1859 rules him out of later appearances by this supposed Victorian demon.

After surviving various suicidal stunts in 1842, Waterford married Louisa Stuart, daughter of the 1st Baron Stuart de Rothesay, abandoned his wild ways and settled down to a life of quiet domesticity in the family estate in Ireland, until he broke his neck and died, while out hunting, aged forty-eight. According to legend, it was the beginnings of a particularly malevolent Waterford family curse. The fifth marquess shot himself in 1895, worn down by years of suffering from injuries caused by a hunting accident, which had left him crippled. The sixth marquess, having narrowly escaped being killed by a lion while big-game hunting in Africa, drowned in a river on his estate in 1911 when he was thirty-six. The seventh marquess died aged thirty-three in a shooting accident in the gunroom at the family seat. Lesser-titled members of the family were not immune from the curse; Lord Delaval Beresford was killed in a railway accident in Texas in 1907 and, in 1910, Captain Beresford lost his life while attempting to stop a runaway horse at Aldershot in England.

A RAKE'S PROGRESS

If most of the upper-crust hellraisers escaped justice for the violence, theft, rape and general mayhem they committed while young men, there was a poetic justice at least in that many came to sad and sorry ends in later life.

Edward FitzGerald, 7th Duke of Leinster, was an early twentieth-century bounder with an appetite for self-destruction that few Georgian rakes could match. His family, the FitzGeralds of Kildare, enjoyed seven centuries of influence and distinction. Their family history is bloody and packed with curious incident. Several of its more unruly members had perished by evisceration, hanging or imprisonment as a result of rebelliousness or just bad fortune. John FitzGerald, 6th Baron of Offaly, was one of the luckier ones. A valiant soldier who assisted King Edward I in his Scottish campaigns, he was created Earl of Kildare in 1316. Legend has it that, during a fire at Woodstock Castle, Kildare, the earl, then a baby, was left forgotten in a turret. He was rescued by the family's pet monkey, which broke loose from its chain, nipped into the burning turret and carried him to safety. As a sign of appreciation the earl adopted the monkey for his family crest.

The 5th Duke of Leinster died of typhoid fever in 1893 when Edward, the youngest of three sons, was eighteen months old. His rebelliousness showed itself early at Eton, where he kept several live snakes in his room. At home his family were disturbed one morning by the sound of repeated gunfire. They rushed outside to find the boy firing a gun into the air; he explained that he was keeping his hands warm. It was a reminder of a much earlier family incident when his ancestor Gerald, the 9th Earl of Kildare, burned down Cashel Cathedral in Tipperary: when asked to explain himself, Gerald replied, 'I thought the bishop was inside.'

Edward was determined to enjoy life on his terms. He spent freely, drove fast cars he couldn't afford and was a soft touch at gambling. In 1919 a receiving order was made against him as a bankrupt – the first of three. Despite his burgeoning career as a playboy, he had fought in the First World War bravely at Gallipoli as captain in the Argyll and

Sutherland Highlanders and was wounded. One of his two older brothers, Desmond, was killed in action in 1916 (he died heroically, throwing himself on a bomb to save the lives of his colleagues), but Edward still thought it unlikely he would ever become duke, because as long as his other brother Maurice was still alive, his own income from the Leinster estate would be negligible.

On that basis, Edward took the biggest gamble of his life. He sold his reversionary life interest in the Leinster estates to a businessman Henry Mallaby-Deeley, who in return paid off all Edward's gambling debts of £67,000 (sixteen million pounds in today's terms) and gave him an annual allowance of one thousand pounds a year for life. In other words, as long as he lived, any income he earned from the entire Leinster estate would go to Mallaby-Deeley and his heirs. The loan would get him out of a scrape now – the future would take care of itself.

In 1922 Edward's eldest brother Maurice died, mad and childless, in the Edinburgh psychiatric institution to which he had been consigned ever since he had tried to kill himself and two members of his household staff. Unexpectedly, Edward FitzGerald was now the 7th Duke of Leinster and entitled to receive eighty thousand pounds a year from the estate, except that, under the agreement he had signed with Mallaby-Deeley, he would never see a penny of it. The Leinster trustees offered to buy back the inheritance for a quarter of a million pounds, but Mallaby-Deeley refused. Edward FitzGerald had ruined himself and there was nothing that he or anyone else could do about it.

A year earlier Edward shocked his family when he married, at Wandsworth Registry Office, an actress called May Etheridge, one of the Pink Pyjama Girls who performed at Shaftesbury Theatre. A year later their only son was born and by the following year they were separated. She explained later that she struggled with the practicalities of sharing the family home with her husband's fifteen monkeys ('the smell was simply horrible,' she recalled) and several snakes that were given the run of the house, not to mention Edward's insistence she carry his pet fox cub under her arm when they went shopping down Regent Street. In 1930 she was found in a gas-filled room in Brixton, but was brought back to life just in time. Prematurely aged and stricken in health, she succeeded in taking her own life in 1935, aged forty-three.

Although beset by crippling financial problems, the seventh duke showed no sign of reining in his spending and he continued to gamble compulsively. In July 1922 he laid a bet for three thousand pounds that he could drive from London to Aberdeen, a distance of 557 miles, in fifteen hours. In an open Rolls-Royce, with his pet wolfhound for company, he completed the journey in fourteen and a half hours – a remarkable feat at the time – along the way picking up two speeding fines for driving at 38.5 and a half and 33 miles an hour.

Leinster was made bankrupt again in 1923 with debts of £25,300. A few months later he was found guilty of obtaining credit under false pretences. The judge reminded him: 'We treat everyone alike in these courts.' He went to America to find himself an heiress to clear his debts. The plan was partically successful when he married the Brooklyn-born Rafaeele Van Neck in 1932. Her injection of cash allowed him to entertain lavishly for a while, but it wasn't enough to save him from bankruptcy again four years later.

Although debauched and down at heel, Leinster still kept all of his powerful aristocratic connections, including King Edward VIII, despite suspicions that Leinster had an affair with Wallis Simpson around the time of the abdication crisis. Leinster's remorseless downward trajectory continued and the debts mounted until he was reduced to selling his life story, 'My Forty Years of Folly', to a national newspaper, in which he described his road to penury, with 'mad parties, reckless friends and lovely women'.

Unlike William Hogarth's eighteenth-century rake Tom Rakewell, at least, the 7th Duke of Leinster was spared the asylum. He married two more times. His third was another actress; his fourth wife was a housekeeper of the tiny bedsit in Westminster where he spent the final years of his life. After spending most of his eighty-three years on the run from creditors, this was where he took his own life in 1976 by swallowing an overdose of pentobarbital. According to the press, at the time he was living mostly on tins of baked beans.

2

Playing Deep

Henry Bromley, 1st Lord Montfort and MP for Gloucestershire, was reckoned by many to be one of the shrewdest men of his day. One evening in 1754, while at his gentleman's club White's, he bet his friend Sir John Bland, 7th Lord Kippax, one hundred guineas that Beau Nash would outlive Colly Cibber. The wager referred to Cibber the aged thespian and the equally venerable Nash, notorious gambler and for many years a prominent figure around the spa town of Bath. Bromley had a liking for strange bets; he had already struck around sixty wagers with fellow club members – worth a total of £5,500 – mostly about matters of birth, death and marriage.

His latest wager was never settled. On New Year's Eve that year Montfort spent an evening at his club, enjoying supper and playing whist until 1 a.m., before retiring to bed 'in a strange mood'. The next morning he made his will in front of his lawyer and witnesses, then walked into the next room and shot himself. Sir John Bland followed suit in September that year. After losing every penny of his fortune playing hazard at his club – thirty-one thousand pounds at one sitting – he shot himself on the road from Calais to Paris. Both men had chosen suicide to escape ruinous gambling debts.

High-stakes gambling was to the Georgian aristocracy what gin was to the poor: the ruination of families and a frequent cause for suicide. Reckless displays of obscene wealth such as placing the modern-day equivalent of £200,000 on the roll of a single dice may strike us today as insane but for the nobility, the casual disposal of wealth was a badge of virility. How you won and lost was much more important than how much you won and lost.

From the middle of the eighteenth century the gambling habits of the great British aristocratic families revolved around the fashionable gambling clubs – or hells, as they were known – which were springing up around St James's in London. The club was where gentlemen could discuss affairs and relax in comfort and privacy in their leisure time, of which there was usually a great deal. Most of all, they offered opportunities to gamble recklessly, to 'play deep', in the parlance of the time – a safe haven from the world of racing hustlers, bent jockeys and doped horses.

The first clubs developed out of coffee houses and other existing meeting places for the privileged classes. White's, the oldest and arguably most exclusive gentleman's club, started out as a regular meeting of wealthy men at a chocolate house. Only five or six new members were admitted to White's every year with no adjustment made for deaths of existing members. According to Horace Walpole, when an heir was born to a great house, the family sent the butler to put the boy's name down for White's first, then to record the birth at the registry office second. It was and still is an exclusively male domain. The only woman ever to have visited White's was one Elizabeth Windsor in 1991. There were several other clubs, including Almack's, Boodle's, Brooks's and Crockford's, each of which made up for in luxury what they lacked in imaginative names.

'Hell', the inner gaming room at White's, was the great destroyer of fortunes. Jonathan Swift called it 'the bane of half the English nobility'. It is shown in all its debauched glory in the sixth episode of William Hogarth's *The Rake's Progress*. Tom Rakewell, wigless and cursing his fate, has just gambled away all of his money. He's not the only loser in the room – a dejected highwayman, with his pistol and his mask sticking out from his pocket, sits by the fire while a nobleman, desperate to continue playing, pleads with a moneylender for an advance. Only the two croupiers have noticed the smoke curling in from behind the panelling. Everyone else gambles on, unaware of the impending danger.

Anything worth talking about was worth a bet at White's. Like most gentlemen's clubs they kept a record book because one or more parties to a bet might be too drunk to remember the terms the next day. Their archive of wagers placed between 1743 to 1878 reads like a list of morbid and bizarre predictions: a typical entry states: 'Mr Howard bets Colonel Cooke six guineas that six members of White's Club die between this day of July 1818 and this day of 1819' (Colonel Cooke won). Two White's members bet fifteen hundred pounds on whether or not a man could hold his breath under water for twelve hours. Allegedly the men hired a 'desperate fellow', sunk a ship with him on board, and never heard from him again.

Bets were placed on a change in weather, the birth of a child or the colour of a horse. The war in Europe was the subject of many wagers. In January 1809 Lord Sefton bet Sir Joseph Copley fifty guineas 'that Lisbon and Cadiz will be in Bonaparte's possession on or before the 1 April next year'. Bets on current affairs were wide-ranging. On 13 April 1809: 'Lord Henry Moore bets Sir Joseph Conley that the man who shot at Lord Palmerston will be hanged'.*

The sums of money gambled at White's were staggering. The twenty-year-old Lord Stavordale lost eleven thousand pounds on the roll of two dice, but recovered it with one hand at hazard. Stavordale didn't learn any lessons from this slice of good fortune, merely noting: 'If I had been playing deep, I might have won millions.' Many of the young aristos who gambled away their fortunes were moneyed simpletons – not an accusation you could level against Stavordale's cousin, Charles James Fox. The second son of Lord Holland and Foreign Secretary

---

* One not recorded in White's betting book was the possibly apocryphal, but frequently told story about a man who had a seizure on White's doorstep and was carried inside by passers-by. The assembled company of dukes, earls and lords made bets as to whether he was dead or not. When some members rushed to his assistance, the wagerers intervened, complaining that it would affect the outcome of the bet; the man died shortly afterwards.

three times, Fox was thought to be the most brilliant man of his day, except when it came to gambling. On 6 February 1772 it was reported that he had performed poorly in a debate in the House of Commons: this was hardly surprising, as he had just gambled continuously for forty-eight hours with no sleep at Almack's and White's, losing eleven thousand pounds in the process. He was so broke that he had to borrow money from the club waiters and at one point his friend the Earl of Carlisle was contributing one-sixth of his own income to help pay off the interests on Fox's debts. His gambling addiction was sadly reflected in a bet made on 2 March 1774 at Brooks's. 'Lord Clermont has given Mr. Crawford ten guineas upon the condition of receiving £500 from him, whenever Mr. Charles Fox shall be worth £100,000 clear of debts.' Crawford knew his money was safe. Bankrupted twice through gambling, Fox lost an estimated two hundred thousand pounds over his lifetime (around twenty million pounds in today's values).

Some clubs were highly political. White's was the play-pen of the Tory Party, while across the road Brooks's performed the same function for the Whigs. Brooks's had an average age of just twenty-five when it was founded in 1764 and by 1780 it had fifteen dukes on its books. Losing heavily was the mark of a true Brooks's gentleman, and if you didn't gamble consistently or hard enough you could be blackballed. In the 1770s the baronet Henry Frederick Thynne made the shameful mistake of cutting and running from Brooks's with twelve thousand pounds, not realising that he was meant to stay and get rid of it. Alongside his name in the club book was written: 'That he may never return is the ardent wish of the members.'

Brooks's betting book is full of wagers made to combat boredom. For example: 'April 1819. Sir Joseph Copley bets Mr Horace Seymour five guineas, that Lord Temple has a legitimate child before Mr. Neville.' Some of the wagers had a much darker side. On 28 February 1782 Brooks's book records: 'Lord Craven bets Mr. Crewe and Sr. C. Davies one Guinea that Sr. W. Dobson either shoots or hangs himself before this day twelve months.' The book doesn't record who won the bet.

Surprisingly, given the obvious temptations to fix the outcome, mortality was the subject of many wagers. On 22 June 1771, Mr Boothby bet Mr Fawkner five guineas at odds of 20-1 'that the Duke of Queensbury would be dead before half an hour after five on the afternoon of the 27 of June 1773'.* More ominously, Lord Alverny bet Mr Goddard five guineas that Mr Talbot 'does not die a natural death'. Brooks's membership had a robust attitude towards death. When an announcement was posted on the notice board that two members had shot themselves with a gun borrowed from the club wall, splattering the wallpaper with blood and brains, a member remarked, 'I see we've got a right and a left'. Gambling on premature death was outlawed in 1774.

Some bets were considerably more eccentric. One listed in the Brooks's betting book from 1785 records: 'Ld. Cholmondeley has given two guineas to Ld. Derby, to receive 500 Gs whenever his lordship fucks a woman in a balloon one thousand yards from the Earth.' There is no further indication as to whether Lord Cholmondeley ever

* Mr Fawkner kept the five guineas. The duke inconveniently lived on five years longer than Mr Boothby predicted.

joined the thousand-yard-high club, or how they would check to see if he managed it, nor is there any indication of how the following bet played out in 1748: 'Mr. Boone bet Mr. Rigby that his penis was within an inch as long as Mr. Hardy's.'

The high-class brothels of St James's, within walking distance of White's and Brook's, offered even more risk-taking opportunities. On their way to the bawdy houses, gentlemen would bet on their likelihood of catching venereal disease. One member tried to fix the odds by deliberately seeking out a diseased prostitute to make sure he caught the pox and won his bet.

THE FISHMONGER

The 1820s saw a surge in high-stakes gambling as peace returned to Europe after four decades of war and a generation of bored young aristocrats found themselves with far too much time on their hands. The biggest beneficiary was a former East End tradesman called William Crockford. His extraordinary rags-to-riches story was funded entirely by his ability to fleece the English aristocracy at the gaming tables. At the height of his success in 1830 he was said to be worth the equivalent of around £120 million today, all of it straight from the pockets of the lords he had lured into his eponymous gambling den, Crockford's.

'Crocky' was born in 1776 in Temple Bar, London, the son and grandson of fishmongers. Schooled in the family trade of gutting, scaling and selling fish, in his teens he discovered he had a near-genius head for figures, especially for rapidly calculating odds. By the late 1790s he had become a professional gambler and a regular at the races and London's small-time gambling clubs. It was in this corrupt and viciously cutthroat environment that Crocky learned a valuable lesson. You didn't need to cheat a nobleman to take his money; careful calculation of the odds alone will ensure that the house inevitably triumphs.

There are various accounts of how he came to raise the capital to launch his new enterprise. According to one version he won it in a single twenty-four-hour game of hazard from three men who went on to become founder members: Lord Thanet, Lord Granville and Edward Hughes Ball Hughes.* Before long Crocky had roughly tripled that amount and was able to put up the five thousand pounds nightly bank demanded by his membership committee.

Crockford's was slightly more democratic in its membership than White's or Brooks's – and less stuffy. The club's senior member was the Duke of Wellington, by some distance the most respected man in the country at the time. The victor of Waterloo was in his early sixties when Crockford's opened and was far from typical of the club's regular clientele because he never gambled, but having the revered Iron Duke as a member helped attract the cream of London society. The new club also had the star attraction of the celebrated French chef Louis Eustache Ude, recognised as the finest cook in Europe. While the more

---

* Edward Hughes Ball Hughes was so wealthy that he was known as 'the Golden Ball'. Having been given the middle name of Hughes after his uncle and benefactor, he then added it again on the end to become 'Edward Hughes Ball Hughes'. Whether this was an act of gratitude or a condition of the legacy is not clear.

exclusive London clubs were offering an endlessly bland diet of boiled meat, boiled vegetables and boiled puddings, Ude plied his customers with the best food and the most comprehensive wine list in London, making it much easier to lure them into the gaming room, where Crocky was waiting to part them from their fortunes.

One of Crocky's strengths was his apparently encyclopaedic knowledge of the financial resources of his victims. It was said he knew more about the prospects of Britain's young aristocrats than they did. He could predict, to the pound and to the hour, exactly when prospective members would come into their inheritances and so could send invitations for the newly rich to visit his luxurious premises.

A generation of hapless young men were destroyed on the gaming tables of Crockford's. Among the biggest of the many big losers was Sackville Tufton, 9th Earl of Thanet, who lost two hundred thousand pounds (about £16 million today). William Molyneux, Earl of Sefton lost over two hundred thousand pounds at the club's tables over two years and died owing Crockford forty thousand pounds, a debt that his son was obliged to clear. Crocky would often take payment in kind in lieu of a gambling debt; Lord Seagrave had to settle by handing over the keys to his house in Bruton Street.

Another of his victims was the dandy Viscount 'King' Allen, whose only exercise, according to the diarist and dandy Captain Gronow, was 'his usual walk ... from White's to Crockford's and from Crockford's to White's'. Allen was a terrible snob who always referred to rich bankers as 'tradesmen' and blackballed them every time one tried to join a club of which he was a member. It was a tactic he lived to regret: when he ran into debt through gambling, the bankers foreclosed on his estates and he was forced to flee the country. 'King' Allen died destitute in 1845.

For Crocky it was never about social advancement, it was all about making money. In manners and dress he was very careful to assume social inferiority to the people he fleeced, like Uriah Heep: 'wholly without grace or elegance, his manner servile, his gaze shifty and suspicious and his bow clumsy and absurd'. He also understood the value of discretion. At the time gambling houses were illegal and their owners could have faced prison or transportation, but attempts at enforcement were sporadic at best. Every now and then, however, the authorities would get serious about it. In 1844 Crocky was hauled before a House of Commons Committee and quizzed about alleged illegal gambling at his club. He stonewalled his interrogators: 'I do not feel myself at liberty to answer that question to divulge the pursuits of private gentlemen.'

Crockford's didn't keep any written records and its members were far too posh to record their losses, so we can't know for sure how much was won and lost there, but according to a contemporary estimate the club could turn over a million pounds (£120 million today) in a single evening of eight hours' play. The club was so successful at separating its members from their fortunes that there are many eminent British families today still feeling the effects of their ancestors' encounters with the oleaginous 'Crocky'.

Crockford's reign lasted for just twelve years. By the time he retired in 1840, according to Gronow having 'won the whole of the ready money of the then existing generation', the former fishmonger was living in the second grandest house in the Mall after Buckingham Palace and his fourteen children, including four by his mistress, were going to Harrow and Oxford and Cambridge. He died four years later following a fit of apoplexy, it was said, because of the enormous losses he incurred in the famously crooked running of that year's Derby.*

Gambling was often also seen as an honourable means by which cash-strapped grandees could make some money without lowering themselves to actually work for a living. Among them were Lord Robert Spencer and General Fitzpatrick, who after being almost 'cleaned out' put their funds together and set up their own faro bank. As the bank always won, Spencer found himself one hundred thousand pounds in credit; he was wise enough to spend his winnings on an estate at Woolbidding, Suffolk, and never gambled again.

Lord Rivers, a skilled player at whist, lost £3,400 playing at White's after a costly loss of concentration when he forgot the seven of hearts had already been played, but went on to win over one hundred thousand pounds over his short membership at the club. Lord Carlisle allegedly funded a third of the construction of Castle Howard from winnings at the card table in Brooks's.

* Crockford's untimely death was bad news for his gambling friends as he also had a heavily backed filly entered for the Oaks flat race. If his death became public, the filly would be disqualified. According to legend, they got around the problem by propping the body up at a window in his house overlooking the racecourse, where, clearly visible to the crowd, it might discredit rumours of his death. Crockford's filly won the race and, the story goes, the punters collected their winnings before their ruse was discovered.

Carlisle's allegedly brilliant card career, however, was one of the very few exceptions. The 3rd Duke of Bedford, in a single evening, lost almost a quarter-of-a-million pounds to the infamous gambler Jansen at White's, a sum unsurpassed as a gambling loss for forty years. Another big loser was Admiral Harvey, hero of Trafalgar, who lost one hundred thousand pounds at White's on the throw of a dice, only to win most of it back on the following throw, then lose it all again with the next. He volunteered his estate as payment, but the Irishman to whom he lost generously agreed to settle for ten thousand pounds.

Lower down the scale of losses, during the prosecution of a gambling club proprietor in 1844, the 3rd Marquess of Conyngham, a twenty-four-year-old officer in the Life Guards, admitted to twice losing five hundred pounds in an evening's play. His losses may have shocked his Irish tenants but their rents contributed to his annual income of fifty thousand pounds, so his bad luck at the tables didn't really lose him any sleep.

Wealthy gamblers were subject to the gentleman's code of honour. A gentleman might gamble away a fortune, but he must do it without losing his temper or integrity. Not everyone took his losses lightly. The baronet St Vincent Cotton, a familiar presence in the gentlemen's clubs of St James's, gambled his way through a large fortune. One evening, believing that he had been cheated, he smashed up all the furniture in his club, laid out a couple of croupiers, then departed the mayhem with a stolen decanter of brandy in his hand.

Gambling losses were not recoverable in law so paying out on huge losses depended on gentlemanly honour. Debts were maintained on a man-to-man basis and were completed in a cooperative manner without hint of dispute from either side.

Lord Douglas once placed a bet on the death of a man he knew was already dead. His wager was accepted, but the man who took it refused to pay up when he found out about Douglas's deception. Douglas took the case to the King's Bench claiming that the bet was still valid and demanded payment. He won the case but it cost him his club membership; he had disgraced himself by disputing another gentleman's judgement of the bet.

Gambling debts took precedence over all others. Tradesmen were made to wait for their money for years, even if their businesses went bankrupt because of it, but betting debts had to be paid promptly. Voluntary exile or suicide was preferable to the disgrace of an unsettled debt at the gaming table. When the Baronet Berkeley Craven lost heavily on the 1836 Derby, he went home to his house in Connaught Terrace, sat down on the sofa and blew his brains out with a duelling pistol. His losses, around eight thousand pounds, were later described by his friends as 'trifling': they would have paid them for him had they only known. Gambling stories rarely had a happy ending. Another victim, the Polish Count Miecislas Jaraczewski, was a close friend of the Prince of Wales. In 1881 he gave a midnight supper party at the Turf Club, then retired to bed and swallowed a lethal dose of prussic acid rather than face arrest for fraud and bad gambling debts.

The only thing worse than defaulting on a gambling debt was being caught cheating. One of the great talking points of London society in the 1830s was an accusation levelled against Lord Henry de Ros, one of England's premier barons. De Ros was clearly something of a rotter.

In 1818 he was caught *in flagrante delicto* with Harriet, daughter of the poet William Spencer. He disowned the child she was expecting, claiming Spencer's daughter was 'as common as the street' and had invited him to her father's house on the strength of a casual encounter. In 1836 de Ros was in trouble again, rumoured to be cheating at cards by marking the deck with his thumbnail. It was assumed that he would do the decent thing and leave the country, but a report in *The Satirist* made the matter public. He sued his accusers for libel, but lost the case, in spite of providing a medical witness who testified that de Ros had 'a painful stiffness in his finger-joints, which prevents him from playing tricks with cards'. The disgraced baron died not long after, commemorated by the Georgian man of letters Theodore Hook with the punning epitaph, 'Here lies the premier baron of England, patiently awaiting the last trump.'

LADY LUCK

Aristocratic ladies were as susceptible as men to the gambling virus, but as they were excluded from the all-male clubs where the really big-money games usually took place they ran their own illegal high-stakes card tables in private houses.

The boredom of long evenings in draughty mansions made 'play' at cards a universal pastime among European ladies of leisure. In pre-Revolutionary France, the size and frequency of their wagers passed into popular folklore. Madame de Montespan lost four million livres (about £175,000 today) in a single evening at cards.

The most popular eighteenth-century diversion for

women gamblers was faro, a card game infamously open to rampant rigging of the dealing box. Several titled ladies were well known for the illegal faro tables they hosted late into the night, among them Lady Buckingham, who was said to actually sleep in the parlour with a blunderbuss and a pair of pistols at her side to protect her faro bank. Her gaming house in St James's Square was considered to be particularly disreputable and was noted for the frequent and unaccountable disappearance of golden snuffboxes and purses.

One of the heaviest losers of the era was Georgiana, Duchess of Devonshire. Married on her seventeenth birthday and finding herself with an indifferent husband who already had several mistresses on the go, the bored duchess filled her days and evenings playing faro with her sister Harriet, Countess of Bessborough, both aided and abetted by their mother, another heavy gambler. She had taught them how to play cards when they were small children.

Duchess Georgiana turned Devonshire House in Piccadilly into London's most exclusive illegal gambling club, even charging professional faro dealers fifty guineas a night for the right to set up tables there. The only thing she managed to gain from these activities, however, was enormous debts. Even ownership of one the largest fortunes in England was not enough to insulate her against crippling losses. Within two years of her marriage her gambling arrears had risen to three thousand pounds, the equivalent of three-quarters of the annual allowance given to her by the duke; to put that figure into context, at the time a well-off parson could raise his family on two hundred pounds a year.

The duchess borrowed from a moneylender and

continued as before, running up enormous debts, sublimely indifferent to the consequences and without so much as a word to her husband, who seems to have been not in the least curious about what she was doing when he wasn't around. She died in 1806, aged forty-eight, after a brief, painful bout of jaundice, hounded by her creditors. When informed that his wife had died with debts equivalent to three and a quarter million pounds, the Duke of Devonshire replied, 'Is that all?'

Lady Sykes, wife of the eccentric Sir Tatton Sykes of Sledmere House in Yorkshire, was also addicted to drink and heavy gambling, earning her the nickname 'Lady Satin Tights'. When she ran up heavy debts her husband placed an advertisement in all the national newspapers:

I, SIR TATTON SYKES, hereby give notice that I will NOT be RESPONSIBLE for any DEBTS or ENGAGEMENTS which my wife, LADY JESSICA CHRISTINA SYKES, may contract, whether purporting to be on my behalf or by my authority or otherwise.

His refusal to settle her debts led to an infamous legal dispute in 1897. When the case came to court, Lady Sykes' counsel revealed that Sir Tatton had once ordered his servants to hang his son's pet terriers by their necks from a tree in order to teach his wife a lesson for drinking and spending too much money.

By the middle of the nineteenth century the dangerous gambling addiction that could, and did ruin whole families had largely fallen out of favour in London, but it continued to wreak havoc elsewhere in Europe. In Paris, the Salon des Etrangers offered aristocratic visitors plenty of opportunities for kamikaze betting. One of the Salon's victims was Lord Thanet, who lost his entire income of fifty thousand pounds a year. One evening he lost £120,000 and, when told that there had probably been cheating, he replied laconically, 'Then I consider myself lucky in not having lost twice that sum'.

Another frequent visitor was the Hungarian Count Hunyadi, famous for his good looks, manners and wealth. For a while his luck seemed invincible; at one time his winnings were reckoned to amount to two million francs. He had two gendarmes who regularly escorted him to his home to guard against robbery. To all outward appearance he was the most poker-faced of players. He would sit impassively, his right hand inside the breast of his jacket, while fortunes were at stake on the turn of a card or a die; his valet, however, said that in the morning he found deep, bloody marks on his master's chest where he had dug his nails into his flesh. The count's luck turned eventually and he lost not only his winnings, but also his entire family fortune, and had to borrow fifty pounds to carry him home to Hungary.

The days of the aristocracy playing 'deep' have long since gone, but the ghosts of aristocratic excess still haunt London, although today the chips being played are purchased by new money, not old, and it's more likely to be Chinese, Russians and Arabs doing the serious gambling.*

---

* In Mayfair the spirit of Crockford's lives on at The Clermont, which follows the style of a Georgian gaming house and where another generation of English aristocrats, including, famously, the 7th Lord Lucan, risked fortunes.

3

Lords of the Bizarre

The French Marquis de Bacqueville had little experience of flying, nor for that matter did anyone else in 1742. You can imagine everyone's surprise when the sixty-two-year-old aristocrat emerged from his Paris hotel one spring morning and announced his intention to fly a distance of about 600 feet across the River Seine. As a large crowd watched, the nobleman attached a pair of paddle-shaped wings to his hands and feet, and then launched himself from the roof of his hotel. For a couple of seconds he appeared to hover, before falling onto the deck of a passing washerwoman's barge, breaking his leg. A couple of years later, the marquis convinced himself that it was possible to live without eating. He abandoned this theory after first trying it out on his horses.

There's nothing quite like being insulated from the real world by vast wealth, rolling acres and great social status to cultivate absolute, barking weirdness. In fact eccentricity is an important part of the aristocracy's mystique; they *are* different and they want you to know it.

Some, like Lord Berners, who dyed his Farringdon house pigeons in vibrant colours and had a horse as a tea companion, even worked hard at maintaining their reputation for eccentricity. Many – arguably the only *true* eccentrics – had no idea how out of step their behaviour was and didn't give a damn. Into this category falls Edward King 4th Viscount Kingsborough, who spent his entire family fortune attempting to prove that the tribes of Israel had settled in Mexico; and the Somerset baron Sir Richard Paget, inventor of a sign language for the deaf, who tested it on his daughters by stuffing their ears with treacle, then in the spirit of scientific enquiry threw them off the back of a moving bus to test his theory that the force of the air behind them would ensure that they landed on their feet.*

Perhaps eccentricity is in the eye of the beholder. Was Lord Seymour, who fed his dinner guests laxatives and gave them exploding cigars, charmingly eccentric, or just a loutish practical joker with enough money not to care? How should we view the second Lord Rothschild, who

---

* Fortunately it did, although one of his daughters, Pamela, ended up with a broken arm. His child safety awareness did not improve; later, when electricity was installed at the family home, Sylvia, his nine-year-old, was given the job of doing the wiring.

spent weeks training a team of zebra to pull his carriage up the Mall? Was he eccentric, or actually insane? You decide. Perhaps if there is one thing we can agree on, it is that all these people have one thing in common: they make for a good story, because an eccentric without a few decent anecdotes isn't deserving of the name.

Love me, love my dogma

Very often aristocratic eccentricity has an animal theme. Take the Czech Baron Georg Haas, Jr, who kept over eighty mistresses. However, it isn't his sex life he is remembered for as much as his obsession with his pets. The baron's single goal in life was to make sure they never left his side, even in death. Haas had a menagerie of stuffed pets, including fifty-one dogs, several badgers, cats and a collection of stuffed squirrels, each inexplicably dressed in tiny fezzes. The only pet he didn't fill with sawdust was his fully gown lioness Mietzi-Mausi, which was given free rein to prowl around his castle, terrorising visitors. Her only duty was to take lunch with Haas every day. The baron's story didn't end well, although it was not, as one might expect, in the jaws of a lioness. In 1945, aged sixty-eight, he said farewell to his stuffed companions for the last time when he was forced to leave Czechoslovakia at the end of the Second World War. A few days later he was found dead near the Austrian border, killed by a self-inflicted gunshot wound to the head.

If you look up Francis Henry Egerton, eighth and last Earl of Bridgewater, it won't be long before the subject turns to dogs. Egerton's more famous ancestor, the 6th Earl, was a deeply eccentric misogynist known as the

'Canal Duke' after he bankrolled the construction of a twenty-eight-mile engineering marvel to transport coal from his mines at Worsley to the industrial areas of Manchester, yielding him an astonishing eighty thousand pounds a year (after which the miserable sixth earl became a famous 'canal bore' and would talk about nothing else).

His nephew took pleasure in the finer things in life, like throwing elaborate dinner parties for his pets, for example. The Egerton dogs lived like aristocrats in his family mansion, Ashridge House in Hertfordshire. Every evening he enjoyed a candlelit dinner with fifteen of them at his table, each dressed in the latest fashions, including little handmade leather boots. Every dog wore a linen napkin and ate off silver dishes and had its own footman.

Another of Egerton's obsessions was footwear. He had a different pair of boots or shoes for each day of the year; every night he would remove them and place them next to the pair he had worn the day before, until he had rows and rows of shoes in chronological order. The shoes were never cleaned and left exactly as they were. He boasted that he could work out the date and the weather conditions on any particular day by observing the state of the shoes.

Egerton spent the last thirty years of his life living in Paris (a city he claimed he despised) and, during all his time there, refused to speak a word of French. He missed home, especially the English hunting and shooting season, which he made up for by recreating it in his Paris garden, staging miniature hunts and keeping it stocked with partridges and pigeons with their wings clipped so that, in spite of his failing eyesight, he could shoot them for sport. At huge expense he hired one of France's top chefs, who was instructed to cook him (to the chef's disgust) boiled beef and potatoes. One year Egerton set off to spend the summer in the French countryside, accompanied by his usual retinue of thirty servants and sixteen carriages full of luggage. He returned after a few hours because he couldn't find a restaurant that served boiled beef and potatoes. When his dentist, Monsieur Chemans, mentioned one day that his young son had been stricken with scarlet fever, Egerton ran out of the room, stripped naked and threw his clothes on the fire to escape contamination. All of his servants were instructed to do the same.

To be fair, there was more to Egerton than cranky, reclusive, hypochondrial, dog-bothering, footwear fetishist. Far from being a feckless, uneducated upper-class twit, he was remarkably well-read and compiled one of the finest collections of historical manuscripts in Europe. In his ample spare time, he was a writer, a translator and scholar. He wrote quirkily and extensively, chiefly on the narrow field of Bridgewater genealogy and, putting his classical education at Eton and Christ Church Oxford to good use, he translated Milton's 'Comus' into French and Italian and wrote an annotated edition of Eurypides' *Hippolytus* with a facing translation in Latin. Inspired by his industrious namesake, the 'Canal Duke', he also wrote a pamphlet urging the benefits of similar works on France. But you throw a few dinner parties for your dogs . . .

The misanthropic earl died in Paris in 1829, unmarried and surrounded by soiled footwear and pampered pooches. There was, however, one more unusual legacy – his lengthy and constantly changing will, which he used to cheer himself up by having his secretary read aloud extracts. He also made a number of legacies to his servants with the instruction that they were to be regarded as void if he should be 'assassinated or poisoned'. The earl was one of many creationists who were alarmed by the heretical new theories being advanced by science and in his will he left eight thousand pounds to the Royal Society to fund the writing of a book that would 'prove the power, wisdom and goodness of God manifested in the Creation' – known to posterity as the *Bridgewater Treatises*.* Accordingly, eight sympathetic 'experts' were chosen from various branches of British science to write an essay proving the existence of God. Unfortunately the thousand bound volumes of printed essays were far too expensive for most people and proved even harder to shift than the steaming piles of dog shit around Egerton's stately homes.

Excessive sentimentality for dogs is something you find frequently among the British aristocracy. So it was with the 2nd Earl of Massereene, Clotworthy Skeffington, whose name alone should qualify him as an eccentric. When the fabulously wealthy Irish aristocrat's beloved pet dog passed away at his Dublin residence, it received all the privileges that would be bestowed on any family member. The dog was laid in state on the drawing-room floor then removed to the earl's wife's bed as people arrived for the wake. The dog was then taken to the earl's estate in County Antrim for burial, where the local people were commanded to follow the procession with their pet dogs, each dog wearing a back scarf for a doggy guard of honour.

To be fair, sentimentality for dogs was the least of Skeffington's quirks. He inherited his fortune when he was fifteen, then settled in Paris, leaving the management of his

* But mocked by Darwin's supporters as the *Bilgewater Treatises*.

family estates in the hands of his mother. His allowance of two hundred pounds a month didn't go anywhere near covering his tailor's bills, gambling losses and the demands of his many mistresses. His shortage of ready cash led him to get involved in a disastrous financial speculation. When he was twenty-seven he joined with a crooked merchant in a mad business venture that was supposed to import salt from the Barbary Coast into France and Switzerland. When the business failed, the earl refused to pay his debts and was confined to a debtors' prison. All he had to do to secure his release was admit his guilt, pay the thirty thousand pounds he owed and go home, but Skeffington stubbornly opted to see out his twenty-five-year prison sentence until his debt was cancelled under French law. You might assume that this was just a miserly ruse to save him money, but during his incarceration he spent a fortune on fine wine and sumptuous dinners prepared for him by his private chef.

He spent the next eighteen years in several Parisian jails, including the notorious Conciergerie and the Grand Châtelet. By 1789 he was in his eighth year in a jail known as the Grande-Force, located just a stone's throw from the Bastille. It was there that he met Marie Anne Barcier, the beautiful daughter of the prison governor, who later became his first wife.

On Monday, 13 July 1789, the day before the storming of the Bastille, Skeffington and two dozen fellow inmates escaped from prison, without any assistance from the throngs of Parisian rioters who were taking control of the city, after Marie Anne had bribed someone to force open the gates.

Skeffington returned home, where he was lured into another fraudulent business venture, which again resulted in temporary imprisonment for debt. Back in Ireland he formed his own yeomanry to defend against the anticipated Jacobite uprising, training his men himself in unorthodox fashion; drilled without weapons, they imitated musket fire by clapping their hands and presented arms with a complicated system of hand signals.

When Skeffington died in 1805 he left his entire estate to his second wife, a nineteen-year-old servant girl, whose attention he had caught while nude shadow-boxing at his bedroom window. His family contested the will on the grounds that he was insane: they may have had a point. In the end, the girl and her family were paid off and the estate was restored.

WOBURN WOES

It is a truth universally acknowledged that the British Isles has produced more top-drawer fruitcakes than anywhere else. It's impossible to say why, exactly. Perhaps it was because their inherited fortunes were much greater than anyone else's and made them the most spoilt and indulged class in the whole of Europe.

There were few more spoilt or indulged than the Russell family, Dukes of Bedford, who in the words of the thirteenth duke, 'thought themselves slightly grander than God'. There was no such thing as an 'ordinary' Russell. They either achieved greatness, as politicians, writers or thinkers, or they were legendary oddballs. The vast wealth that facilitated their weirdness came from their London properties: at one time the Russells owned huge tracts of land in London's West End including Covent Garden – as the 9th Duke of Bedford once put it: 'If one hadn't a few acres in London in these times of agricultural depression, I don't know what one would do.'

It could have turned out quite differently for them. Wriothesley Russell, the 3rd Duke, was easy prey for every gambling den in London. He lost almost a quarter of a million pounds at White's in one evening – a record gambling debt in 1731. Wriothesley's marriage was not a great success either. The aristocratic letter writer Mary Wortley Montagu recorded that he was 'so much disappointed by his fair bride . . . that he already pukes at the very name of her, and determines to let his estate go to his brother rather than go through the filthy drudgery of getting an heir to it'. Lady Mary blamed this on his having 'living until sixteen without a competent knowledge either of practical or speculative anatomy' and thus formed the erroneous view that women were 'composed of lilies and roses'. As it happens Wriothesley got his wish. He was well on his way to blowing the entire Russell fortune when his grandmother packed him off to Spain, away from the temptations of London's gaming tables, where he did his family a huge favour by dropping dead aged twenty-four.

His titles and estates passed to his younger brother John, who as 4th Duke was much more careful with his money. He refused to heat his family home properly and when his wife hosted grand balls at Woburn Abbey their guests would freeze. At one of these house parties three of the invited, Lord Thorn, George Selwyn and Horace Walpole, were so cold that they took themselves off to a small room they had found which had a fire in the grate. The duchess followed them silently and left; a few minutes later a workman appeared and removed the door from its hinges.

Francis Russell, the 5th Duke of Bedford, succeeded to his title at the age of six when his father died in a fall from his horse. Francis was one of the few Russells who knew how to enjoy himself; by the age of twenty-four he had hardly ever opened a book. He died in 1802 aged thirty-six from a strangulated hernia incurred while playing tennis, leaving a bevy of mistresses to be kept, including the notorious prostitute Nancy Parsons.

Lord William Russell, younger brother to the 5th and 6th Dukes of Bedford and uncle to the future prime minister Lord John Russell was a tight-fisted, paranoid employee who regarded of all his servants as thieves and considered having all of the cutlery in their quarters stamped with the words 'stolen from Lord Russell'. He eventually drove his valet to murder.

In May 1840, the seventy-three-year-old lord was found dead in his bed at his house, No. 14, Norfolk Street, Park Lane, with his throat slit from ear to ear. Jewellery and other items were missing and there were signs of forced entry at the rear of the house. The police treated it as a burglary that had turned violent, but within a matter of days suspicion fell on the duke's twenty-three-year-old Swiss valet François Courvoisier, who had recently quarrelled with his employer and given his notice.

Courvoisier later made a sensational written confession, in which he explained how he had carefully stripped himself naked to avoid bloodstains on his clothes and slit his master's throat as he slept. Around four thousand people turned up to see Courvoisier hanged outside Newgate prison, Dickens and Thackeray among them. Russell's murder caused a huge panic; Charles Greville wrote: '[it] has frightened all London out of its wits. Half the world go to sleep expecting to have their throats cut in the morning.'

The incredibly wealthy Francis Russell, 7th Duke of Bedford, was a miserly misanthrope who grew steadily more miserable as his vast income increased. He got up at 5 a.m. every morning, it was said, so he could spend the day worrying about his colossal fortune and 'never retired to rest satisfied unless he could trace that he had saved that day at least a five pound note'.* The 7th duke's younger brother, the British prime minister Lord John Russell, was similarly renowned for his cold, unfriendly and often offensive manner. Queen Victoria made a point of avoiding him whenever possible.

William, 8th Duke of Bedford, was even more sullen and reclusive than his father. Lord Grey described him as 'the most impenetrable person I have ever met with . . . more silent even than [Prime Minister] Russell . . . it is impossible to get a word out of him'. The duke and his wife led separate lives, but frequently quarrelled by letter. In time he became terrified of any kind of social interaction and only ever left his home with the windows on his carriage tightly shuttered. His son Francis, the 9th Duke of Bedford, also a man of few words, was a morose hypochondriac. He and his wife were widely known as 'the Icebergs'. The duke died in 1891 'having shot himself, while temporarily insane, during pneumonia', according to his death certificate.

The record for not being on 'speakers' is probably held by the 11th and 12th Dukes of Bedford, two legendary eccentrics who, after some long-forgotten argument, didn't exchange a word for more than twenty years.

* Benjamin Disraeli in a letter to Queen Victoria.

The elder, Herbrand Arthur Russell, was another mean-minded misanthrope who hardly spoke more than a few words throughout his entire life, a peculiarity that went largely unnoticed by his wife, who was stone deaf. According to their eldest son, Herbrand lived 'a cold, aloof existence, isolated from the outside world by a mass of servants, sycophants and an eleven-mile wall'. His main pleasure in life was a daily cup of beef soup made from nine-and-a-half pounds of shin of beef, always prepared by the same kitchen maid. He had a staff of over two hundred, including fifty footmen with powdered wigs and eight chauffeurs, most of whom he never saw: his workmen and gardeners would station themselves at strategic intervals on the family estate so that they could signal each other to hide at the duke's approach to spare his lordship the unpleasantness of seeing a workman. His wife, the duchess, waited until she was a pensioner before learning to fly; aged seventy-one, she took off in an aeroplane and was never seen again. She was assumed to have taken a wrong turn somewhere on her way home to Woburn Abbey, where a servant had helpfully stencilled the word 'Woburn' on the roof to guide her.

Like many well-born children, heirs to the Russell dukedom were starved of parental affection, supposedly to teach them self-reliance. The 11th duke's only son and heir was never allowed to breakfast with his parents. He stood in a corner while his parents ate in silence; when they had finished eating the duke would dismiss him with the words, 'Tavistock, you may leave now.'* When the duchess died,

* The name was a title traditionally carried by the eldest son of the Duke of Bedford, Marquess of Tavistock.

his grandson, in a rare, spontaneous display of family affection, visited the bereaved duke to express his condolences. The old man stiffly observed that the grandson did not have an appointment and after a five-minute audience the young visitor set off to catch the first train back to London.

The twelfth and arguably the most peculiar of all the Bedford dukes, Hastings Russell, known as 'Spinach', was an expert on parrots. He kept large numbers of them, along with a flock of budgerigars, which he fed daily with chocolates: his starving children meanwhile were reduced to stealing the birds' food. The duke was a germophobic and Woburn Abbey was permanently drenched in antiseptic germ-killing sprays. He changed his underwear three times a day and carried with him at all times a bottle of TCP lozenges, which he would suck furiously if anyone coughed or sneezed.

Spinach was also known for controversial political views. He was a pacifist during the First World War, giving the rest of the Russell family, not the most communicative at the best of times, an excuse not to speak to him at all. This theme continued in the House of Lords, where his views were considered so annoying that resolutions were passed that 'the Duke of Bedford be no longer heard'. His pacifism earned him a national reputation as a heretic and a crank, especially his conviction that Adolf Hitler would behave himself if only he was shown a little patience and understanding. He was investigated by MI5, which concluded that the peer was 'a sexual pervert, a physical coward' and probable Nazi sympathiser. In his spare time Spinach wrote articles about parrots and budgerigars for *Country Life*. He died in 1953 after accidentally shooting himself with his 12-bore while aiming at a bird of prey that was threatening one of his precious budgies.*

The 11th and 12th dukes were so uncommunicative that the 13th Duke, John Russell, didn't know of his grandfather's existence or that he was heir to the dukedom until he was sixteen, when a servant let the information slip. When he inherited the title in 1953, facing massive death duties, he saved Woburn from being sold by opening it to the public. Believing that his ancestral possessions were 'plain boring' he offered visitors a shooting gallery and bingo hall. Weekends were laid on for nudists while 50 guineas would buy a bed for the night, with what his lordship described as 'tea in golden teapots and that sort of thing'.

The Russell family did at least produce one great talent. Bertrand Russell, pacifist and Nobel Prize winner for literature, was one of the greatest philosophers of the century and, on his days off from thinking about life and stuff, one of its most furious womanisers. The three-times-divorced philosopher had a string of high-profile affairs with married women, including the mad wife of the poet T. S. Eliot. He was still enjoying extramarital affairs in his seventies and enjoyed his fourth honeymoon at the age of eighty; all this in spite of a childhood accident when he damaged his penis while falling out of a moving carriage. On one of his lecture tours of America, the principal of a respectable girls' college was thrilled to find herself seated next to the great man at a dinner party and enquired: 'Why did you give up philosophy?' Russell replied: 'Because I discovered fucking.'

* The coroner's verdict of accidental death was disputed by his eldest son, who was quite certain it was suicide.

TUNNEL VISION

The seventeenth-century jurist Sir Edward Coke asserted that 'an Englishman's home is his castle'. This was literally true for the wealthiest of the titled classes, who did whatever they wanted behind the walls of their actual castles, no matter how depraved or eccentric the project.

For the first fifty-odd years of his existence there was nothing strikingly odd about the 5th Duke of Portland, William Cavendish-Bentinck-Scott. Born in 1800 into one of the English aristocracy's most ancient families, as a young man he served in the army, reaching the rank of captain in the Grenadier Guards, and then, following in the family tradition, he went into politics, serving as MP for King's Lynn. He was a keen hunter and shooter and was said to be one of the best judges of a horse in England.

He was also fond of the opera. His problems began after a night out in Covent Garden when he fell for the strikingly beautiful singer Adelaide Kemble, younger daughter of the famous actor Charles Kemble. Portland was obsessed. He stalked Adelaide wherever she was performing and showered her with gifts and letters. He even paid the artist John Hayter to paint her portrait from every possible angle, loaning his private box at the Opera House to Hayter so he could study his subject. Sadly, Portland's passion for the diva was unrequited. When he eventually plucked up the courage to propose marriage, she turned him down, not unreasonably as it turned out, because she was already secretly married to a wealthy businessman called Edward John Sartoris.

Portland took rejection badly. While still recovering from his knock-back from Adelaide Kemble he was involved in a serious street accident, when the wheel of a horse-drawn cab actually passed over his head, causing him severe injuries. From that day on he couldn't bear to sit on a horse or listen to music.

No one has been quite able to pinpoint the exact origin of his apparent meltdown, whether it stemmed from the rebuffal by his beloved actress, or the physical and psychological damage caused by the cab accident, or whether it was stress-related on the assumption of his duties when his father died. One way or another, in 1854 he retired to his bedroom at Welbeck Abbey, where he remained more or less permanently for the next quarter of a century until his death in 1879.

Portland had his bedroom fitted with two letterboxes, one for incoming and one for outgoing correspondence. The only person who was allowed to enter the bedroom was a much-put-upon valet, who served him his meals – a chicken a day, half at lunch and half at dinner. This valet was also a go-between for Portland and his doctors, who were denied actual physical contact with him. When Portland felt ill the doctor was made to stand outside his bedroom while the servant took his master's pulse and reported his condition. On the rare occasions when he left his room and ventured out, his staff were instructed to ignore him 'as they would a tree'.

The first thing people noticed were Portland's clothes. He wore anything up to six coats at the same time, all made by his London tailor, who supplied them in six sizes: the second coat had to be slightly bigger than the first, the third slightly bigger than the second, and so on, so he could add extra layers according to the weather. They were worn over a pair of old trousers tied above the ankle by pieces of string. Completing this ensemble was a very tall stovepipe hat perched on top of his long brown wig, and an umbrella which he carried everywhere to shield himself from prying eyes.

He only travelled at night and was always preceded by a woman holding a lantern; she was under strict instructions to walk fifty paces in front of him and to never turn round on pain of dismissal.

Portland's withdrawal from the outside world naturally led to speculation about his mental and physical wellbeing. Some thought that his road accident might have left him with permanent brain damage. There were numerous references to his 'unhealthy pallor' and it was rumoured that he was afflicted by some terrible disfiguring skin disease.

The main source of local gossip, however, was Portland's obsessive building operations. Over a period of twenty-five years, he built a vast network of tunnels and underground chambers beneath Welbeck Abbey, including a huge ballroom said to be the biggest room in Europe. There was also a massive library and a games room large enough to take a dozen snooker tables. In all there were about fifteen miles of pink-walled tunnels running underneath his home, linking the subterranean rooms with the abbey and with each other, so that he could travel like a mole, unseen. One tunnel was a mile and a quarter long and led directly to the local railway station at Worksop and was used when he needed to catch a train to visit his town house in Cavendish Square, London. Another went to the kitchen, where a chicken was always roasting and ready to be eaten: it was placed in a heated cart and pushed on rails to Portland's room.

The duke was constantly surrounded by workmen, who did his burrowing for him, but they were all under instructions never to look at or speak to their employer. One worker made the mistake of saluting his painfully shy boss and was sacked on the spot.

The tunnelling went on until his death in 1879. With hindsight it seems likely that Portland's famously sallow complexion was just a consequence of hanging around in underground tunnels for a quarter of a century; the reason for his obsessive building programme, however, was never made clear. You could argue that he was just creating more space in which to enjoy his solitude, but the abbey wasn't small to begin with and the building works meant that his home was constantly crowded with workmen – up to 1,500 at a time. Why would someone who couldn't stand listening to music and never entertained build himself a ballroom capable of holding two thousand guests, or for that matter, construct an underground riding school when he had a fear of horses?

By the time of Portland's death much of his deluxe burrow had fallen into a state of neglect. When his cousin arrived at Welbeck Abbey to take up his inheritance he found the grounds overgrown and strewn with rubble. When the front door was forced open, the new duke was surprised to discover that the floor was missing from the main hall. The only habitable rooms were the four or five used by the late occupant in the west wing, all painted pink, with little or no furniture apart from the odd commode in the corner. One of the rooms was lined with cupboards filled with green boxes, each containing several dark brown wigs.

Portland's death also resulted in an unexpected legal battle over his estate. In 1896, a middle-aged widow, Mrs

Anna Druce, petitioned the home secretary to have her late father-in-law's coffin opened, on the grounds that his funeral in 1864 had been a sham. Mr Druce had not died at all; he had simply wanted to revert to his other identity as the 5th Duke of Portland.

According to Mrs Druce, every now and then the nobleman became bored with his life as the Duke of Portland, so he would put on a false beard, enter a tunnel built under his London townhouse and re-emerge as Thomas Charles Druce, dealer in second-hand furniture at the Baker Street Bazaar in London. When the fun of being a simple salesman began to pall, he would reverse the process and re-duke himself. Eventually he grew tired of leading a secret double life and needed to kill off 'Mr Druce' to concentrate his energies on important construction work at Welbeck Abbey. Ergo, Mrs Druce's son was the rightful 6th Duke of Portland, heir to uncountable millions in cash.

Mrs Druce's astonishing and rather complicated story was not dismissed out of hand because there were a few bizarre coincidences that lent it a degree of plausibility. Thomas Druce and the duke had a couple of shared characteristics. Both men suffered from strange skin complaints, which apparently erupted in large boils on the nose. They were both antisocial, suspicious types who liked to travel in closed carriages with the blinds drawn. In fact, there was nobody in the country better placed to lead a double life than the duke, because there were very few who could swear what he looked like. Even if anyone did catch sight of him he was usually hidden under several overcoats and behind a huge umbrella. What's more, the dates fitted. Whenever Portland's movements are detectable, Thomas Druce becomes scarce, and vice versa. After the funeral of

Druce in 1864, the Duke of Portland was permanently in residence at Welbeck Abbey.

The newspaper-reading public lapped it up and the Druce story became the media sensation of the day. The case dragged on for years, long after Mrs Druce, consumed by her obsession, ended up in a lunatic asylum, so other members of the Druce clan took up the baton. A company was set up to support her claim, with capital of over thirty thousand pounds subscribed by various members of the public in expectation of huge profits, and a succession of witnesses was brought forward to establish that the duke and the businessman were one and the same. In the end the authorities called their audacious bluff. In December 1907 the Druce coffin was opened and found to contain the body of the real T. C. Druce, sufficiently preserved to be immediately recognisable. The Druce-Portland Company, and the legal case, collapsed.

Another socially phobic grandee, the reclusive and depressive 4th Duke of Marlborough, George Spencer, was said to have gone for three years at a stretch without uttering a single word. He was jolted out of his silence at the beginning of the fourth year by the imminent arrival of the Frenchwoman Madame de Stael; when informed of her visit he said simply, 'I'm off.'

The actual double life of George Edward Dering received less public attention than the alleged one of the Duke of Portland's but was also deeply odd. Dering inherited two large estates on either side of the Irish Sea at Lockleys, in Hertfordshire, in 1859 and in 1870 in Dunmore, County Galway. He spent most of his time inventing electrical devices and took out seventeen patents over a period of thirty-one years. When he was at work he demanded absolute silence. He spent twenty thousand pounds on having roads diverted because they ran too near his house. Even the bleating of newborn lambs disturbed his concentration and when he found a flock of sheep grazing in the park near his home he had them removed. Noisy pheasant and partridge were also culled from the estate.

Besides electronics, his other hobby was acquiring books. For several years he had an arrangement with a local bookseller who was paid to buy every single book on the subject of electricity he came across, in any language. When Dering died his home was found to house a vast library, of which around fourteen thousand volumes had never been opened by him. For years his staff at his Lockleys estate hardly ever saw him, except on Christmas Eve when he would suddenly drop in unannounced, read his mail, then vanish again on Christmas morning. His servants had instructions to have a mutton chop handy at all times, just in case. Dering returned to Lockleys permanently in 1907 and became reclusive, occupying only one room of his mansion, never allowing anyone in to clean it. It turned that he had been living in Brighton as 'Mr Dale' and had a wife and daughter who had no knowledge of his real name and fortune. Dering's reputation for eccentricity was reinforced by the fact that in the only known photograph of him he is perched on a tightrope.

Books were also the passion of Richard Monckton Milnes, 1st Baron Houghton. As far as history is concerned, he was the sole romantic interest of Florence Nightingale, with whom he had a frustrating seven-year courtship ending in her refusal to marry. In certain literary circles he is better known as the aristocratic author of the spanking classic 'The Rodiad', a pornographic poem on the subject of flagellation. Monckton was obsessed with publishers of, and dealers in, erotica and befriended fellow connoisseurs such as the deeply creepy Sir Frederick Hankey, who once attended a public hanging with a friend and took along two girls so that he and his pal could have sex while witnessing the event, and whose ambition was to have a Bible bound with skin cut from the private parts of virgins.* Milnes's almost unsurpassed collection of erotic literature, containing the most extensive collection of writings by the Marquis de Sade and even a human skin bookmark, now in the British Library, was known to few in his lifetime.

A CLASS ACT

Dame Edith Sitwell, a granddaughter of the 7th Duke of Beaufort, wrote one of the classic reference books of the genre called *English Eccentrics*. She didn't need to look very far for inspiration. The Sitwell family in the early twentieth century were known for their artistic inclinations, producing three notable writers – Osbert, Sacheverell and Edith – but their family's wealth was built on something much more practical. George Sitwell, founder of Renishaw Hall in Derbyshire in 1625, made his living from coal and iron ore and went on to become the country's biggest manufacturer of nails. The family earned their title

---

* Sir Frederick's sadistic tastes were not confined to books. In London he patronised a flagellant brothel run by Mrs Jenkins, who provided facilities for flogging girls as young as thirteen. He admitted that he enjoyed sticking needles into the girls – but not very far, he said, indicating the tip of his finger.

in 1808 when Sitwell Sitwell, an early adopter of the family fetish for weird Christian names, organised a lavish ball for the Prince of Wales, for which he was rewarded with a baronetcy.

The family tree had more than its share of eccentrics. Edith Sitwell's great-grandmother the Dowager Duchess of Beaufort insisted on having her coachman take her and her beloved pet parrot for a different run-out in the New Forest each day, oblivious to the fact that the coachman always took the same route, or that her parrot had been dead for several years and now sat stuffed beside her on the carriage seat. Edith's maternal grandmother Lady Londesborough required her children to wear gloves at all times, even indoors, so that they could grow up with perfectly smooth hands.

Edith's other grandmother, Lady Louisa Sitwell, was a very religious woman whose hobby was driving through the streets of Scarborough in her coach, rescuing prostitutes. Or, more accurately, she kidnapped women she thought looked as though they *might* be prostitutes, then drove then off to a home for fallen women she had funded, where they were forcibly stripped naked, hosed down, then dressed in uniforms and put to work as laundresses behind locked doors. Edith Sitwell's cousin, the famous botanist Reginald Farrer, became a vegetarian and a Buddhist after accidentally dining on his beloved Siamese cat while visiting Japan.

Some episodes in Edith's extraordinary and occasionally comic life read as if they had been scripted by P. G. Wodehouse. Her father, Sir George Reresby Sitwell, was rabidly reactionary. Visitors to his home were given a taste of what to expect by a sign on the front door which read: 'I must ask anyone entering the house never to contradict me in any way, as it interferes with the functioning of my gastric juices and prevents me sleeping at night.' Sir George filled seven rooms with his books and papers, while writing profoundly obscure epics such as *The History of the Fork*; *The Black Death at Rotherham*; *The Use of the Bed*; *My Advice on Poetry*; *The History of the Cold*; and *The Errors of Modern Parents*. Other works in progress included *Wool-Gathering in Medieval Times and Since*; *Lepers' Squints*; *Domestic Manners in Sheffield in the Year 1250*; and *Acorns as an Article of Medieval Diet*. As befitting a lifelong hypochondriac, he wrote up the results of his analysis for curing insomnia, entitled *The Twenty-Seven Postures of Sir George R. Sitwell*. The only one that found a publisher was *On the Making of Gardens* in 1909. His advice to his readers wasn't always practical: 'The great secret of success in garden-making is that we should abandon the struggle to make nature beautiful round the house and should rather move the house to where nature is beautiful.'

Sir George thought a lot about landscape gardening. He employed four thousand men to dig him an artificial lake in the grounds of his home, with a wooden tower sticking out of the water from where he could ponder on various expensive projects, most of them never finished. Lawns were raised or lowered, lakes appeared then disappeared, large trees were relocated. To improve the view from his study window he had Chinese willow patterns painted onto his herd of white cows. His landscaping ambitions included the homes of his children. 'I don't propose to do much here,' Sir George announced when visiting his son's house in 1924, 'just a sheet of water and a line of statues.'

The Sitwell household was policed by an imperturbable butler called Henry Moat who, according to Edith Sitwell, was 'an enormous purple man like a benevolent hippopotamus'. He saw a lot of strange things in his time, not least of which were Sir George's inventions, which included a musical toothbrush that played 'Annie Laurie' and a small revolver designed for shooting wasps. Sir George also discovered a way of making knife handles from condensed milk, prompting an enquiry from Moat: 'But what if the cat gets them?' There was also a Sitwell Egg, comprising a yolk of smoked salmon embedded in a white of rice in a synthetic shell – a boon to arctic explorers because it would never go 'off'. Sir George arrived unannounced in the office of Mr Gordon Selfridge, founder of the Oxford Street store, and declared: 'I'm George Sitwell and I have my egg with me.' Mr Selfridge's response can only be guessed at. Plans to market the egg were quietly shelved and it was never mentioned again.

Sir George stubbornly resisted the conventions of modern life. He banned electricity from his household until well into the 1940s, restricting guests to just two candles each. He tried to pay one son's school fees at Eton College in pigs and potatoes and calculated another's allowance based on the amount that a forebear paid his eldest son at the time of the Black Death. A friend of Sir George had told him that he would 'give him a ring on Thursday'. Sir George waited and then complained bitterly about his friend's lack of consideration: 'Such a pity to promise people things and then forget about them. It is not considerate – really inexcusable.' He'd been expecting a piece of jewellery.

He travelled extensively around Europe, always

accompanied by his devoted butler and an extensive collection of self-medication, deliberately mislabelled to stop anyone else using it. To save money they often dossed down with tramps in dormitories. He lived on a diet of roast chicken, which he always ate alone, wearing full evening dress, no matter where he was or how inauspicious the surroundings.

Sir George's approach to procreation was equally eccentric. In order to achieve the best result he would read a long book before declaring, 'Ida, I am ready.' Otherwise he had little time for his beautiful, outstandingly extravagant wife. While Sir George was cooped up in his study thinking about topiary, Lady Ida spent her days drinking, gambling and running up debts. She lavished a small fortune on her 'psychic' pig and once sent her seventeen-year-old daughter to pawn her false teeth.

Lady Ida was afraid to tell her husband about her debts and so became a target for unscrupulous moneylenders. Her predicament was resolved at the Old Bailey where she was sent for a three-month stretch in Holloway for fraud. Her husband could have easily settled the matter out of court but chose not to, much to the disgust of his family.* Lady Ida herself, however, proved to be a very resilient prisoner. When a local doctor's wife proposed calling on her, Lady Ida refused to see the woman, saying that she was someone whom she would never have received at Renishaw Hall, and did not see why she should do so at

---

* The sentence was such a shock that the family forgot to tell her son Sacheverell. While studying at Eton he saw on the front page of the *Sunday Express* that his mother had been sent to prison.

Holloway. When Lady Ida died in 1937, their butler noted: 'Well, at least Sir George will know where Her Ladyship spends her afternoons.'

Sir George's children were a disappointment to him. When he discovered that Osbert was writing a novel, he told his son: 'You'd better drop that idea at once. My cousin had a friend who utterly ruined his health writing a novel.' Edith was also told to give up her literary ambitions and take up gymnastics instead, with the valuable advice: 'There's nothing a man likes so much as a girl who's good on the parallel bars.' The junior Sitwells were so anxious to avoid their father that they invented an imaginary round-the-world cruise on a yacht called *The Rover*, then had some fake headed notepaper made up on which they wrote to him explaining that the yacht's itinerary had yet to be finalised so they couldn't provide a forwarding address at which they could be contacted. All the while they were living in London, confident their ruse wouldn't be rumbled, because Sir George was incapable of recognising his own children when he passed them on the street.

MITFORD FAMILY VALUES

The eccentricities surrounding the household of David Bertram Ogilvy Freeman-Mitford, 2nd Baron of Redesdale, were much less charming. Redesdale was a brave army officer who fought with distinction and lost a lung in the Boer War. His career took an unexpected sideways move when he became editor of the upmarket women's weekly *The Lady*. This came as a surprise to many people, not just because he took a mongoose to work with him to catch rats, but also because he was an avowed chauvinist and semi-literate, having boasted that he had only ever read one book in his life. When his wife read *Tess of the D'Urbervilles* to him he found it so upsetting she had to explain that it was a work of fiction. Redesdale was dumbstruck. 'What! The damned feller made it up?' The writer in the family, his brother Clement, was the author of one book, a privately printed volume of his letters to *The Times* and other publications, mostly on the subject of manure.*

Lord Redesdale inherited his title on the death of his eldest brother in the First World War, then moved his family several times from one large residence to another, finally settling at Swinbrook House, near Chipping Norton. His family renamed it 'Swinebrook' because it was cold, draughty and had a plumbing system that had not been updated since the Black Death. Swinbrook was built as a fortress, according to his daughter Jessica, to keep out 'Huns, Frogs, Americans, blacks and all other foreigners'.

Lord Redesdale was a hard-bitten xenophobic. 'Abroad is unutterably bloody and foreigners are fiends,' he explained. 'I loathe abroad, nothing would induce me to live there. As for foreigners they are all the same, and they all make me sick.' His bigotry made no distinction between race or colour: when one of his nephews married an Argentinian of Spanish origin he remarked, 'I hear that Robin's married a black.'

The Redesdales had some novel ideas about raising children. They didn't believe in formal education; their only son Tom was sent to school because he was a boy, but their six

---

* According to Clement Redesdale, the success of Elizabethan England was founded on the widespread use of sheep droppings in producing an organic diet and, therefore, a sound society.

daughters received none at all, apart from some French delivered to them by a string of hapless governesses. Lady Redesdale, meanwhile, held strong opinions about diet and modern medicine, especially vaccination, which she described as 'pumping disgusting dead germs into the good body'. She once met Adolf Hitler and lectured him at length about the health benefits of wholemeal bread, while her daughter Unity translated. She refrained from sharing her other dietary rules with the Führer; although neither she nor her husband practised the Jewish faith, the Mitford children were not allowed to eat pork, rabbit, hare or shellfish 'as dictated by Moses in the Old Testament'. School meals were a great relief to Tom, who wrote home from Eton: 'We have sossages every day.' One day the children burst into the morning room, where their mother was writing letters, to inform her that their sister Diana was threatening to commit suicide by throwing herself from the roof. Lady Redesdale replied without looking up: 'Tell her it's her favourite pudding for lunch, that's sure to get her down.'

Redesdale was a high-profile supporter of the policy of appeasement towards Nazi Germany and in 1938 he and his wife attended the Nuremberg Rally and met Hitler, with whom his daughters were already acquainted, and was won over by Hitler's charm. His wife went further, writing articles in praise of Hitler ('such very good manners') and Nazism. Redesdale's hatred of foreigners, however, won the day and when war was declared in 1939 he was once again virulently 'anti-Hun'.* The couple split up after more

---

* Redesdale appears as fearsome Uncle Matthew, Lord Alconleigh of Alconleigh, in his daughter Nancy's novel *The Pursuit of Love*. Uncle Matthew bludgeoned eight Germans to

than thirty-five years of marriage over the crucial question of whether Hitler would be welcome as a son-in-law; Lord Redesdale was against, his wife all for it.

When Redesdale died in 1958, his obituary in *The Times* noted with understatement, he 'adhered to somewhat old-fashioned views with tenacity and boisterousness'. His daughter Diana put it more bluntly, describing him as 'one of nature's fascists'. Only two of his daughters inherited their father's right-wing politics to an extreme. Unity Mitford became a friend – and possibly a lover – of Hitler, who described her as 'a perfect specimen of Aryan woman-hood', while Diana Mitford married the fascist Sir Oswald Mosley. Their sister Jessica took the opposite political route, joining the Communist Party.

THE QUIET LIFE

For some members of the Victorian aristocracy politics was an interesting diversion from managing their estates, shooting grouse and catching venereal disease from high-class prostitutes.

Lord Robert Gascogne-Cecil, the 3rd Marquess of Salisbury, expressed his gratitude for being elected British prime minister three times by describing the democratic system as 'a dangerous and irrational creed by which two day-labourers shall outvote Baron Rothschild'.* To be fair,

---

death with his spade, which he then kept on display above the fireplace complete with human blood and hair. The book is thought to be largely autobiographical.

* Salisbury especially hated having to tour the country in search of votes and having to put up with 'screwed up smiles and

Salisbury's disdain for the people who put him in power was matched by his indifference to politics in general. He was a spectacularly lazy prime minister, so disinterested in running the country that the few reforms that did take place generally happened while he was away on holiday. He kept a penknife in his pocket, which he used to jab into his leg to keep himself awake during business in the House of Commons.

Salisbury was the type of old-school aristocratic eccentric that tended to be scruffy, unembarrassable and unmotivated by money. He often wore a skullcap to protect his bald head from draughts, but when he lost the cap he took to wearing a grey woollen glove on top of his head instead. He was once arrested by a farmer who thought he was a poacher and was refused admission to the casino at Monte Carlo because he was taken for a tramp.

Life at Salisbury's home, Hatfield House, was chaotic. He was a keen amateur scientist and liked to dabble in his private laboratory in the basement, connected to his study by a spiral staircase, from where guests heard regular explosions. He once emerged from his lab, covered in blood, explaining that he had been 'experimenting with sodium in an insufficiently dried retort'. Hatfield House was one of the first houses to have electric lighting installed. The overloaded and completely uninsulated wiring ran the

---

laboured courtesy, the mock geniality, the hearty shake of the filthy hand, the chuckling reply that must be made to the coarse joke, the loathsome, choking compliment that must be paid to the grimy wife and sluttish daughter, the indispensable flattery of the vilest religious prejudices, the wholesale deglutition of hypocritical pledges . . .'

length of the ceiling above the dining-room table and frequently burst into flame, to the alarm of dinner guests. Salisbury and his family coped by occasionally lobbing a cushion at the ceiling to put out the fire.

Salisbury was also notoriously forgetful. Despite having filled the government with so many of his relations that it was nicknamed 'Hotel Cecil', he couldn't remember the names or faces of half his cabinet ministers. On one occasion he was standing behind the throne at a court ceremony when he saw a young man smiling at him. He asked a colleague, 'Who's that?' The reply came, 'He's your eldest son.' Salisbury's appointment of the wholly talentless Alfred Austin to the post of poet laureate in 1896 was considered one of the oddest ever. When asked why he had chosen such a terrible poet, Salisbury explained, 'I don't think anyone else applied.' Queen Victoria was said to be very fond of Salisbury, despite his 'peculiarities'. He was the only man she ever asked to sit down.

In a highly competitive field, the most reactionary Tory to have sat in Parliament during the Victorian era was the preposterous Charles de Laet Waldo Sibthorp. Long before he became MP for Lincoln, 'the Colonel' was a curiosity figure in his local constituency thanks to his bushy dragoon's whiskers and anachronistic style of dress, including Regency-style blue frock-coat, cravat, antique quizzing glasses and top-boots. He became known to the wider public in the elections of 1826 when he stood up to speak at his very first hustings and was felled by a large brick thrown from the crowd.

His fellow MPs got the gist of his political leanings from his maiden parliamentary speech. He was opposed to any form of social progress: this included trains, water closets, taxation, anti-bribery laws, Catholics and 'the lamentable influx into this country of foreigners talking gibberish'. He particularly hated railways – 'the Steam Humbug' – which he predicted would bring an array of disasters ranging from moral ruin to wholesale slaughter. Sibthorp enjoyed the support of at least one important sympathiser, the old Duke of Wellington, who was also deeply suspicious of railways because 'they encourage lower classes to move about'. Sibthorp enjoyed one major triumph when, to the annoyance of Lincoln's businessmen, he stopped the Great Northern Railway from running through his constituency.

Most of all, Sibthorp loathed foreigners: 'It would take ninety-nine foreigners to make one thorough good Englishman', he said, and the only excuse for an Englishman to travel abroad was to wage war against them. Sibthorp's xenophobia extended to Queen Victoria's German husband Albert – one of those 'nasty foreigners who live on brown bread and sauerkraut'. Sibthorp called for Albert's proposed annual allowance of fifty thousand pounds to be halved. To the huge embarrassment of the Tory prime minister Lord Melbourne, who had given the queen his personal assurance that Albert's allowance would go through on the nod, Sibthorp won the day by 104 votes. Sibthorp also opposed Albert's most famous project, the 1851 Great Exhibition, on the grounds that it would attract foreigners, advising people living near the Crystal Palace to 'keep a sharp lookout after their silver forks and spoons and servant maids'. The queen vowed never to go anywhere near Lincoln again so long as Sibthorp was MP. She had to wait a long time because his constituents kept re-electing him as MP for Lincoln right up until his early death in 1855. Sibthorp worked himself into a strop for the last time when he rose in the House to accuse his old foe Lord John Russell of fiddling his expenses on a trip to Vienna. He died of a stroke soon after.

The political affiliations of some aristocrats were far less predictable. The 3rd Baronet Sir Hugh Charles Rhys Rankin joined the Labour Party in 1939 and was subsequently a Dominion Home Ruler for Scotland, a Scottish nationalist, a Scottish communist and a Welsh republican nationalist. In *Who's Who* he described himself as having 'extreme political views' and 'now left-side Labour'. In 1950 he was elected to Perthshire County Council, one of the most solidly Conservative areas of Scotland, where no one seems to have noticed that he was, in his words, 'a blood-red militant communist in every possible way'.

Away from politics, in the late 1950s he and Lady Rankin had a couple of unsettling encounters with the Abominable Snowman, one during a trip in the Himalayas, then another in Scotland. While cycling through the Lairig Ghru Pass they suddenly felt 'the Presence' behind them. They turned and saw a big, olive-complexioned man dressed in a long robe and sandals, with long flowing hair. 'We were not in the least afraid,' Rankin explained later, because, 'being Buddhists we at once knew who he was'. Rankin later explained that they had instantly recognised the hairy stranger as a Bodhisattva, 'one of five Perfected Men who control the destinies of this world, and meet once a year in a cave in the Himalayas . . . one of them lives permanently in the Scottish Cairngorms'.

In 1965 Rankin claimed that he was 'the only baronet in the United Kingdom who is living on national assistance'. When asked what job he would like to do, he replied: 'Anything except being a butler. I hate snobbishness.' He listed his hobbies as 'golf, sheep-shearing and crawling under fir trees'.

Martin Attlee, 2nd Earl Attlee and son of former British prime minister Clement, campaigned vigorously in the House of Lords against drug abuse, demanding that dealers should be forcibly injected with heroin 'to give them a taste of their own medicine'. Attlee told the lordships he spoke as an authority, having experienced drugs at first hand. On holiday in Portugal, he had accidentally smoked cannabis and found himself on a 'high' – a sensation he found to be disagreeable. Shortly before he died Attlee took up another campaign, this time drawing attention to the brutality of the Metropolitan Police force, citing 'horrific stories of police arrogance, especially when it comes to picking up boys with a public school accent'. It later transpired that Attlee had fallen asleep on a London underground train and had been bundled into a police cell and charged with being drunk and disorderly.

Throughout the 1950s, half the speeches made in the House of Lords by the 6th Duke of Sutherland were on the subject of deer, which was arguably more useful than the two contributions of the 8th Earl of Arran – one on badgers, the other on buggers. 'On the whole', he reflected, 'I rather think their lordships were more interested in the badgers.' Thomas Coke, 5th Earl of Leicester, sat through twenty-two years of debate before finally speaking, maintaining a great family tradition; his father maintained thirty-two consecutive years of restrained silence, while his grandfather held out for an impressive sixty-seven. The family motto is: 'He is prudent who is patient.'

In 1796, 1st Baronet of Netherby, Sir James Graham pleaded with Henry Dundas, the Secretary of State for

War, for a safe government constituency, reminding his friend 'my sole object for coming into Parliament would be to obtain a peerage'. Graham's hopes were raised in 1798 when he was elected for Ripon in Yorkshire, which he represented for the next nine years. Graham was asthmatic, which may explain why he never once spoke in debates. Sadly his silent support for successive ministries did not win him a peerage.

Spencer Cavendish, 8th Duke of Devonshire, was said to be the most boring speaker ever to set foot in the House of Lords. His long-winded monologues were 'the finest example of pile-driving the world has ever known', according to a friend. He was once caught yawning in the middle of one of his own speeches. He apologised immediately: 'I can't help it because what I have to say is so damned dull.' He related a nightmare he experienced at Westminster. 'I dreamed I was making a speech in the House of Lords and woke up to find I actually was.'

Unlike his philosopher father Bertrand Russell, John Conrad, the 4th Earl Russell, was a less than gifted freethinker, renowned for his rambling and often spectacularly confused speeches in the House of Lords. In 1978 he startled the slumbering peers by demanding the total abolition of law and order and called for the police to 'stop raping young people in their cells'. Russell went on to propose 'there should be universal leisure for all and a standing wage sufficient to provide life without working ought to be supplied ... so that everybody becomes a leisured aristocrat ... aristocrats are Marxists'. He added that 'women's lib would be realised by girls being given a house of their own by the age of twelve and three quarters of the wealth of the State being given to the girls so that marriage would be abolished and the girl could have as many husbands as she liked'. He finally advised that 'Mr. [Leonid] Brezhnev and Mr. [Jimmy] Carter are really the same person,' before suddenly exiting the Chamber without further comment. The full text of this speech, published in *Hansard*, became a collector's item. Russell retired from politics to take up writing and crocheting. He once made himself a pair of trousers out of string. 'It took a very long time,' he explained later, 'because I didn't have a pattern.'

UPPER-CLASS ALIEN

According to *Burke's Peerage*, the Irish Earldom of Clancarty was created for the first time in 1658 by King Charles II. William Brinsley Le Poer Trench, 8th Earl of Clancarty, believed he could trace his descent from much further back – from 63000 BC, around the time beings from other planets had landed on Earth in spaceships.

Lord Clancarty was both Irish peer and a member of the Dutch nobility, having succeeded to the earldom in 1975 on the death of his half-brother when he took his seat in the House of Lords. In his spare time he wrote several books about UFO's including *Secret of the Ages: UFOs from inside the Earth* in which he claimed that mankind emerged from inside a hollow Earth. He spent several years in the House of Lords trying to expose a government cover-up of the existence of UFOs and of beings living in the interior of the Earth.

In earlier books he postulated that a number of the 'Elchim' (gods) had indulged in a breeding experiment. This went wrong and they were expelled, along with the race of Adam; these were the 'fallen angels', 'giants', 'Anunnaki' – the Nephilim of the Bible. 'It is my firm view', he explained, 'that the ground work has now been prepared for a take-over of this planet by those who live inside it.' Most humans were descended from these aliens: 'This accounts for all the different colour skins we've got here,' he said in 1981. A few of these early aliens did not come from space, but emerged through tunnels from a civilisation, which 'still existed beneath the Earth's crust'. There were seven or eight of these tunnels altogether, one at the North Pole, another at the South Pole, and others in such places as Tibet. 'I haven't been down there myself,' his lordship admitted, 'but from what I gather these beings are very advanced.'

In Clancarty's book *The Sky People* he elaborated on his theory that several biblical characters including Adam and Eve and Noah had originated from Mars, Adam and Eve (and the Garden of Eden) being the experimental creations of extra-terrestrials. When the Martian north polar ice cap melted, that's when descendants of Adam and Eve moved to Earth.

In January 1979, which in Britain was a time of strikes and unrest, fuel shortages and lay-offs – the winter of discontent – Clancarty organised the House of Lords' first ever debate on UFOs, calling for a government investigation. It attracted speeches on both sides, including one from Lord Gainford, who described a personal sighting of a UFO, and the Bishop of Norwich, who wondered if aliens from other planets had souls. Clancarty confessed disappointment at never having actually spotted a flying saucer, despite having installed a UFO detector in the bedroom of his South Kensington flat.

Clancarty's unique contribution to House of Lords debates was a motivating factor when the Labour government decided in 1999 to ration the number of hereditary peers who would automatically be allowed to retain their seats. Pending the verdict on who would make the cut, their lordships were invited to submit brief manifestos stating what they could contribute and what measures they favoured. The 2nd Viscount Monckton of Brenchley rose to the occasion by demanding that all cats should be made to wear muzzles when let outside. He said it was in order to prevent 'the agonising torture of mice and small birds'. Charles Francis Topham de Vere Beauclerk, Earl of Burford, meanwhile achieved his fifteen minutes of infamy by leaping onto the Woolsack (the Lord's Chancellor's throne in the House of Lords) – to denounce the abolition of voting rights for hereditary peers.

LADY LIGHT-FINGERS

Aristocrats are expected to entertain generously, a serious duty, which can result in social disgrace if performed inadequately. Not that this worried the London society hostess Venetia Cavendish-Bentinck. She was so tight-fisted that she recycled milk from the cat's bowl for her guests. She would send her butler a note with the acronym 'DCSC': it stood for 'don't cut second chicken' – her ladyship having decided that her guests had already had enough to eat. She also bought bacon on a sale-or-return basis and when members of her household fell ill, hired a vet because their fees were lower.

Lady Mary, wife of the 7th Earl of Cork, Edmund Boyle, was a much more generous Regency-period hostess, whose London house became a favourite meeting place for some of the most famous people of the day including Dr Johnson, Lord Byron, Sir Walter Scott and the Prince of Wales. The diarist Fanny Burney described her as 'very short, very fat but handsome, splendidly and fantastically dressed, rouged not unbecomingly yet evidently and palpably desirous of gaining notice and admiration'.

Old Lady Cork continued to entertain in style until she was well into her nineties. The favour was rarely returned because she was also a notorious kleptomaniac. Friends and acquaintances anticipated her visits by hiding their best silver and replacing it with cheap pewter. It made little difference; Lady Cork scooped it up and hid it in her muff anyway. When she got home her servants would gather together any items they didn't recognise and send them back with an apology. It wasn't just cutlery that Lady Cork stole: she took flowers from gardens and once made off with a live hedgehog in her handbag.

Between bouts of thievery she kept a famous macaw that once nibbled George IV's stocking and bit a chunk out of Lady Darlington's leg. The bird's reputation reached a peak when Lady Cork's conservatory was fitted out to look like a Brazilian rainforest with tin palm trees and a stuffed alligator, in which the macaw would practise his party trick of drawing out, clipping and smoking a cigar.

On the subject of odd pets, we should also mention the 16th Baroness Strange (by name and by nature) who lived at Megginch, a medieval castle in Perthshire, where she read tea-leaves and wrote romantic novels under the pseudonym Cherry Evans. She was at a supper party when a pet mongoose was observed to emerge from her cleavage, approach her plate, gnaw at a lamb chop, then return to its refuge. The other guests continued to eat without remark.

In her later years, Lady Sybil Primrose, daughter of the 5th Earl of Rosebery, British prime minister in the 1890s, spent much of her time living in a tree house in one of her homes, Pitchford House in Shropshire. From her perch up in the foliage she could often be heard shouting instructions to her butler through a megaphone. During one period, she took to dyeing her hair orange, wearing orange clothes, applying orange lipstick and living in her orangery, which at least was an entirely consistent form of demented behaviour. Lady Sybil was considered quite normal, however, compared to Lady Katherine, wife of the 1st Viscount Tredegar, who came to believe that she was a kingfisher and built herself a bird's nests big enough for her to sit in. Severely agoraphobic, she did not attend her daughter's funeral or her son's wedding and was very rarely seen in public. She would sometimes sit in complete darkness, or even in a closet, to shut out the outside world. She did, however, maintain her passion for art and patronised such figures as Augustus John, Ambrose McEvoy and Gaudier-Brzeska.

Like many of her class, the famous hostess Lady Diana Cooper, youngest daughter of the 8th Duke of Rutland (but more likely of Henry Cust, a womanising MP with whom her mother had a long affair) was a stranger to life's practicalities. She once contacted the War Office during the Blitz advising them to place large magnets in London's parks to attract Hitler's bombs. In later years she liked to warm her plate, and everyone else's, by holding them over her breasts. She carried with her everywhere a small dog in a basket; if it was somewhere dogs weren't allowed, she smuggled it in within a large muff.

Lady Cooper's driving skills were legendary. She ran

red lights freely and abandoned her car wherever the mood took her, leaving a message in her windscreen, which read: 'Please have pity on a poor blind lame old lady.' At a reception the elderly Lady Cooper fell into conversation with a friendly woman who looked vaguely familiar. Her failing eyesight prevented her from recognising her fellow guest, until she peered more closely at the magnificent diamonds and realised she was talking to the queen. 'I'm terribly sorry, Ma'am,' said Lady Cooper breaking into a curtsey, 'I didn't recognise you without your crown on.'

It's appropriate to end a chapter about eccentricity with a randomly eccentric death. The Marchioness of Salisbury, wife of the first marquess, was a charismatic eighteenth-century society hostess who entertained lavishly with enormous parties at her town house in London or at Hatfield House. She was particularly fond of gambling and her scandalous Sunday card parties would go on all night, leaving the long gallery ankle deep in playing cards by morning. She refused to grow old gracefully and still wore the fashion of her youth, with her hair piled high and deco-rated with feathers, into her eighties. She died when a fire ripped through the west wing of her home at Hatfield House on the evening of 22 November 1835. It was several hours before the blaze was brought under control, by which time all that remained of Lady Salisbury were her dentures and a few charred bones.

At the inquest, it was established that the fire had started at the top of her ladyship's head, when her hair caught alight in a chandelier candle.

4

Pride and Prejudice

There are many different ways for the aristocracy to display rank and wealth. Some are for the benefit of the lower classes, others so finely calibrated that only other aristocrats can grasp their meaning, as if to say 'Just between us, I'm richer than you.'

Among the more subtle status symbols were the height and general turnout of footmen, known as 'fart catchers', so called because they walked behind their employees with no discernible occupation. Some of these retainers were paid by height – extra for every inch over six foot – so a row of towering footmen was a clear signal of superiority.

In the 1920s, the footmen at Blenheim Palace, home of the Duke of Marlborough, were hard to ignore: all well over six feet tall, they wore maroon coats covered in silver braid, their hair powdered with a mixture of violet powder and flour: the violet powder came out of their own wages.

As well as height and impressive bearing, footmen required speed and stamina. The 4th Duke of Marlborough was one of many aristocrats who employed a running footman – a servant dressed in full livery paid to run alongside his lordship's coach. A good running footman could average about seven miles per hour – more, it was said, if they were fed white wine and eggs. Noblemen amused themselves by arranging and betting on races between these footmen and horse-drawn coaches. One of the last recorded races of this kind was staged between Marlborough's footman and the duke himself, riding in a carriage and four, from Windsor to London. The duke won by a narrow margin; the footman died from his efforts.

The 4th Duke of Queensberry kept a running footman who was employed to run messages and errands for him and to beat a path before him in heavy crowds. He interviewed prospective candidates by making them do a test run up and down Piccadilly in London, dressed in full ducal livery, while he watched from the balcony of his home overlooking the busy street. One candidate ran so quickly that Queensberry called down to him, 'You'll do very well for me!' 'And your lordship's livery will do very well for me,' the man replied, as he disappeared from view.

For some reason Irish footmen were all the rage in English aristocratic circles, but how much this had to do with innate athleticism and how much with economics is unclear. Fynes Moryson, English travel writer and bigot, thought that Irish footmen performed best when treated poorly. It was definitely a mistake, he suggested, ever to let them sit on a horse, or they would never run again. There were running footmen in other parts of Europe too. The almanac *Chambers Book of Days* quotes 'Mrs St George', a traveller in Vienna around 1800, who was appalled at their treatment. 'They seldom live more than three or four years and usually die of consumption,' she noted.

There were many hazards for footmen. The 5th Earl of Lonsdale's London residence had a particularly dangerous antique lift to the upper floors. The lift was completely open at the sides and was no more than a caged platform offering no protection from the walls on either side. One day Lady Lonsdale, who was on her way to the races at Newmarket, was waiting on the ground floor for her footman to bring down her trunk in the lift. On the way down he got wedged between the trunk and the walls and by the time the lift arrived at the ground floor the footman was dead. This was very awkward for her ladyship; not only had she lost a footman, she also very nearly missed her train. No tragedy, however great, was allowed to interrupt the ducal routine.

In British country houses of the 1700s it was fashionable to keep a black servant. Some were well treated, but many were not. Often they were regarded as slaves and paid no wages. Some, like the Duchess of Kingston's black servant Sambo, once they reached adolescence and lost their appeal as fashion accessories, were sold back into slavery on a plantation. Others remained as family retainers. At Knole in Kent the Earls of Dorset kept a succession of black servants who, regardless of their real names, were known as John Morocco.

One of the more eccentric status symbols enjoyed by the English aristocracy was the acquisition of real, mechanical or occasionally stuffed 'ornamental hermits'. In the 1830s Lord Hill installed a human hermit in the grounds of his home at Hawkstone in Shropshire. The bare-footed 'Father Francis' was required to sit in a cave with an hourglass in his hand and exchange *bon mots* with passing visitors. He was eventually replaced by an automaton that would nod its head whenever someone came by, but according to regulars, the effect was disappointing. Charles Hamilton, a younger son of the 6th Earl of Abercorn, advertised for a hermit for his estate at Pains Hall, near Cobham, Surrey. The conditions of employment were stringent: 'He shall be provided with a Bible, optical glasses, a mat for his feet, a hassock for his pillow, an hourglass for timepiece, water for his beverage, and food from the house. He must wear a camlet robe, and never under any circumstances, must he cut his hair, beard, or nails, stray beyond the limits of Mr. Hamilton's grounds, or exchange one word with the servants.' Sadly, real people were not as reliable as mechanical hermits. They got rheumatism, became bad-tempered and often failed to nod when required. Hamilton's first hermit lasted three weeks before running away and being found drunk in a nearby hostelry.

By the eighteenth century, every self-respecting aristocrat with a scientific bent had a private menagerie of exotic animals. The Duke of Richmond had a private zoo at Goodwood, comprising five wolves, two tigers, one lion, two leopards, three bears, monkeys, eagles, and 'a woman Tyger' and 'a new animal he is very fond of which he calls a mangoose'. The Duchess of Portland collected animals so frantically that friends wondered if she was anticipating another biblical deluge. The Earl of Shelburne, later to become prime minister, kept an orangutan and an allegedly tame leopard in his orangery at Bowood House. Sir Robert Walpole's pet flamingo warmed itself by his kitchen fire, while Sir Hans Sloane was followed round his Chelsea home by a tame, one-eyed wolverine; it kept his opossum and his porcupine company. The 4th Duke of Marlborough kept a tigress in his grounds in a cage, fed by regular orders made to the local butcher's shop. Records show that the tigress cost the same as three servants to feed.

Parrot ownership was all the rage, but you had to be seriously rich. In the mid-1700s a macaw would cost you the equivalent of a domestic servant's annual salary. Sadly, attitudes towards animal welfare were not very enlightened. One polar bear was fed on bread and milk and a rhinoceros was given three bottles of wine a day, while a baiting contest pitched twelve dogs against a panther.*

Exotic animals were also luxury ingredients. In Georgian Britain, turtle feasts were something of an obsession among the affluent classes and no high-society dinner was complete without copious servings of the freshly prepared reptile. A gentleman who wanted to show off would generously donate a turtle to his club. It isn't clear why the ruling classes developed a taste for this unlikely delicacy (people who have sampled it describe its flavour as muddy,

---

* These aristocratic menageries, rebranded 'safari parks', proved just as popular in the twentieth century. Lions and later other creatures drew visitors to the Marquess of Bath's house at Longleat and the Duke of Bedford established a zoo at Woburn in Bedfordshire.

dirty, mushy and chewy: if you must, general consensus seems to be to go for the innards and flippers). Perhaps it was simply because they could. Turtles were incredibly difficult and expensive to come by because they were caught in the West Indies and had to be kept alive during the long voyage across the Atlantic before being slaughtered in Britain. Vast turtle warehouses sprang up in Bristol, where the turtle boats usually docked.* It is an indication of how gastronomic taste has changed over the past 200 years that oysters were then so cheap that servants refused to eat them more than a couple of times a week. Now oysters are an expensive luxury and turtles are relegated to tinned soup.

Perhaps equally baffling was the upper-class mania for having their wigs dressed in bear grease. Thousands of barrels of bear grease were exported from Arkansas to London to keep pace with demand, decimating the state's population of bears in the process. Live bears were imported from Russia to be fattened up for slaughter by London hairdressers and wig-makers. Customers were invited to watch the removal of the fat from a recently slaughtered bear so as to prove that they were not being fobbed off with pig fat.

In London and Paris, high-class perfumers, apothecaries and grocers traded in goods prepared from either living or dead turtles, bears or civet cats. The scented glandular secretion extracted from the anal glands of the civet cat

---

* Turtles were kept in water alive until the night before they were on the menu. Then they would be turned on their backs, decapitated, scalded and then hung to drain of blood. *Bon appétit.*

was one of the most expensive materials employed by seventeenth- and eighteenth-century perfumers and was used to scent linen, pomades and handkerchiefs and as an ingredient in perfumes or even as a treatment for sexual and hysteric disorders. One expensive eighteenth-century treatment for erectile dysfunction utilised twenty-five grains of civet (four shillings) for a single dose.

TOO POSH TO WASH

Clothes were an obvious way of showing off rank and status. In the fifteenth and sixteenth centuries there were even laws to prevent commoners wearing certain types of clothing thought suitable only for noblemen. In France, the red heels fashionable at King Louis XIV's court were synonymous for nobility for many generations, long after the fad had passed. In the Regency era, clean linen, precision grooming and good manners were the hallmark of a gentleman. What went on beneath this façade was slightly less glamorous. A gentleman would change his shirt a couple of times a day to keep the louse population down, but only his hands and face saw soap and water. The standard for most male noblemen was a dirty body and filthy hair, both heavily doused with perfume in an attempt to mask, usually unsuccessfully, massive body odour. The Austrian Prince of Kaunitz-Rietberg, for instance, spent a part of every morning pacing up and down his room while four valets puffed a cloud of scented powder in his direction, each with a different colour.

'Filthy rich' was a literal description of Charles Howard 11th Duke of Norfolk, said to be richest and the smelliest man in England. When his body odour became unbearable his servants waited until he was drunk then washed him while he lay comatose on the floor.* The notoriously unsanitary Topham Beauclerk, great-grandson of Charles II and his mistress Nell Gwynne, was said to be so filthy that, according to the diarist Horace Walpole, he 'generated vermin'.

Rotting teeth and bad breath were extremely common and painful problems for the rich because only they could afford sugar, sticky fruits and sweetmeats. A lot of damage was also done by contemporary tooth-cleaning methods such as the use of coarse powders and chalk or soda whitening agents that wore away tooth enamel and irritated gums. Lord Chesterfield completely destroyed his teeth through the overly energetic use of sticks and irons.

In the summer, the well-heeled decamped to the spas at Bath and Cheltenham where the alleged medicinal properties of the local spring water had been attracting invalids for centuries. These spas, however, were run on such unsanitary principles that they must have created many more health problems than they solved. Communal bathing in what was basically a small swimming pool full of warm water created a bacterial soup where people with infected wounds and running sores bathed alongside people with contagious diseases.

Even among the wealthiest, standards of hygiene were, by modern standards, abysmally poor. Although Queen Caroline brought the German bathing regimen with her

---

* Norfolk suffered terribly from rheumatism and complained to his friend, Dudley North, that he had tried everything to relieve the pain without effect. North replied, 'Did you ever try a clean shirt?'

from Ansbach when she came to the throne in 1727 and immediately ordered a set of bathtubs for the royal family, the British aristocracy were notoriously reluctant to convert to 'foreign' bathing habits. Although the flushing water closet was invented during the reign of Queen Elizabeth I, most English aristocratic dwellings didn't catch up with the technology until the 1780s. One or two of the great houses, such as Chatsworth and Blenheim, had a bathroom but most did not – even Buckingham Palace didn't have one when Queen Victoria inherited it in 1837. The top London gentlemen's club, Brooks's, didn't have a lavatory, only a cesspit that was emptied when it started to overflow. In French aristocratic homes sanitary conditions were even worse. The flushing toilet, referred to as *les lieux à l'anglaise* and the inbuilt plumbing they required were not considered a necessity until the later nineteenth century.

CONSPICUOUS CONSUMPTION

In the eighteenth century there was no greater indication of wealth than the amount of food you were prepared to eat. For gentlemen it was also a test of virility; gluttony was manly, not greedy. In Britain, where the fare was considerably more basic than on the continent, this usually meant vast consumption of beefsteaks. The most legendary of all the beefsteak eaters, the afore-mentioned Charles, 11th Duke of Norfolk, once ate fifteen huge steaks at a single sitting and his meal breaks often went on from 3 p.m. until well after midnight. Surprisingly, he lived into his seventieth year.

Lavish dinners were expected of the nobility. It was customary to provide more food than the company could feasibly eat (unless the Duke of Norfolk was a guest, obviously) so a society hostess would be expected to lay on at least fifteen courses and often many more. Some aristocratic epicures had appetites that were worthy of the Roman emperors. Richard Sackville, 3rd Earl of Dorset, died in agony on Easter Sunday when his digestive system failed to keep pace with his massive intake of potato pies. The 4th Duke of Rutland was also famous for spectacular overindulgence. He began each day with a breakfast of six or seven turkey eggs then spent the rest of the day washing them down with port. He died aged thirty-three of liver disease.

Just occasionally, the upper classes would try to lose weight for reasons of health or vanity. Lord Byron, whose tendency to put on weight didn't sit easily with his image as a romantic hero, tried various fad diets and once threw a strop at a dinner party to which he had been invited because there was too much fatty food and demanded 'nothing but hard biscuits and soda water'. There was none available, so he settled for a plate of potatoes drowned in vinegar.

Sir Tatton Sykes, 5th Baronet, was a miserable hypochondriac who obsessively followed various bizarre health-fads of his own invention. He lived almost exclusively on a diet of cold rice pudding and, so the story goes, in 1911 refused to leave his 250-year-old mansion Sledmere House during a blazing fire until he had finished his bowl. 'I must eat my pudding!' he told his fleeing servants as the flames consumed his property. Helena, the Comtesse de Noailles – a thoroughly English lady despite her French title – lived on a diet of milk, champagne, fresh herring roe (to prevent bronchitis) and methane. She encouraged her cows to graze near open windows because she thought the farts they produced were good for her health.

Surviving a country house dinner party required a strong constitution – and that's where alcohol helped. Gentlemen were encouraged to drink; in fact, part of being a gentleman meant holding your liquor. William Hogarth's painting *A Modern Midnight Conversation* shows a typical upper-class drinking bout in full swing. Under a side table is a pile of empty bottles and on top, more bottles and a bowl of punch. The participants are in varying states of disarray. One has fallen over, smashing the bottle he was holding, another is staggering around the room while two others have fallen asleep.

According to Thackeray, the English nobility spent at least a quarter of their lives drinking and were rarely entirely sober. Dr Johnson noted: 'Claret is the liquor for boys, port for men: but he who aspires to be a hero must drink brandy.' The 11th Duke of Norfolk had an astonishing capacity for alcohol and was said to be capable of drinking five or six times more than any normal person – including his good friend the Prince Regent, who was partial to the odd gallon of cherry brandy. Sir Beaumont Dixie's devotion to alcohol earned for himself and his wife the nicknames Sir Always and Lady Sometimes Tipsy.* Sir William Paxton, who built a tower in Carmarthenshire high enough for him to keep an eye on his horses in a field near Tenby, thirty-six miles away, drank 406 bottles of

* A spendthrift, a hopeless gambler and a heavy drinker, his debts forced him to sell the family seat, Bosworth Hall in Leicestershire.

sherry in a single year. Another legendary toper, William Thoms Eardley-Twisleton-Fiennes, 15th Baron Saye and Sele, breakfasted on omelettes made from golden pheasants' eggs, and drank wines and spirits, including absinthe, in truly frightening amounts. A new manservant, on being appointed, approached Fiennes as he was going out to dinner and asked his master if he had any orders. Fiennes replied: 'Place two bottles of sherry by my bedside and call me the day after tomorrow.' Ladies drank heavily too. Lady Caroline Lamb downed at least one bottle of sherry every day of her adult life, which ended when she was forty-one.

The Georgian aristocracy was drowned in port, which explains why so many of them died of gout or liver disease. It was the age of the 'three-bottle man'. The ability for a young man, in a single sitting, to be able to drink three bottles of port, was a sign that you were someone to be reckoned with. To be fair, the standard size of a bottle of port or wine was smaller than it is today, but it still represented a truly alarming intake of alcohol. The Regency diarist Captain Gronow claimed he knew of four-, five- and even six-bottle men – although we can't be absolutely sure to what degree Gronow's own recollections were seen through an alcoholic haze.

The growth in popularity of port as the young gentleman's tipple of choice was partly born of necessity. While the Napoleonic Wars raged on the continent, the vineyards of France, Italy and Spain were denied and the only available trading nation to Britain was its oldest ally, Portugal. Port had been Britain's wartime drink of choice since the seventeenth century and there was even a degree of patriotism to be seen in the drinking of it.

It was also ostensibly very good for you; according to most informed medical opinion of the time, a regular infusion of port would drive other less welcome toxins out of the body. William Pitt the Younger, prime minister and son of the 1st Earl of Chatham, was referred to his father's physician, Dr Addington, who gave him a piece of medical advice that probably contributed to his early death. Addington recommended diet, regular exercise on horseback and a daily quantity of port wine, variously recorded as 'a bottle a day' or 'liberal potations' – at any rate, it was a lot of port. Pitt stuck to this advice throughout the rest of his life, especially the bit about drinking. Coincidentally, he enjoyed a substantial improvement in his health and shook off the illnesses that had plagued him as a child, so he could be forgiven for thinking that the port was doing the job.* Drinking a quantity a day for medicinal purposes, however, was still a long way from knocking back three bottles in a single sitting. It also explains why, during speeches in the House of Commons, he often had to dodge behind the Speaker's Chair to throw up.

After the Napoleonic Wars the British aristocracy took to their fine wines with a vengeance. Wine consumption was directly related to wealth: the more you could afford, the more you drank. To ensure there was always plenty to go around, most estates kept large cellars with very detailed books. It was not unusual for aristocratic families to have several thousand bottles in stock. It's perhaps only

---

* Although to be fair he was rather luckier than Lord Fermanagh, who fell ill for fifteen days in 1716 and his doctor advised him to drink 'horse dung possit daily'.

fair to point out that that compared to their Russian counterparts, British aristocrats were lightweights. The test of
a true St Petersburg nobleman was to be able to drink
vodka by the pail-full. When Friedrich Wilhelm, the teenage Duke of Courland, unwisely got himself involved in a
drinking contest at his wedding ceremony with his new
Russian in-laws, he dropped dead from alcohol poisoning
on his way home.

Throughout Britain's war with France, which had lasted
continuously for almost twenty-two years, the British
public was vehemently anti-French, as the cartoons of the
day show, but the aristocracy stuck to their fondness for all
things French and saw no reason to change their ways. The
upper classes continued to pepper their conversation with
French, filled their homes with French furniture, ate
French food, drank French wine (when they could get it)
and generally hankered after a return to Paris. When war
with France was briefly interrupted by the Treaty of
Amiens in 1802 the British upper classes stampeded to
Paris *en masse*. You can imagine the public reaction if in
1940 the British upper classes had spoken in German to
each other at parties about how they couldn't wait to revisit
Berlin.

After Britain's defeat of Napoleon, however, Europe's
nobility became determinedly Anglophile. The dress,
manners and habits of the British elite were slavishly
copied right across the continent. In St Petersburg, luxury
shops were crammed with British goods and fashionable
Russians even sent their laundry to London. Austrian and
Hungarian counts were served English breakfast,
Transylvanian ladies ate cucumber sandwiches cut in the
English style, French noblemen took up polo and

horse-racing and Sicilian noblemen ordered shaving soap from Piccadilly.

CLASS ACTS

Some aristocrats are so grand that their grandeur never occurs to them. They see no need to assume airs and graces because their identity is a given; they know other people will respect them because of their name and pedigree.

Others, however, needed to lay it on with a trowel. One of the most wildly ostentatious aristocrats of the early nineteenth century was the eccentric and possibly mad Charles, Duke of Brunswick, who fled political turmoil in Germany in 1830 and decamped to Paris, then London where he maintained his reputation as 'the wealthiest lunatic who ever lived'. He was chiefly famous for his ludicrous appearance. He stayed in bed until the late afternoon, then began his elaborate preparations for going out around 4 p.m.; he rarely saw the sun during winter months. He used an enormous amount of face paint, dyed his beard every day and had a range of silk wigs, long after the fashion for them had died out, worn according to the hue of facial colouring he assumed. He was also regularly festooned with gems, 'rescued' from the Brunswick crown treasury, right down to, or so he claimed, diamond-encrusted underpants.

The duke was also known for his passion for lawsuits. He filed hundreds of them, once suing a washerwoman over a seven-franc bill, and including at least twelve lawsuits over the repair of a watch. His most famous legal battle was with the publisher of *The Satirist* over a series of libellous articles, including one claiming that he had murdered a London prostitute. He consumed vast amounts of sweets, sometimes paying sweetshop owners large sums of money for the privilege of going into their premises and eating as many sweets as he could stomach at once, contributing to his 'extreme corpulence' in later years. In 1873 in the middle of a chess game, the bizarre nobleman excused himself, instructing his opponent not to cheat while he was away, then went to his room and died.

Some aristocrats were more determined than others to flaunt their rank and were very touchy about matters of precedence. The 6th Duke of Devonshire, who liked to appear at the races with a coach and twelve outriders, was furious when Lord Fitzwilliam, of inferior rank, turned up with two coaches and sixteen outriders. John de la Pole, 2nd Duke of Suffolk, once refused to ride from his seat at Ewelme in Oxfordshire with just twelve servants, all that were then available to him. The truly grandiose would insist on having horses all of the same colour: the 9th Duke of Marlborough only tolerated greys. The 6th Duke of Devonshire kept a private orchestra on permanent standby and always travelled with his personal pianist, Charles Coote, which was probably a bit too much, especially when you consider that the duke was deaf.

The extraordinarily arrogant Charles Seymour, 6th Duke of Somerset, was known as 'the Proud Duke' on account of his obsession with rank and protocol: according to the historian Thomas Macauley he was 'a man in whom the pride of birth and rank amounted almost to a disease'. Somerset was such a snob that he refused to communicate with his servants except by sign language. Whenever he travelled from London to his country estates he sent outriders ahead of his carriage to clear the roads of riff-raff and had a series of houses built at convenient points along the route so that he wouldn't have to stop overnight in a public inn and mingle with the lower classes.

Even members of his own family weren't spared his insufferably imperious manner. Somerset insisted that his children always stand in his presence and he cut off the inheritance of one of his daughters when he fell asleep and woke up to find her sitting down.

It was quite normal for the aristocracy to expect deference from their own children, although not everyone went to the extremes taken by the Italian Duke Vespasiano Gonzaga, who kicked his only son Luigi in the testicles when he failed to doff his cap to him in the street. Within a week the son died of internal rupturing.*

The 3rd Baron Crewe couldn't bear the sight of his own servants. Any member of staff he encountered after 10 a.m. was liable for instant dismissal. This was possibly why, in 1866, no one told him about the blaze that destroyed most of Crewe Hall until it was too late. John James Hamilton, Marquess of Abercorn, was so overbearingly aristocratic that it was said even the king was afraid to speak to him. Hamilton wore his ceremonial blue ribbon of the Knights of the Garter everywhere he went, even when out hunting. Servants were required to wear white kid gloves when they changed his bed linen and his footmen had to dip their hands in a bowl of rose water before handing him a dish. The novelist Walter Scott once came across

---

* More tragedy ensued. At the age of sixty the duke was suffering from some neurological disease and to cure him doctors drilled a hole in his skull. After the trepanation he sat up in bed, and said, 'I am cured', before he fell back and died.

a procession of five carriages with twenty outriders; it turned out to be Hamilton, off for a spot of informal lunch at the local inn. In 1816 Hamilton's youngest daughter died of consumption. He was grief-stricken, but too proud to admit that a member of his family had died of a disease he associated with poverty and the working classes, so he begged the doctor to write a letter to *The Times* announcing that the death had been caused by something 'less common'. Hamilton was scrupulous in his insistence that correct conventions were observed at all times. When he found out that his second wife was about to run off with another man, he insisted that she use the family carriage, so that it could never be said that Lady Abercorn 'left her husband's roof in a hack chaise'.

Those aristocrats who could afford it thought nothing of buying vast objects from abroad and paying for them to be shipped home to ornament their estates.* Lord Abercorn's namesake and distant relative Alexander, the 10th Duke of Hamilton, outbid the British Museum by paying eleven thousand pounds for a sarcophagus originally made for an Egyptian princess, then housed it in a colossal and ridiculous mausoleum. He would often visit his expensive coffin and imagine himself lying in it; he even bought the spices he was planning to have himself embalmed in.

There was, however, one small problem; it had been

---

* In 1915 the Shrewsbury millionaire Baronet Sir Cecil Chubb bought Stonehenge for his wife on a whim. She wasn't keen, so three years later he gave it to the nation instead. On a slightly smaller scale, Michael Onslow, the 7th Earl of Onslow, once bought a Roman artefact – a stone testicle – which he placed under his wife's pillow.

made for someone much smaller than Hamilton. It was also made from a piece of rare Egyptian marble, so it couldn't be altered. It wasn't until his death in 1852 that it was discovered that he was too tall to fit inside it: the only way they could get his lordship in was by sawing his legs off.

The 11th duke, son of the fake pharaoh, had his fair share of Hamilton's love of excess. He never travelled abroad with a lesser retinue than two hundred horses, carriages and servants. In Paris he used to drive down the Champs-Élysées in a carriage drawn by twelve horses and six postilions, in contravention of the law which banned anyone but the Emperor Napoleon himself to drive with more than eight horses and postilions. Hamilton, of course, considered himself at least the equal of Napoleon and above such petty legislations.

A BRIDGES TOO FAR

The ultimate signifier of status is, of course, a title. Technically, it is illegal to buy a British peerage, but this hasn't stopped people from going to absurd lengths to acquire one by any means.

There were none quite as desperate as Samuel Egerton Bridges, self-styled 13th Baron Chandos. Bridges, antiquarian and part-time poet, was born in 1762 into a comfortable family from Kent who were distant relatives of Jane Austen. He came to believe that he was descended from great nobility through his mother's side. He spent his entire life and all of his money trying to prove that he was descended from the Earl of Comyn, who came to England with William the Conqueror. One of Comyn's descendants was created Lord Chandos in 1554. Bridges was convinced that when the then-current holder of this title died, his elder brother Tymewell Bridges would inherit it. Up until now his family had always spelt their surname Bridges, but they changed it to Brydges to show off their newly discovered kinship with the nobility.

In reality, however, Egerton and Tymwell Bridges were descended from much more humble stock, an obscure family of grocers from Harbledown, near Canterbury, completely unconnected with the Chandos family. There were also grounds for suspecting that crucial entries in local parish registers backing the Bridges' claim were insertions, though nothing was ever proven.

After the death of his brother, who left no male heir, Egerton Brydges styled himself 'Baron Chandos' and bought himself a ruined castle at Sudeley in Gloucestershire. In 1808 he was delighted to accept a knighthood from the Swedish order of St Joachim – a totally bogus distinction – and began signing himself 'Sir'.

Sadly for Brydges, it all went peer-shaped. His claim to the Chandos barony was thoroughly investigated by a committee, who concurred that the claim was unfounded. The events that followed were arguably the silliest ever to have wasted the time of the House of Commons. His resubmitted his claim again and again, and each time it was rejected for lack of documentary proof. Brydges simply decided to invent some. He 'found' a small black box in an attic, which he said was full of documents supporting his claim to the peerage. This discovery, however, was undermined by his long refusal to let anyone else study them. In 1803, after thirteen and a half years during which the Committee of Privileges sat twenty-seven times, they decided that Brydges 'has not made out his Claim to be the said Baron' and the case was closed for good. Brydges, however, was not going to give up his title without a fight. He proceeded to bombard every peer in the House of Lords with letters urging them to vote against the Committee's recommendation – a gross breach of parliamentary etiquette, which resulted in a humiliating public rebuke.

Still Brydges persisted. When he compiled the new edition of *Collin's Peerage*, the standard reference of its kind for the Georgian era, he dedicated thirty-six pages of it to his own family. Brydges spent the rest of his life struggling to prove that his title was valid, in a single year writing thirty-three letters to the prime minister, only one of which was answered. He published at his own expense a book *Lex Terrae* is which he argued that the House of Lords had limited powers, which he was not obliged to take any notice of. Finally he published another book, *Stemmata Illustria*, that tried to prove that he was descended from the Merovingian kings of the fifth century. In 1814, after what the *Dictionary of National Biography* calls 'intense pressure', he was created a baronet in his own right. Brydges died in 1837 aged seventy-five, the last of a line that didn't actually exist. His absurd pursuit of a title had cost him an estimated one hundred thousand pounds – almost six million pounds at today's values.

5

There's Nowt so Hard as Toffs

An eighteenth-century gentleman was required to have what was known as 'bottom'. It was a shipping metaphor and referred to stability. Today we would call it 'guts'.

Bottom implied courage, fortitude and coolness under pressure and was the most admirable quality a man of breeding could possess. Gambling far more than you could possibly afford was one way of showing you had bottom; drinking vast quantities of port was another. Taking part in a duel was the boldest statement that you had bottom because it showed you had the courage to risk your life over a matter of honour.

No one could argue that William Petty, 2nd Earl of Shelburne, didn't have bottom, if not a complete set of gonads. In March 1780 he traded insults in the House of Commons with Colonel Fullarton, MP for Plympton. Shelburne had maligned Fullarton's regiment – a red rag to a bull for a serving officer. Fullarton countered with a provocative remark about Shelburne's 'aristocratic insolence'. The earl responded in the only way proper and challenged Fullarton to a pistol duel. The two men and their seconds met in the grey dawn of Hyde Park. Both men missed with their first round of shots, but the colonel fired again and shot off Shelburne's right testicle. Despite this, Shelburne deliberately discharged his second shot in the air. When asked how he was, the injured earl, coolly observing his wound, replied: 'I don't think Lady Shelburne will be the worse for it.'

As a method of settling differences, the duel of honour had its origins in medieval trial by combat and the cult of chivalry, with its tournaments and jousts.* The private duel first emerged in Italy in the fifteenth century, then spread like an epidemic across Europe. France embraced the lethal fad with the most enthusiasm, then took it to new levels of butchery. Duelling was illegal and it usually took place in private, so no one knows exactly how many took place, but it has been estimated that during the brief reign

---

* Although these events were supposed to be a celebration of the ideals of chivalry and the rituals of knighthood, they weren't always conducted in a gentlemanly fashion. In Flanders, when Herman 'the Iron' defeated fellow knight Guy in trial by combat, after being kicked from his horse, Herman pretended he was dead then reached up and tore off Guy's testicles.

of Henry IV from 1589 to 1607 as many as eight thousand French aristocrats died fighting private duels. Some took place brazenly in public. The Place Royale in Paris was so popular among duellists that spectators would hang around the balconies and windows surrounding the square waiting for the next one. On a single day, on 12 May 1627, the blood of six dead young French noblemen was spilled on the Place Royal cobblestones.

French noblemen could pick a quarrel at the drop of a hat – literally, in the case of the notorious 'duel of the hat' between Vallon Lagarde and Bazanez. The latter was jealous of Vallon's fame as a duellist so he sent him a hat, along with a note daring him to wear it in public. The two men met and exchanged insults, and duelling commenced, Lagarde supposedly bashing his tormentor over the head with the pommel of his sword before stabbing him several times: each stab was accompanied by a curse – 'this is for the hat' and 'this is for the feathers' and 'this is for the tassels', and so on (evidently this was a very fancy hat). After being pierced by multiple sword thrusts, Bazanez knocked Lagarde to the ground, stabbed him fourteen times, then bit a chunk out of his opponent's chin. Despite considerable loss of blood, both men lived to fight again.

One notorious French duellist, the Duc de Guise, was famous for killing a father and son in successive encounters in 1613. The first duel with the elderly Baron de Luz was fought over a point of historical fact – as good a reason as any at the time. The second duel was with the baron's avenging son, fought with swords on horseback; this dispute was concluded when the Duc grabbed his opponent's sword arm and drove the weapon through the young man's throat.

The prize for the highest number of duels fought at this time by a single man goes to the lunatic Frenchman Chevalier d'Andrieux, who killed seventy-two men in duels before his thirtieth birthday. One of his victims boasted, rashly: 'Chevalier, you will be the tenth man I have killed', to which d'Andrieux replied, 'and you will be my seventy-second', before killing him on the spot.

Despite Louis XIV's efforts to put an end to it by threatening to torture, exile or execute anyone who took part in one, duelling continued to flourish in France. One of the most vexatious Frenchmen of the period was the Duc de Richelieu, who seems have been almost permanently engaged in *affaires d'honneur*. In 1734 he killed one of his own relatives, the Prince de Lixen, after a minor squabble over the dress code at the siege of Phillipsburg. Richelieu was also the cause of an unprecedented duel between two females over *him*; Madame de Polignac and Madame de Nesle fought with pistols in the Bois de Boulogne, resulting in minor injuries on both sides.

The history of French swordplay was rich in eccentrics. The foppish Count d'Orsay, an early nineteenth-century French dandy of ambiguous sexual orientation, took part in several duels but was always careful to ask his opponents not to wound him in the face: for the count this would be a fate considerably worse than dishonour or death. Another character, known as Chevalier d'Éon, has to date been the subject of at least sixteen biographies. He entered the service of King Louis XV, first as a soldier, then later as diplomat and spy. D'Éon also had a key role in negotiating the Peace of Paris in 1763, ending the seven years' war between France and Britain. After that he lived in London for about thirteen years making a living from demonstration fencing matches. The Chevalier was a transvestite who not only carried out his spying missions disguised as a woman, but also wore dresses in his daily life. London society, which at the time was not especially known for its tolerance of Frenchmen, let alone French secret agents in frocks, was confounded and fascinated by the Chevalier. There were several bets made on the subject of his sexuality, including £120,000 in a single wager. In 1777 there was even a judicial enquiry held into it at the Guildhall in London: this investigation, not having an actual person, let alone an anatomical examination to fall back on, failed to arrive at a conclusion. It wasn't until 1810, when he died at the age of eighty-one, that a post-mortem confirmed to public satisfaction that the Chevalier was indeed a fella.

One theory offered for his open cross-dressing was that he had threatened to publish secret correspondence and blow the lid off his work as a spy for the French King. The Chevalier, it was said, had to remain dressed as a woman to avoid being arrested and deported back to a French prison – some kind of Bonnie Prince Charlie-style disguise that extended for the remainder of his life out of necessity. A more likely explanation is that he just enjoyed it. By all accounts he was such a remarkably convincing woman that he even managed to fool Casanova, who you would expect to have been an expert in such matters. The National Portrait Gallery in London, however, has a portrait of a rather butch-looking middle-aged woman, which for many years was catalogued as 'Portrait of a Woman with a Feather in Her Hat', but in 2012 was identified as a long-lost portrait of the Chevalier. It was spotted by an eagle-eyed art collector who couldn't help noticing that it was clearly 'a bloke in a dress'. The stubble was a dead giveaway.

In England, as in most of Europe, duels occupied a strange position in law. James I made duelling illegal in 1613 but the authorities were usually willing to turn a blind eye. Even when prosecutions were brought, juries were reluctant to convict. If you killed someone in a duel, at worst you would face a manslaughter charge, but usually you would be acquitted outright – unless you infringed the rules of duelling through cheating. If you were a nobleman you were more or less guaranteed to avoid prison, thanks to an anachronistic legal loophole. Until it was abolished in the 1840s, any English peer of the realm charged with manslaughter could plead 'benefit of the clergy'. If a noble-man could read or recite a verse from the New Testament, he could walk out of court a free man. Benefit of the clergy was only available on charges of manslaughter, but if you were unlucky enough to be convicted of murder there was always the likelihood of a royal pardon to fall back on. In the case of Earl Talbot, who duelled with John Wilkes, the earl received his pardon from King George III beforehand and carried it in his pocket, just in case.

The British were never quite as fanatical as the French about duelling but they had their moments. The first recorded duel in England took place in 1609 between Sir Henry Wharton and Sir James Stewart. We don't know the cause but we know the outcome was a score-draw – they both ended up dead. There followed an explosion of duel-ling among the British nobility, which peaked between 1610 and 1619. For some reason 1613 was a particularly violent year. The best-known duel of that summer, and of the whole period, was between Edward Sackville, the future 4th Earl of Dorset, and Edward Bruce, 2nd Lord Kinross. The two twenty-three-year-olds were good friends but fell out over a society beauty called Venetia Stanley. They agreed to duel to decide who should become her husband, but to avoid punishment by the authorities they went to Bergen in Holland to fight. Both men were seriously injured and Bruce died from his wounds a few days later.

Unfortunately, this grand gesture was completely lost on Miss Stanley. Sackville arrived back in England to claim his bride only to discover that she had decided to marry someone else. Over time, France became the most popular destination for English duellists hoping to avoid prosecution. In 1839 Lord Loftus and Lord Hardy went to Boulogne in the morning, exchanged shots and were home in time for tea.

The interregnum saw a decline in duelling but the return from exile of King Charles II in 1660 restored some colour and glamour to a nation starved of both. With the king came a group of young aristocrats who had shared the hard times and were now keen to have some fun, and there was a surge in binge drinking and duelling, the two combining with often deadly consequences. Young noblemen provoked quarrels by being rude to women at the theatre or shoving one another off the pavement: it was fashionable at the time for gentlemen to wear a dress sword, which should have served as a constant reminder where the argument was likely to go next. One of the biggest offenders was the king's close friend, the Duke of Buckingham. In 1667 Buckingham fought and killed the Earl of Shrewsbury on Putney Heath. Samuel Pepys takes up the story:

My Lord Shrewsbury is run through the body, from the right breast through the shoulder . . . this will make the world think that the King hath good councillors about him, when the Duke of Buckingham, the greatest man about him, is a fellow of no more sobriety than to fight about a whore.

The 'whore' in question was Shrewsbury's wife, with whom Buckingham was having an affair. It was rumoured that on the night after the duel, Buckingham slept with Lady Shrewsbury in the same bloodstained shirt he had worn while killing her husband.

Accusations of cheating and non-payment of gambling debts were among the commonest causes of duels. Affronts to honour varied from the trivial to the ridiculous. In 1731 a challenge arose from 'allegations of effeminacy', another in 1777 was sparked by 'marks of rudeness' including 'picking teeth and lounging at a table with his feet in the challenger's face'. One duel in 1824 was a consequence of a squabble over a game of billiards, another was over 'unjustifiable assertions against a gentleman's sister': in the latter case, the challenger thought it was worth travelling all the way from Madras to England to put a bullet in the thigh of the man who had traduced his sibling. In 1765, Lord Byron, great uncle of the poet, ran a sword through the stomach of his neighbour and cousin William Chaworth during a dispute over the most efficient method of hanging game. Unusually, the duel was fought indoors, in a dimly lit backroom in the Stars and Garter Tavern in London. Chaworth, incontrovertibly, showed 'bottom'. Before succumbing to his fatal injury, he lamented his failure to pick his fight somewhere with better lighting, then dictated a letter which stated that the duel was a fair fight.

THE DUELLING CODE

In their purest form, duels were so regulated that they had everything except an offside rule. Let's suppose you are an eighteenth-century aristocrat and you are looking forward to a duel. Perhaps someone has just trod on your dog or made an offensive remark about your mistress.

First comes the challenge. It is a bit more complicated than slapping your opponent in the face with a glove (although slapping a nobleman in the face with a glove would have done the trick). If someone has insulted you, step back from the situation; decide if it's really serious. If it is and you still want a duel, you should issue your challenge in writing. Try to keep it as civil as possible. That's not to say that lots of challenges weren't rude or that all of them were written down.

You're under no obligation to accept a challenge from someone you don't consider your social equal. For example, when the future Viscount Townshend challenged the Earl of Leicester to a duel in 1759 over a dispute about killing foxes on their estates, the earl refused to fight because he outranked his challenger. It had nothing to do with the fact that the earl was also elderly, infirm, couldn't hit a barn door with a pistol and hadn't handled a sword for twenty years. A gentleman's refusal to accept your challenge can also be deeply humiliating. In 1741, when Lord Windsor refused Charles Nourse's challenge to a duel on the grounds that Nourse was too old, the challenger went home and cut his own throat.

The next rule of duelling is to get a second – a gentleman's gentleman – someone you can trust with your life. The primary job of your second is to try to prevent the duel from taking place. Ideally he should talk to your opponent and the other second and try to reach an agreement about an apology. The preliminaries can take weeks or months; a letter requesting an apology is sent, more letters are exchanged. If after all that a peaceful resolution can't be reached, plans for the duel can commence.

A good second will make sure that your weapons are in good working order and that your opponent doesn't quietly stab you in the back or shoot you in the back of the head while you are looking the other way. Until the eighteenth century it was also normal for the seconds to get involved in the fighting if necessary.* Of course it is also very possible that you won't have any friends willing to risk prison for you: it is, after all, illegal to fight a duel or act as a second even if no one is hurt or killed.

And so to the day of the duel. An English duelling manual written in 1838 advised participants to take coffee and a biscuit before their duel, but to avoid a big breakfast. Once battle commences, it has to proceed in accordance with the duelling code. Entire manuals were published on the protocol and mechanics of the duel. According to the duelling code of honour, the *Code Duello*, a duellist must not 'wear light-coloured clothing, ruffles, military

---

* When the Duc de Beaufort killed his brother-in-law the Duc de Nemours in 1652 their seconds followed the fashion of the day by piling into each other. Accordingly, the Marquis de Villars shot dead his opposite number d'Héricourt, who he had never met before.

decorations, or any other . . . attractive object, upon which the eye of his antagonist [could] . . . rest'. as it could affect the outcome of the duel. In the Kaiser's Germany, black frock-coats were the order of the day, often worn with black top hats, to reflect the gravity of the occasion, like duelling undertakers.

The good news is that the *Code Duello* does not require duelling 'to the death', although this might be the ultimate end to your duel. Duelling is about recovering honour, not about killing. When duels with pistols became popular some duellists deliberately fired into the air or the ground, although, confusingly, the code forbade this.

THE KILLING FIELD

In England there was little or no public protest about duelling, until the outrage caused by a spectacularly brutal contest fought between two leading scions of the British aristocracy, the Whig Lord Mohun (pronounced Moon) and the Tory Duke of Hamilton in 1712. It was the bloodiest and most horrific duel ever fought on British soil.

Lord Charles Mohun's life wouldn't look out of place in a Gothic novel. His father was killed in a duel when Charles was five months old (a sword thrust through the stomach) leaving his mother a widow with a mass of debts. As a result, young Mohun was never schooled and in his teens turned to gambling to pay for an increasingly spendthrift lifestyle. He was married off to his legal guardian's daughter when he was just fourteen, but was disappointed to discover that his new wife didn't come with a substantial dowry, so he dumped her.

He fought his first duel when he was fifteen, after

quarrelling with the twenty-year-old Lord Kennedy: minor wounds were inflicted on both sides. A few months later he was implicated in his first murder. In 1692 while binge drinking in London with a friend, Richard Hill, they decided to kidnap the object of Hill's teenage crush, Anne Bracegirdle, a respectable actress. Hill convinced himself that Anne's stage partner, the upstanding and happily married William Mountford, was a real-life love rival. When Mohun and Hill accosted the actress, Mountford, who happened to be nearby, stepped in to help her. As Mohun watched (or, according to some eyewitness accounts, pinned Mountford's arms back) Hill stabbed him through the chest. Not yet sixteen, Mohun was sensationally tried for murder and acquitted at Westminster Hall. He celebrated his court victory by attacking a coachman on Pall Mall, then later walked into a London coffee house and beat a writer named Dyer around the head with a wooden cudgel for writing unflattering things about him in a pamphlet.

In 1697 Mohun was involved in a drunken brawl in a tavern in which Captain William Hill of the Coldstream Guards was stabbed to death. Once again he was indicted for murder, again the House of Lords acquitted him. To celebrate once more escaping the noose, Mohun and his friend Edward Rich, 6th Earl of Warwick, drank heavily at a Charing Cross tavern and later that evening engaged in a drunken brawl in the pitch-black of Leicester Fields with another army officer, Captain Richard Coote, resulting in the death of the latter. Mohun was tried for accessory to murder but acquitted again.

His luck had held so far because he was a friend of King William III and had important connections in the Whig Party. In Mohun's dealings with James Douglas, 4th Duke of Hamilton, he was less fortunate.

Hamilton's reputation was only marginally better than Mohun's. He was by all accounts a pleasure-seeking, bone-headed wastrel who spent his life drinking and whoring. He fathered several illegitimate children and was virtually disowned by his parents for his debauchery and for using the Hamilton estate as a cash machine to fund his rakish lifestyle. Although related by marriage – both had married nieces of the 2nd Earl of Macclesfield – there was a long history of bad blood between Hamilton and Mohun. The origins of their duel were very complicated (to date there have been two books written on the subject) but the main source of their grievance was a disputed inheritance and a harsh exchange of words spoken in the course of a Chancery suit. There was also a much deeper political dimension and it has long been speculated that the duel was part of a massive conspiracy orchestrated to prevent a Stuart restoration.

Mohun was a diehard Whig, committed to the expulsion of the Stuart dynasty and the Hanoverian succession. Hamilton was on the Jacobite wing of the Tory Party and had connections with James, the 'Old Pretender', at his court in France. In 1712 the Stuart Queen Anne appointed Hamilton her ambassador to France with orders to make peace with Louis XIV after ten indecisive years of the War of Spanish Succession. This rang alarm bells in the Whig camp, because in the event of a Stuart restoration, the likes of Mohun, who had staked everything on the Whigs and the Hanoverian succession, would be ruined. Hamilton had to be stopped at all costs from going to France and making the final arrangements with Louis XIV and the Pretender that would doom the Whigs to exile. So Mohun had another reason for attempting the desperate tactic of picking a fight and provoking Hamilton to a duel.

Their quarrel was resolved in the manner of a classic western, an eighteenth-century High Noon, or in their case, High Dawn. Mohun was thirty-seven years old. Hamilton, although the more experienced swordsman, was fifty-four, overweight and out of shape. They met in Hyde Park at 7 a.m. on the Sunday morning of 15 November 1712. Mohun arrived for the duel directly from a brothel with his second, General George MacCartney, a seedy character and convicted rapist who was said to be living off Mohun's handouts. On the way, Mohun ordered his coachman to wake up a local innkeeper so that he could enjoy a jug of ale before the fight. The duke arrived shortly after, seconded by his illegitimate son, Colonel John Hamilton.

At the time it was still accepted practice for a second to cross swords with his opposite number, should both be inclined. Mohun proposed that the quarrel be settled between the principals and the seconds should stand aside, but MacCartney, who was said to have personal issues with John Hamilton, was up for a fight and the duke's second felt the same way. At this, the participants drew their swords.

As accounts made clear, there was nothing remotely gentlemanly about the fight and nor was there any pretence at clever swordplay. It was a brutal, no-holds-barred bloodbath. Mohun and Hamilton charged at each other and set about slashing, hacking and grabbing like wild animals. Hamilton drew first blood by slicing open a six-inch gash in Mohun's left side. Mohun slashed back, opening an eight-inch cut in Hamilton's right leg, exposing the bone, then cut into Hamilton's elbow, slicing through a main artery. Despite devastating blood loss, Hamilton fought back, skewering

144

Mohun below the lower right ribcage, the point of the sword emerging from his left hip. As Mohun fell backwards he slashed into the left side of Hamilton's chest, across the lung. Hamilton wasn't quite finished yet. He stood over the fallen Mohun and thrust his sword through Mohun's groin, the tip exiting through his left buttock. Mohun, who lost three fingers trying to grab Hamilton's blade, was meanwhile desperately hacking at Hamilton's foot.

At this point some early morning Hyde Park strollers came across the scene and gaped in astonishment at the sight of two peers of the realm cutting each other into ribbons, pouring blood from multiple wounds like the Black Knight sketch in Monty's Python's *Holy Grail*. As Mohun lay dying, the mortally wounded Hamilton staggered to a nearby tree, where he collapsed. The whole event had taken less than a couple of minutes. Several bystanders pounced on the tree and began stripping away pieces of bark for souvenirs.

It says something about how swiftly and shockingly the scene unfolded that none of the onlookers could agree exactly who took part in the fighting. Some said that the seconds Colonel Hamilton and MacCartney joined in, but according to another report some bystanders confiscated their swords and bent them double, rendering them useless. There was lingering suspicion that Mohun's second finished the duke off after his principal had been put out of action. One of Mohun's footmen may have also joined in and attacked the duke. If true, this put a completely different complexion on the whole business; rather than being a spat between two gentlemen to settle private differences, it was looking more like a murderous conspiracy with possible political motives.

Both of the seconds went into hiding immediately afterwards. Colonel Hamilton was later cleared of murder but found guilty of manslaughter and was punished by branding on his hand. MacCartney was tried a few years later after returning from self-imposed exile in Holland. He was also cleared of murder but found guilty of manslaughter.

Polite society was deeply shocked by the ferocity of the duel, although on a personal level the deaths of two noblemen, one a well-known thug and the other a buffoon, didn't elicit too much sympathy. The following year a bill was introduced in the House of Commons to toughen up sanctions against duelists, especially those who fought to satisfy gentlemanly honour. It was lost after two readings, but in a watered-down version the government passed legislation banning the use of seconds. Whatever the law said about it, until health and safety took hold in the nineteenth century, duelling continued to be an entirely acceptable and respectable way of settling gentlemanly disputes and noblemen continued to maim and kill each other with impunity.

Some quick-tempered aristocrats couldn't be bothered to wait for a properly organised duel to settle their differences. Looked at another way, a 'duel' was very often just a convenient cover for murder. For example, in 1776 the 3rd Earl of Kingston killed his son-in-law Richard Fitzgerald in a supposed duel after Fitzgerald eloped with Kingston's daughter Mary. Kingston and his son sought Fitzgerald out and a brawl followed during which the latter was shot dead. It was generally agreed that this was stretching the definition of a duel beyond reasonable limits and Knighton was charged with murder. He elected to be tried by his peers in the House of Lords but was acquitted, no evidence offered against him.

Duelling was not entirely the preserve of gentlemen. Known as 'petticoat duels', several affairs of honour between ladies took place in France during the mid-1600s. Just like their male counterparts, female duellists fought over the trivial. Two highborn French ladies crossed swords because one thought she was entitled to precedence of place at a society event. In 1792 *Carlton-House Magazine* ran an article with an accompanying illustration of two English female petticoat duellists identified as Lady Almeria Braddock and Mrs Elphinstone. They crossed swords after the latter paid a social call to the home of Lady Braddock and insulted her host over a cup of tea with a casual comment about her age. Lady B couldn't let the catty remark go and challenged her guest to a duel in Hyde Park. They started with pistols; Mrs Elphinstone came nearest to inflicting injury by knocking Lady Braddock's hat off. They switched to swords and Lady Braddock struck a light wound to her opponent's arm. Honour satisfied, both ladies went home.*

One of the most intriguing duels fought between women (OK, *the* most intriguing) was the only one featuring exposed breasts. It took place in August 1892 in Liechtenstein, between Princess Pauline Metternich and the Countess Kielmannsegg, arising from a disagreement over the floral arrangements for an upcoming musical exhibition. The confrontation was refereed by Baroness Lubinska, who had a degree in medicine (a rarity for a woman in those days) and whose job it was to minister to any wounds incurred. Before the proceedings began, the

* This story, repeated often over the intervening two centuries, may be apocryphal. Apart from the single magazine article there is no other contemporary account of the duel being fought.

147

baroness pointed out that many insignificant injuries in duels often became septic due to strips of clothing being driven into the wound by the point of a sword, so she advised both parties to strip to the waist.

Both women obediently disrobed, footmen and coachmen meanwhile ordered to observe decorum and stand some distance away with their backs to the action. In the ensuing swordplay both ladies drew blood, the sight of which caused the respective lady seconds to faint. At this, the male servants rushed to offer assistance but Baroness Lubinska saw them off with her furled umbrella, shouting, 'Avert your eyes you lustful wretches!' *Pall Mall Gazette* reported that, after both combatants had received wounds, their seconds 'advised them to embrace, kiss, and make friends'; which they accordingly did.

Topless female fencing did not catch on; you can imagine the TV bidding wars for coverage of clothing-optional female Olympic fencing if it had.

FEUDING FITZGERALD

In Regency London, young noblemen would go to the playhouse just to insult some woman, thereby provoking a duel that might further their reputation among their peers. The theatre was a dangerous place; rowdiness got so out of hand that some owners discouraged members of the audience from attacking the actors by arranging a row of spikes in front of the stage. In 1787 the Duke of Leinster impaled himself on one of these and was maimed for life.

The master of the 'Did you spill my pint?' method of provoking duels was George Robert 'Fighting' Fitzgerald, a descendant of the great Desmond dynasty. Raised in

Ireland and schooled at Eton, Fitzgerald fought his first duel when he was fifteen and went on to fight at least twelve – and possibly as many as twenty-seven – duels in his short lifetime, provoking them by rudeness, or on one occasion by shooting a man's wig off his head. Fitzgerald was mad, bad and dangerous to know – or even to bump into by accident. In an English coffee house, he sliced the nose off a student who claimed he could 'smell a Catholic'. In Paris, he ran his rapier through a man who accidentally stood on his dog. On this occasion, however, an enraged mob followed him back to his lodgings, trashed his carriage and killed his valet. He also kept a pet bear, dressed it in clothes and took it on the Castlebar–Dublin stagecoach to terrorise other passengers. Loose comment about Fitzgerald's bear, of course, was also grounds for a duel.

Surprisingly, Fitzgerald wasn't an especially good marksman or swordsman; his skill was in surviving duels when he was on the losing side. He didn't care much for duelling etiquette and was open to any ruse that might save his skin. He would crouch low to present a smaller target, or wear armour under his outer clothing, or simply flee the duelling ground if he didn't fancy his chances of winning. He was badly injured several times and, on one occasion, had part of his head shot away in a duel, replaced by a silver plate inserted in his skull. As the surgeon worked to remove the bullet, Fitzgerald, in agony and streaming with blood, begged him not to damage his wig.*

---

* Short fuses ran in the Fitzgerald family. Once, when prematurely informed that his son lay dying as a result of a duel, George Fitzgerald senior was so upset that he ran his sword through the first man who offered his condolences.

This injury, however, clearly affected his judgement: whereas in his youth he had been merely violent, Fitzgerald became increasingly psychotic. He would lash out at complete strangers on the street or snatch their ring or watch. If he failed to pick a fight in a bar or a theatre he would stand in the middle of a narrow street waiting for someone to jostle him.

Fitzgerald's appetite for random violence finally caught up with him in 1786 when he got involved in another deadly dispute with a neighbour, Patrick McDonnell. By this time the authorities in County Mayo had grown impatient of the thirty-eight-year-old nobleman's habit of using his family connections to flout the law and they tried him for murder. While he was lying in Castlebar jail awaiting trial, McDonnell's relatives broke in and gave him a savage beating, leaving Fitzgerald for dead. He survived, not that it mattered much because he was hanged for murder the next morning. On the first attempt the rope broke, at which he quipped that the courts of Mayo were too mean to buy a rope strong enough to hang him. The replacement, however, proved more than adequate. After the execution, a Dublin newspaper reported, 'Every part of Fitzgerald's body was scarred with wounds, which he had received in the various duels he had been engaged in [including] . . . a large hole where a ball had lodged in one of his hips and another in the small of one of his legs.' Fitzgerald left a young daughter, who survived her father by eight years before dying suddenly and unexpectedly. It was said she died of shock after reading an account of her father's execution in *Gentleman's Magazine*.

POLITE EXCHANGES OF BULLETS

The duel in the Star and Garter between Lord Byron's uncle and William Chaworth in 1765 was one of the last encounters in England fought with swords. From now on the pistol would be the weapon of choice in settling disputes.

In theory, pistols should have made duelling more deadly. The rules required that each participant stand their ground while an opponent fired at them from just thirty to forty feet away. A lead ball burying itself anywhere in a body generally proved fatal, if not instantly then later from infection. In practice, however, pistols led to a rise in the number of duels, but a surprising reduction in the number of fatalities. In the hands of an unskilled marksman, even at close range, the pistols of the time were far from accurate. They also offered duellists opportunities to refuse to fire, or to fire in the air, thus ending the contest. More often than not, pistol duels were a symbolic show of arms to demonstrate that honour has been satisfied. You turned up, fired in the air, or wide, shook hands and everyone went home happy.

Of course, you had to be very sure that your opponent would do the same. In Germany, where they tended to take their duels more seriously, firing over an opponent's head was frowned on. When a German and a Spanish diplomat duelled at The Hague in 1892, the Marquis de Vallarda fired in the air and was more than a little annoyed when he was promptly shot in the hip by Freiherr von Gärtner-Griebenow. If the offended party was still not satisfied, in theory they could carry on firing at each other until someone got hit, but more than three exchanges of fire was considered not only ungentlemanly but frankly embarrassing for both parties.

In many cases pistol duels were (from a spectator's point of view) disappointingly bloodless affairs. The poor level of marksmanship of eighteenth-century combat was striking. In 1770 Lord George Germaine and Governor Johnstone emerged without a scratch after both men fired twice, aiming to hit. Three years later Lord Bellamont received only a slight graze from his duel with Lord Townshend. In 1786 Lord MacCartney, governor of Madras, fell out with his commander-in-chief and fellow Scot, James Stuart. The two men kept their differences under wraps until they returned to Britain, then Stuart insisted on a duel. Having only one leg he had to be propped up against a tree. MacCartney, however, was short-sighted and, although Stuart was slightly injured, neither was able to do the other significant harm. In 1822 the Duke of Buckingham called out the Duke of Bedford, who had accused him of political snobbery. This rare encounter between a pair of England's highest-ranking noblemen was not as thrilling as some might have hoped. Bedford fired in the air, Buckingham didn't fire at all. Not a drop of ducal blood was spilled.

Although most pistol duels were non-fatal it was always a good idea to bring a doctor with you, just in case. The balls of lead shot travelled slowly and often didn't pass all the way through the body, so the physician would attempt to extract them where the victim fell, without anaesthetic. Seconds and onlookers on Brighton beach in 1806 were surprised when Humphrey Howarth, MP for Evesham, arrived for a duel with Lord Barrymore, then removed all his clothes and presented himself for combat stark naked. Howarth had been an army surgeon in India and knew that gunshot wounds were often aggravated by pieces of clothing being driven by the ball into the wound, so he took the sensible precaution of stripping off to reduce the risk of infection. In the event no blood was spilt. Lord Barrymore flatly refused to duel with a naked man and the two parted without further discussion. Howarth's thinking was way ahead of his time because it would be another sixty-four years before the theories of the British surgeon Joseph Lister revolutionised surgical procedures with the introduction of antiseptic.

Duels were fought usually with either swords or pistols, but on rare occasions, both. In November 1773 the Irishman Count Rice and the Frenchman Viscount du Barry fell out over an unknown lady while taking the waters at Bath. A duel was arranged and they set off for nearby Claverton Down. They started with pistols and both men took a bullet, Rice in his thigh, du Barry in the chest. Both fired again and missed. At this they both threw away their pistols and drew their swords. Du Barry collapsed to the ground and begged for mercy, but then a few moments later fell back and died. The matter caused quite a sensation, as du Barry was the nephew of the famous Madame du Barry, mistress of King Louis XV.

Disputes over women were one of the most common pretexts for duels. Russia's greatest poet, Alexander Pushkin, didn't need much of an excuse to call someone out. Born into Moscow nobility, Pushkin was notoriously touchy about matters of honour and fought at least twenty-nine duels over slights about his writing, insults directed at his friends, women he was courting, arguments at the dinner table, comments about his terrible manners – he even fought a duel over the weather. He once fought an army officer after accusing him of cheating at cards. Pushkin calmly stood eating cherries while his opponent took aim and missed his target; he then contemptuously refused to return fire because he thought his opponent wasn't worth the powder and shot.

Pushkin died at the age of thirty-seven, at the peak of his career, after being fatally wounded in the stomach by a French cavalry officer, Georges D'Anthès, having convinced himself that his killer was flirting with his wife. Curiously, Pushkin's death imitated that of the hero of his book *Eugene Onegin*. It was all the more ironic because a major theme of the book is the relationship between literature and real life. The poet's last home, where he lay dying for two days after the duel, is now a popular museum, displaying his death mask and the very last waistcoat he ever wore, complete with bullet hole.

Another notoriously quarrelsome Russian duellist was Count Fyodor Tolstoy, a heavy drinker with a hair-trigger temper. He fought his first duel when he was seventeen and went on to kill eleven men in duels: he boasted that every one had been fought for trivial reasons.* Tolstoy was a natural fencer and an accurate shot. One of his adversaries, a naval officer wary of Tolstoy's reputation with the sword and the pistol, insisted on fighting in the naval manner – that is, grabbing hold of each other and jumping into the water, victory going to the party who escaped drowning. Tolstoy rejected his terms because he couldn't swim, but the man taunted him, at which Tolstoy rushed at him, dragging both of them into the sea. Both men were pulled out of the water but the officer died from his injuries days later.

---

* His cousin Leo Tolstoy, who called him an 'extraordinary, criminal, and attractive man', fictionalised him as Dolokhov in *War and Peace*.

One of the most unusual duels of Napoleon's reign took place in, or rather, over Paris in 1808. Two French gentlemen, Monsieurs de Grandpre and de Pique, chose to fight from balloons after quarrelling over a dancer, Mademoiselle Tirevit. Watched by a huge crowd, the duellists climbed into their aircraft near the Tuileries Palace and rose to two thousand feet. With the balloons about eighty yards apart, de Pique fired his blunderbuss and missed. De Grandpre aimed his more effectively: de Pique's balloon collapsed and he and his second fell head-first to their deaths on the rooftops below.

The prize for duelling oddness, however, goes to the Prussian Rudolf Virchow, who was challenged by his Chancellor Otto von Bismarck in 1865 and exercised his right to choose weapons by opting for sausages. The idea was that he and Bismarck would be presented with a choice of pork sausages to eat. One was a regular sausage, the other infected with the larvae of a trichinella parasite: whoever consumed the tainted sausage would suffer a terrible and possibly fatal bout of food poisoning. Bismarck declined to take part: he was a born soldier trained for combat, but he was not prepared for a slow death in a puddle of his own faeces.

Today, few politicians would even think of resigning on a point of principle let alone put their lives on the line over one, but a bad-tempered exchange in parliament was once a routine excuse for pistols at dawn. In the eighteenth century the House of Commons was considerably more testosterone-charged than modern-day Westminster and MPs regularly called each other out in disputes arising from parliamentary business.

In May 1798, Britain's prime minister, William Pitt,

upset MP George Tierney, treasurer of the navy, when he suggested that Tierney had been unpatriotic in debates about the French. Tierney called Pitt out and the two men met twelve paces apart on Putney Common a day before Pitt's thirty-ninth birthday. Observers noted that Pitt had an unfair advantage; he was so skinny a strong breeze might knock him over, whereas Tierney was very fat and presented much the larger target. Both fired twice and missed. Satisfaction met on both sides, the two men withdrew unscathed. Even at the time people thought it absurd that Britain's war leader, just when the country's conflict with France was at a crucial stage, had chosen to risk his life in a trivial dispute with an obscure MP. King George III, enjoying one of his sane spells, was said to be furious.

Just over thirty years later another prime minister was at it. This time it was Britain's war hero the Duke of Wellington, conqueror of Napoleon. The Iron Duke said he was against duelling because it led to indiscipline in the ranks and was a waste of good officers, but it didn't stop him rising to the bait when he was called out in 1829 at the ripe old age of sixty-one. Wellington was angered by some allegations of political skulduggery by Lord Winchilsea and the two men agreed to settle their differences with pistols at dawn in a cabbage patch on Battersea Fields. Despite all his wartime trophies, Wellington didn't actually own a set of duelling pistols, although most aristocrats at the time had a pair for show even if they had no intention of using them, so he asked his second Sir Henry Hardinge if he could borrow his. Embarrassingly, Hardinge didn't own a set either, so they had to ask the attendant physician John Hume if he wouldn't mind bringing his along. Hardinge proved to be a useless second. His other job was to load Wellington's pistol for him, which he couldn't do, on account of his left hand having been blown off fourteen years earlier at Waterloo, so it fell to Dr Hulme to sort this out for them as well. It doesn't seem to have occurred to them that requiring a medical practitioner to bring and load the guns for a duel was asking above and beyond his job description, but Hulme did as he was told.

In the event Winchilsea arrived late, to the great annoyance of Wellington, who turned to his second and snapped: 'Now then Hardinge, look sharp and step out the ground. I have no time to waste. Damn it! Don't stick him so near the ditch. If I hit him, he will tumble in.' Winchilsea, out of gentlemanly honour, or more likely, realising that shooting the prime minister might be a move he'd live to regret, pointed his pistol at the ground. Seeing this, Wellington fired wide, but was such a useless shot that he almost hit his opponent's leg. Winchilsea fired in the air and apologised.

Once again, a British prime minister was held up to public ridicule for taking part in a silly dispute that could have had dire consequences. The respective reactions of Pitt and Wellington to the criticism, however, couldn't have been more different. After Pitt's duel he was quite rattled by the whole business, took to his sickbed and wasn't seen publicly or in the Commons for weeks afterwards. The elderly Iron Duke, however, found it all quite arousing. That evening he rushed to see his latest mistress, Mrs Arbuthnot, and greeted her with, 'Well, what do you think of a gentleman who has been fighting a duel?'

British MPs were still duelling over insults traded in the House of Commons as late as 1835. Lord Alvanley, overweight Regency buck and close friend of the Prince

Regent, was insulted by the Irish political leader Daniel O'Connell, who called him 'a bloated buffoon, a liar, a disgrace to his species'. Alvanley demanded satisfaction and, after a good deal of haggling, O'Connell, who had once duelled and sworn never to do it again, sent a substitute – his son, Morgan. The two men met and exchanged shots, but both walked away unscathed. On the way home Alvanley tipped the coachman a guinea. The honest driver, embarrassed by the size of the tip, protested that he had only taken him a short way out, but Alvanley corrected him. 'My friend, the guinea is for bringing me back, not for taking me out.'

By the end of the 1830s the tide of British public opinion had turned against duelling and by the 1850s it had died out completely, but there was still some hankering after the old ways. In 1881 Winston Churchill's father, Lord Randolph, challenged Lord Hartington to a duel after the latter called him 'vile, contumacious, and lying'. Hartington apologised and the matter was forgotten.

Germany was one of the last European countries to abandon the private duel. Well-bred Germans were in the habit of copying French fashion and they adopted duelling with enthusiasm despite having some of the toughest and oddest anti-duelling laws in Europe: typically, in 1695 a sixty-year-old survivor of a duel and the corpse of his victim were both hanged in Berlin. As in England and elsewhere, however, German courts were reluctant to prosecute the aristocracy. The word *satisfaktionfähig* entered the German vocabulary to indicate those people worthy of carrying a sword – mostly the nobility – indicating a mindset that would remain unaltered for the next 250 years. In the late nineteenth century support came from the very top, because the Kaiser himself was said to be a keen duellist. Most people have come to associate these aristocratic spats with the Prussian duelling scar caused by rapiers but in fact most German duels were fought with pistols at close range. The First World War virtually ended duelling in Germany. A few German aristocrats were calling each other out during the war years but afterwards there was a general backlash against anything regarded as Prussian.

In 1913 the Hungarian aristocrat and ex-prime minister Count Tisza fought a duel with the Marquis Pallavicini over an allegation of witness tampering in a political trial. They used heavy cavalry sabres and wore minimal protective equipment. According to the rules of engagement they were to fight until one of them was completely disabled – *hors de combat*. They fought for eleven minutes until a surgeon stepped in and stopped the duel. Both men had cuts to the forehead and neither could see for blood. It was the veteran Count Tisza's third duel that year.

Public duels between noblemen were still taking place in Paris into the 1920s. In September 1921 the Comte de Poret fought an unusually savage duel with Camile Lafarge. They began by firing at each other at a distance of twenty-five paces but, having both failed to hit their targets, they took to their swords. The contest was stopped when the Comte's forearm was completely sliced open from wrist to elbow and he could no longer hold his sword. It was the most publicised duel in France for years and the authorities were stung into action, bringing charges against both duellists and their seconds, the first time this had happened following a non-fatal duel for more than fifty years.

The British aristocratic impulse to rush to weapons in

matter of honour, however, was not quite forgotten either. In 1957 an Italian monarchist challenged the British peer Lord Altrincham to a duel 'to defend the honour of monarchy the world over' after Altrincham made some disparaging remarks about the Queen. The 3rd Baron Moynihan, who happened to be in Italy at the time, offered to take on the uppity Italian, remarking, 'I'll fight this Renato. He cannot be allowed to get away with this blow to British prestige.' Sadly, the Italian police intervened before it got tasty.

6

Sex and Snobbery

In 1767, the 2nd Viscount Bolingbroke, having spent all of his fortune on horses, cards and prostitutes, decided to marry a 'rich monster' to get himself out of a financial hole. First, however, he had to rid himself of his wife, Lady Diana Spencer. The divorce went through, but 'Bully's' heiress escaped his clutches, as did a second, a thirty-year-old lady from Bath called Miss Curtis who was worth about £43,000 a year. The desperate peer died unmarried and insane a few years later. His son George, the 3rd Viscount Bolingbroke, compounded the family's unfolding financial disaster by marrying the penniless daughter of his tutor. It needed only the 5th Viscount Bolingbroke in 1869 to marry the daughter of a blacksmith for the ruination of the family to be complete. In 1942 their fine Wiltshire seat, Lydiard House, home of the Bolingbrokes for more than five hundred years, became a corporation museum.

Marrying 'well' was the one obsession that united all aristocratic families. A good marriage could result in greater wealth or status; a bad match could bring social embarrassment or penury. The idea of marrying for love was generally beneath consideration. When John Spencer, ancestor of Diana, Princess of Wales, was presented with a list of eligible ladies drawn up by his grandmother Sarah, Duchess of Marlborough, in alphabetical order, he simply pointed to the first on the list beginning with a C – job done; her name was Georgina Carteret, daughter of the 2nd Earl Granville, and they were married in 1734.

Noble parents were frequently ruthless in their control of their daughters' marriages. Probably the most famous case of the bullied bride was Lady Jane Grey, who by her own account was beaten into agreeing to marry the Duke of Northumberland's son, Guildford Dudley. The only story to rival that of Lady Jane for parental brutality is that of Sir Edward Coke, seventeenth-century ex-Chief Justice, who forcibly removed his daughter Frances from her mother's household and then had the young woman tied to the bedpost and whipped to make her more amenable to a marriage to the brother of the king's favourite, the Duke of Buckingham, so as to ensure his own return to favour at court. The groom in question was mentally unstable and homosexual and, not surprisingly, the marriage failed and the bride ran off with a lover more to her liking. Marrying off a son or daughter was also a frequent and well-recognised method of clearing debts. The Duke of Richmond wiped out his gambling losses by pledging his eighteen-year-old son and heir to the Earl of Cadogan's thirteen-year-old daughter. This arranged marriage appears to have been much more successful; she bore him twelve children and was pregnant twenty-seven times.

Everyone, it seemed, knew everyone else's finances down to the last penny and who would inherit what and from whom. A wealthy, well-connected widow was a highly sought-after commodity and there were plenty of well-placed gentlemen willing to exploit her financial desirability. The most shockingly mercenary example of this was the marriage of the widowed Elizabeth Cavendish, eldest daughter of the 2nd Duke of Newcastle, known for most of her life as the 'Mad Duchess' of Albemarle. She was so gaga when she wed Ralph Montagu, a relation of the Duke of Manchester in 1692, that she thought she was marrying the Emperor of China.* A title and a lot of money could usually offset even the most serious personal deficiencies. George, 10th Earl of Lindsey, was considered to be 'weak in the head' and something of a family problem. They thought that the solution might well lie in a marriage with a wealthy heiress whose father would be dazzled by the idea of his daughter becoming a countess. On this occasion the scheme failed when the prospective father-in-law got a

---

* Montagu kept her in strict confinement in a couple of rooms at their home, only occasionally wheeling her in public to satisfy her relatives that she was still alive. The shabby deception didn't quite pay off. Much to the amusement of Montagu's critics, Elizabeth went on substantially to outlive her second husband, unaware of the world outside of her 'Chinese' court, until the age of eighty.

sneak preview of the proposed groom and couldn't work out if he was 'drunk or mad'. The tenth earl died unmarried at the age of sixty-two.

A few aristocratic daughters thwarted their family's marriage plans for them by eloping. In 1744 Georgiana Lennox fell in love with Henry Fox, a man not deemed by her parents, the Duke and Duchess of Richmond, to be of sufficiently noble birth to be an appropriate husband. The Richmonds had another suitor in mind and told Georgiana to take 'especial care over her toilette' in preparation for his visit. Georgiana sabotaged the meeting by shaving off her eyebrows, making her unfit to receive visitors. She and Fox had put in place plans to elope, which they soon did and entered into a clandestine union that produced at least three children. The sons of the aristocracy occasionally defied convention as well. The 9th Duke of St Albans caused a scandal by marrying some considerable distance beneath him an Irish woman called Elizabeth Gubbins: she was blamed by the duke's family for bringing insanity to the St Albans' bloodline, but to be fair they were well endowed in that department already.*

The practice of endogamy – 'keeping it in the family' to preserve wealth and status – presented certain problems. Parents who share their ancestry make their offspring more vulnerable to birth defects and harmful DNA

---

* The 3rd Duke of St Albans was known as the 'Simple Duke', his life described by his biographer as 'a glittering crescendo of feats of incompetence'. The 11th Duke spent the last thirty years of his life insane in a secure clinic: his brother joined him soon afterwards after attempting to burn down his old school, Eton College.

mutations. Brian Masters, author of *The Dukes*, calculates that more than a third of Britain's ducal families have one time or another been afflicted by mental instability and some still are. Of the other two-thirds, almost all of them have produced at least one eccentric whose sanity was questionable. According to Masters, without the injection of some different blood through adultery, it's possible that the entire British aristocracy would be mad as hatters.

Aristocratic marriages were generally a business arrangement and financial concerns could make or break a union, but there were occasional attempts to make the process a bit more romantic. Some dynastically approved marriages were actual love matches, although in the case of the 2nd Duke of Manchester, didn't remain so for long. The twenty-three-year-old duke was said to be so madly in love with the Duke of Montagu's daughter Isabella that he shut himself in a room with a pair of loaded pistols and made good on his threat to kill himself if she wouldn't have him. Unfortunately, his aim was poor. The first shot took away his right eye socket, the second shattered his jaw. He then tried to hang himself from the ceiling, but servants came to his rescue. Isabella was so impressed by this display of grim desperation that she consented to marry him on the spot, a hasty decision both parties soon lived to regret. Isabella gave her husband a hard time with her bizarre and uncompromising behaviour, including her habit of coming down to breakfast with a parrot, a monkey and a lapdog. She showed little sign of grief when he died at the age of thirty-nine, leaving her only the furniture of two upstairs rooms and everything else to his brother.

Charles Radclyffe, 5th Earl of Derwentwater, proposed on fifteen occasions to the wealthy but reluctant Charlotte,

Countess of Newburgh, who became so annoyed by the constant harassment that she bolted herself into her home and gave her servants instructions to throw him off the property on sight. The earl finally found a way into her house by climbing onto her roof and lowering himself down the chimney into her drawing room where, black from soot, he made his sixteenth marriage proposal. His persistence paid off and they were married in Brussels in 1724.

CRIMINAL CONVERSATION

As soon as a lady had done her duty and popped out an heir and a spare, she was free to introduce other gentlemen's genes into the baronial bloodline. In most stately homes adultery was taken for granted, provided the affair was conducted with discretion and didn't become a topic of public conversation. It was bad form to cause a scene if and when one's spouse's extramarital affair was discovered. Lord Ranelagh, on drawing back his bed curtains to find his wife naked with Lord Coningsby, simply went downstairs and left them in peace (although later on he had quite a lot to say when Coningsby asked for his daughter's hand in marriage.)

Not everyone was quite as complacent about marital infidelity as Lord Ranelagh. If a gentleman discovered that someone was fooling around with his wife – worse still, he was embarrassed because everyone knew he was being cheated on – he had the option of bringing a charge of Criminal Conversation, or 'crim. con.' as it was generally known. Basically, he could sue his wife's lover for compensation.

The public couldn't get enough juicy details about upper-crust 'rantum-scantum' (eighteenth-century slang for rumpy-pumpy) and crim. con. trials became the tabloid fodder of the Georgian and Regency eras. These trials also involved extraordinary amounts of money, because an aristocrat who debauched a lady could expect to pay compensation to her husband of anything between five and ten thousand pounds, so the rewards for dragging one's affairs through the mud could be well worth the effort.

The most scandalous crim. con. trial of the period took place at Westminster Hall in February 1782, when the baronet Sir Richard Worsley claimed a staggering twenty thousand pounds from his wife's lover. The trial transcript, price one shilling, ran to seven printings in the first year and became an international bestseller (even George Washington owned a copy). Seven years earlier, Worsley had married a rich heiress, seventeen-year-old Seymour Dorothy Fleming, a great-granddaughter of the Duke of Somerset said to be worth fifty-two thousand pounds – over sixty million pounds in today's money, inherited from her father, Sir John Fleming.

The Worsleys appeared to be the perfect power couple. Sir Richard was a rising star in Lord North's Tory government while Lady Worsley was both beautiful and a popular addition to London society. Before marrying Seymour, Sir Richard had set his cap at her equally rich elder sister Jane. The fact that he saw the two sisters as exchangeable gave a hint of what was to come. Another clue was the marriage contract itself, which benefited Worsley much more than might have been expected, given his new wife's considerable wealth, leaving her just four hundred pounds a year pin money and tying up her property until after his death.

To begin with Sir Richard gave his new bride very little attention. The union wasn't consummated for three months and, though they had a son in 1776, soon after, the marital bed, 'like the weather, had grown perfectly cool', according to Lady Worsley.

Her ladyship, however, was not the type to sit around and sew. While her husband was away collecting Roman artefacts, she and two of her friends went on a three-day bender, setting fire to an inn full of the militia, then amusing themselves by urinating through their bedroom window on the heads of some passers-by.

Lady Worsley also took a number of discreet casual lovers. One of these, George Maurice Bisset, a captain in the South Hampshire Militia, next-door neighbour and close friend of the family, became something more. She gave birth to their daughter, Jane. Sir Richard, as was the upper-class custom of the day, claimed the child as his own with little fuss. One night, Seymour and Bisset decided to elope. It was an extraordinarily foolhardy thing to do because she stood to lose not only her fortune, but also her reputation, her children and – crucially, as she was concerned – her clothes and jewels, worth a staggering fifteen million pounds at today's value.

Sir Richard was furious: discreet sexual liaisons were routine among their social circle, but having your wife elope with her lover invited public ridicule. The couple holed up at the Royal Hotel in Piccadilly, where they stayed for several weeks. The staff was suspicious about the identity of their new guests because they were rarely out of bed, partly because Lady Worsley had fled taking only the clothes she stood in.

Faced with the humiliation of a runaway wife, Sir

Richard took his revenge by suing Bisset for twenty thousand pounds in damages – an amount calculated to bankrupt him. Sir Richard also asked only for a legal separation, which meant that his wife would never be free to remarry until he died.

What emerged at the Westminster Hall trial that followed was considerably more shocking than anyone could have expected. To save Bisset from Fleet Prison, Lady Worsley decided to destroy her own reputation by encouraging five of her former lovers to spill the beans about her sex life. Sir Richard, it turned out, was a voyeur who liked to watch his wife having sex with other men and had not only overlooked his wife's affairs, but also actively encouraged them. One of Lady Worsley's partners recalled how, while making his exit after a night of lovemaking, he bumped into Sir Richard in her dressing room, but went unchallenged. Another told how Sir Richard allowed him to watch through a window as his wife dressed, in what appeared to have been an arranged 'show'. Bisset himself had watched Lady Worsley get undressed through the window of the public baths while sitting on Sir Richard's shoulders, and afterwards the threesome had walked away together laughing. No details were spared; Lady Worsley even invited her doctor to testify that he had treated her for a sexually transmitted disease. There was more: the press linked her with a further twenty-one men, making a total of twenty-seven lovers, although these claims were never substantiated and probably based on little more than hearsay.

Lady Worsley's scorched-earth policy worked, because despite finding in favour of Sir Richard, they awarded him just one shilling in damages. His revenge plan had backfired badly because his voyeuristic weirdness had made him a laughing stock. He slunk away to the continent and the scandal continued to dog him for the rest of his days. It was a hollow victory for Lady Worsley as well, because after the trial society turned its well-trained back on her. Their son remained with Sir Richard, as was the law; the baby daughter Jane had died during the trial, not having seen her mother since she eloped. Her relationship with Bisset lasted just eighteen months before he found himself a new wife. Driven from London by growing debts and disapproving glances, she spent a number of years travelling through Europe, supported as a mistress for various wealthy aristocrats.

HIGH LIFE, LOW MORALS

The moral climate of the Regency period was loose and marital fidelity a rarity among the aristocracy, but by any standards the sexual machinations of the so-called 'Devonshire House set', of which Lady Worsley was a member in the early years of her marriage, were mind-boggling.

Devonshire House was the most famous residence in London and the domestic life of its occupants the most talked about. It was home to the beautiful Georgiana, Duchess of Devonshire, ancestor of Diana, Princess of Wales, leader of fashion, social butterfly and heavy gambler. She met her future husband, the fifth duke, when she was sixteen. He was a sexually experienced twenty-four-year-old with at least one child by a mistress. Horrified by her husband's persistent affairs under her own roof, Georgiana had a fling or two of her own and even confessed to her husband that she was pregnant by one of her lovers. The fifth duke, an astonishingly languid character who, apart from taking part in casual adulterous encounters, seems to have cared only for gambling and his dogs, took a very relaxed view of this turns of events and simply suggested he move his long-standing mistress, Lady Elizabeth 'Bess' Foster, into the family home. Georgiana agreed and, perhaps even more surprisingly, the two women soon became firm friends.

For several years, in defiance of public gossip, the duchess, her husband and his mistress lived more or less happily in a threesome along with their assorted children: the duke had three legitimate children by his wife and two by Lady Foster, while the duchess had a couple by the future prime minister, Lord Grey. At one point the duchess and the mistress conceived within days or possibly even hours of each other. It is very likely that Georgiana and Bess were also lovers; the intimate letters they wrote to each were so heavily redacted that we will probably never know. While all this was going on, Devonshire House was host to some of the most famous men and women of the day, including the Prince Regent, Sheridan and Fox, who partied, gambled, danced and gossiped until dawn.

Not surprisingly, the curious morality of Devonshire House attracted widespread speculation. During the election of 1784 Georgiana campaigned for the Whig Charles Fox. The idea of an aristocratic lady taking part in the grubby chaos of a parliamentary election was considered too scandalous for words; it was rumoured that the duchess was exchanging sexual favours for votes. In her defence she could at least point to the fact that only one of the five children conceived by Lady Melbourne, her rival as doyenne of London's fast set, was conceived by her husband. Her son William, the future prime minister Lord Melbourne, was thought to have been fathered by Lord Egremont.

The duchess's pace of life and the pills she took to sustain it saw a rapid and shocking decline in her health. In 1799, when she was only forty-two, she was described as 'painful to see . . . her figure is corpulent, her complexion coarse, one eye gone, and her neck immense'. By the age of forty-eight she was dead from an abscess on the liver. Three years after Georgiana's death, her husband did the honourable thing and married his long-standing mistress Bess, then proceeded to give her a taste of what the late duchess had endured by immediately taking on a new mistress. Bess spent the rest of her days rattling around Devonshire House alone, with only her longed-for new social status for comfort.

The Devonshires weren't the only aristocratic *ménage à trois* keeping tongues wagging in London society. Alfred, Comte d'Orsay, was a French Beau Brummell, an arbiter of fashion and one of the most notorious dandies of his day. Later in life he grew very fat and was known as the 'stout count'. In his youth, however, he was blessed with dazzling good looks, sparkling wit and an exquisite dress sense, which came with a dangerous whiff of adventure (he was a regular duellist) and a pre-Revolutionary title. It was an irresistable combination, and when he made his entry into his adoptive city in 1821, society fell at his perfectly shod feet.

D'Orsay's dandyism was a long way from Brummell's. The latter made a virtue of simplicity, but the bisexual d'Orsay went for high camp, including lots of silk, very tight trousers and so much cologne that his smell announced his arrival several minutes before his loud waistcoats did.

Charles Dickens was just one of the hundreds of young men who studied the count's elaborate appearance in the hope of imitating it on a budget.

D'Orsay was able to finance his lifestyle, including his habit of wearing then discarding half a dozen pairs of gloves a day, thanks to his odd personal arrangement with the very accommodating and also very dim Irish nobleman Charles Gardiner, 1st Earl of Blessington. In 1822 the handsome young d'Orsay took up permanent residence in the Blessington household as the lover of the earl's wife and very possibly the earl himself. With the riches from his Irish estates, Blessington, his wife and their shared lover rambled around Europe in style, periodically setting up camp in some of the most expensive palaces and hotels that the continent had to offer. When the threesome threatened to become too scandalous even for the more open-minded among the upper classes, it was decided that d'Orsay should marry either one of Lord Blessington's two daughters by his first marriage. Having met neither, d'Orsay plumped for the younger, fifteen-year-old Harriet, who was dispatched from Ireland to join his household in France. Lady Blessington, it was reported, insisted that, in the interest of good taste, her stepdaughter's marriage should not be consummated for at least four years after the wedding.

LAMB TO THE SLAUGHTER

Once a wife had given her husband a son to inherit his title and estates she was usually free to go her own way. Her husband meanwhile took his pleasure as he liked.

In the mid-1700s the basic necessities of the fashionable English lord were membership of White's, horses at

Newmarket and a beautiful mistress. When he was ordering his wife's portrait from Joshua Reynolds, the 2nd Lord Bolingbroke instructed the artist to 'give her the eyes of Nelly O'Brien (his mistress), or it will not do'. Nelly O'Brien was one of the most famous courtesans of the day and her relationship with 'Bully' Bolingbroke was far from exclusive; she was rumoured to have had two sons with Sackville Tufton, 8th Earl of the Isle of Thanet. She died in London in 1768, a year after her great rival Kitty Fisher, who was said once to have eaten a one-hundred-pound note between two slices of bread. Successful mistresses like Nelly O'Brien didn't come cheap. They dressed like the best, drove their carriages in Hyde Park at the fashionable hour and competed openly with the fairest society had to offer. The 6th Duke of Devonshire set up his in a London home in fashionable Dorset Square and a second house in Brighton, and then gave her an annual allowance of £1,600 plus carriages, jewellery, fine clothes and various other gifts, including an aviary.

By and large, however, affairs with people of one's social circle were much easier to manage than setting up a household for a mistress or braving an unregulated brothel. Rather more discretion was demanded of a woman than of her husband, naturally, but some aristocratic ladies were less clear on the concept than others. Another addition to Devonshire House's busy nursery was Georgiana's notorious niece, Lady Caroline Ponsonby, aka Lady Caroline Lamb, daughter of her lesser-gambling sister Lady Bessborough. Caroline's upbringing was open-minded, to say the least. All of the grown-ups in her household were lovers and all her playmates were her illegitimate half-brothers and sisters, so no one can have been particularly surprised when she went off the rails.

With her short hair and tomboyish appearance, Caroline was not considered a conventional beauty, but there was no shortage of men attracted to her wit and personality. She was married at nineteen to William Lamb, the second son of Lord Melbourne. Her first affair followed not long afterwards with the notorious rake Sir Godfrey Webster, a reckless gambler with a violent temper. Neither party made much effort to conceal the affair, much to the disgust of Caroline's mother-in-law Lady Melbourne, who was much less shocked by her daughter-in-law's infidelity than by the harm it might be doing to her son's political career. Caroline's unflappable husband put up with her first adulterous affair with commendable restraint, but her next affair tested his patience to the limit.

She was twenty-four when she had a famous four-month fling with Lord Byron through the summer of 1812. He was three years her junior and had just acquired startling overnight success thanks to his romantic poem *Childe Harold's Pilgrimage*. Like many of his lovers, Caroline was introduced to Byron through his verse. The writer Samuel Rogers gave her a copy of *Childe Harold* and said, 'You should know the new poet . . . he has a club-foot and bites his nails.' After she had read it, Lady Caroline said, 'If he was as ugly as Aesop, I must see him.'

She claimed in her journal that she described him 'mad, bad and dangerous to know' after their first meeting, but it's more likely she made the line up much later. It took just one more meeting with Byron for her to be smitten. Soon she was stalking him, disguising herself as a pageboy and lurking outside houses waiting for him to emerge and making a spectacle of herself all over town, much to Byron's annoyance: he was not impressed either when she sent him a lock of her pubic hair as a keepsake. Their passionate four-month affair was conducted very publicly, each jealous for the other's attentions, and the final break was suitably dramatic. At a party given by Lady Heathcote, Byron arrived with Lady Oxford and in front of everyone pointedly ignored Caroline. She collapsed screaming, then tried to slash her wrists with a broken wine glass, then stabbed herself with a pair of scissors. Both Byron and her husband's relations decided that they had had enough of her, but like her distant relation Princess Diana, Caroline was not inclined to go quietly. This included writing novels, the first of which, *Glenarvon*, was a bestselling scandalous exposé of her relationship with Byron. Her in-laws tried to ban any further literary output and took steps to have her certified insane. They failed in this too, but did succeed in separating her from her husband, William, who went on to become prime minister.*

BAD HEIR DAYS

Provided a married woman had secured an heir, no one raised an eyebrow if the younger children in her nursery had hair or eyes of a different colour, or ever commented on a suspicious likeness to a lover. Most upper-class bastards were given the family surname and happily acknowledged, at least legally, in order to save face and avoid scandal. One of Lord Byron's lovers, Lady Jane

* William Lamb's sexual tastes were eccentric. He had a fetish for flogging women and little girls, a topic on which he felt so strongly that he hoped one day to write a treatise describing its virtues.

Harley, Duchess of Oxford, produced a number of children over the course of her marriage to the 5th Earl of Oxford, but no one was ever sure which, if any, were fathered by the earl. Her various children were known as the 'Harleian Miscellany', a play on the book edited by Samuel Jackson. The many mistresses of the 11th Duke of Norfolk gave him more children than he could keep track of. Once, while visiting his northern property Greystoke Castle, he was driving through the small village on the approach to the castle gates when half a dozen children besieged his carriage. He turned to his coachman, enquired who they were and was told, 'So far as I could notice, those that didn't belong to me, belonged to your Grace.'

It was tacitly acknowledged that there were many heirs who were not their father's sons at all. The Duchess of Gordon, who had already married three of her daughters to dukes, struggled to offload the fourth to the heir of Lord Cornwallis, who had grounds to believe that there was insanity in the Gordon family. The duchess was able to put his mind at rest: 'I can solemnly assure you that there is not a single drop of Gordon blood in her veins.' In a strange reversal of this principle, Daisy Warwick was furious with Lord Charles Beresford when she found out that his wife had a baby that looked just like him. How dare he – Beresford was supposed to be having an affair with her!

Some noble bastards, the very embarrassing mistakes, would be born abroad, then mysteriously reappear at a suitable age, when they would suddenly acquire a benevolent 'godfather'. One very fortunate product of disputed parentage was a young girl called Maria Fagnani, known as 'Mie-Mie', daughter of the beautiful Italian Costanzi, Marchesa Fagnani. Mie-Mie was either the daughter of her mother's husband, the Marchese, or of the lecherous 4th Duke of Queensberry, or of his friend George Selwyn. At any rate, all three men claimed paternity and they were all very rich and each left her a great deal of money, despite her disputed lineage, so she became one of the most eligible girls in Europe.

The great gynaecological whodunit of the 1920s was the bizarre 'Russell Baby Case', fought to decide ownership of the Barony of Ampthill and with it the 250-acre Ampthill estate in Bedfordshire.* John Hugo Russell, eighteen-year-old heir of Oliver Russell, 2nd Lord Ampthill, was a gangling, six-foot-six naval officer with a fondness for cross-dressing, known to his friends as 'Stilts'. In 1917 he met nineteen-year-old Christabel Hart, a vivacious blonde who worked in a munitions factory. After a brief courtship he proposed marriage. At first she turned him down on the grounds that she considered herself 'not the marrying kind' but later she relented because, she admitted later, 'I thought it would be nice and peaceful not to be pestered by men asking me to marry them.'

Their marriage got off to an inauspicious start. Lord and Lady Ampthill, who were good friends of George V and Queen Mary, didn't approve of their son's choice on the grounds that their new daughter-in-law danced the tango and shaved her armpits; they refused to attend the wedding. The situation was made even more tricky by the bride's ultimatum on the eve of their big day: she did not want children, so Stilts had to agree to abstain from anything that might cause pregnancy. It got worse. While Stilts was away on his

---

* The Barony of Ampthill was originally created for Lord Odo Russell, a grandson of John Russell, 6th Duke of Bedford.

submarine, his wife wrote him a series of cheery letters about various men she had been seeing while he was away. One read: 'I need hardly say your wife has a vast following of adoring young men. I've four in the Bucks Light Infantry.' She also boasted of being 'in love with a Dago young man' who had 'lovely hands' and of dancing with 'dark sleek Argentinians...Your very naughty wife.'

Russell took this news surprisingly well. In 1919 he bought Christabel a copy of Marie Stopes' *Married Love* with the hopeful suggestion that they might use some form of birth control, a generous offer she declined. In 1920, after almost two years of frustratingly sexless marriage, he charged into her bedroom brandishing a gun and threatened to shoot her cat if she refused to submit to him. When this failed to achieve the desired effect he warned he would blow his own brains out if she didn't change her mind. This didn't work either. From then on the only time he was allowed in her bedroom was while he served her breakfast in bed, while she rudely regaled him with intimate details of her night out.

In June 1921 Russell was very surprised when his wife returned home with the news that she been to see a clairvoyant, who informed her that she was five months pregnant. A doctor confirmed the fact and in October she gave birth to a ten-pound nine-ounce boy, Geoffrey.

Russell sued his wife for divorce on the grounds of adultery. His case was apparently watertight; the child could not possibly be his, because his marriage with Lady Russell was unconsummated. The last time they had shared a bed was when they had been put into the same room while staying with his parents at Oakley the previous December. On that occasion, no physical contact of any kind had taken place. In fact Christabel hadn't even kissed him since August 1920: ergo, the child could not possibly be his.

Lady Russell denied adultery, claiming that her pregnancy was caused by her husband's 'Hunnish practices' (masturbation, presumably: she wasn't specific about what this might have entailed, but agreed that it did not involve full intercourse). She also speculated it might have been caused by a sponge from a bath her husband had recently vacated. Under further cross-examination she claimed she had no idea what a man's penis was for, or even that it could change size.

The jury were left to exercise their imaginations as to the 'Hunnish' events that had taken place, as indeed were the medical profession. Several doctors and gynaecologists testified that Christabel was technically a virgin and had 'never had full intercourse with a man'. The medical men assured the court, however, that conception was possible without 'full penetration'.

The jury found Christabel guilty of adultery with an unknown man and Stilts was granted his divorce. Christabel, however, wasn't going to take it lying down, so to speak. She appealed to the High Court and when that failed she took her case to the House of Lords and won. The divorce was overturned, legitimising Geoffrey the 'Sponge Baby'. He finally succeeded, controversially, to the family title in the 1980s when the Hon. Geoffrey Russell persuaded the House of Lords privileges committee that a few drops of baronial sperm had somehow entered Lady Ampthill, thus making him the rightful heir. Thus, the 4th Lord Ampthill became the only peer who can justly claim to have earned his seat in the House of Lords by proving that his father was a wanker.

NAKED AMBITION

In eighteenth-century Europe divorces were few and far between and difficult to obtain, even for the rich and titled. In Britain, where a divorce required an act of parliament, they were rarer than lottery wins. Only six took place in Queen Anne's reign and only two in George I's. Elizabeth Chudleigh, a covetous tart variously known as the Countess of Bristol or the Duchess of Kingston, depending on where you stood, embarked on an apparently simpler course of action.

Elizabeth's family owned property in Devon but had fallen on hard times when her father, Thomas Chudleigh, invested one thousand pounds in the South Sea Company, only to see the bubble burst on the investment. He took a job as lieutenant-governor of Chelsea Hospital, but then died when Elizabeth was six, leaving her in genteel poverty. As she grew into her teens, however, she realised quite quickly that she could capitalise on her striking beauty. Her first affair was with a much older man when she was fifteen and by the time she was twenty she was sleeping with the Earl of Bath, who secured her a position as Maid of Honour to Augusta, Princess of Wales.

In 1749 she announced her entrance to London society by turning up for a costume ball dressed, or rather undressed, as Iphigenia, daughter of Agamemnon, prepared for sacrifice. She was, an observer remarked, 'so naked that ye High Priest might easily inspect ye entrails of ye victim'. King George II was so impressed that he asked if he might be allowed to fondle her exposed breast. She replied that she knew an even softer place – then guided the royal hand to the bald patch on top of his head.

It appears that Elizabeth Chudleigh's breasts weren't the only things she shared with London high society. At dinner parties she liked to belch and fart her way through piles of food, meanwhile swearing like a trooper, lifting her skirts to fan her backside and blaming the smell on the dogs. Despite her general vulgarity, her beauty and willingness to appear 'next door to nakedness' ensured that men clustered to her like wasps to a picnic. The Dukes of Ancaster and Hamilton wanted to marry her, while the king clearly wanted to do more than just grope her and even gave her an allowance from his personal funds. She was also said to have greatly impressed Frederick the Great with her ability to knock back two bottles of wine.

In 1744 she met Augustus Hervey, grandson and eventual heir to the Earl of Bristol, and after a brief courtship they were married. The ceremony was conducted at night, in secret, with only a few witnesses present. After midnight nuptials, the groom left for his naval duties the next morning. Her husband gone, Elizabeth realised she had made a terrible mistake. As a married woman she would have to give up her position as Maid of Honour and, although she earned only two hundred pounds a year, barely enough for her glamorous lifestyle, her husband's navy salary was even lower – only fifty pounds a year. Between Hervey's long absences at sea the couple spent barely more than a few weeks together. It was soon evident to both parties that the marriage was unworkable. He also was secretly dreading his family finding out that he had just got himself hitched to one of London's premier strumpets, so they conveniently 'forgot' the marriage had ever taken place. The cat almost came out of the bag when she gave birth to a boy in 1746, but the child died in infancy: even this she somehow contrived to keep secret. Their marriage would remain an unsubstantiated rumour for upwards of twenty years.

In 1760 Elizabeth became the mistress of the Duke of Kingston, who seems to have been blissfully and very conveniently unaware of her murky past. In the meantime Hervey came a step closer to inheriting the earldom of Bristol when his older brother died. When Elizabeth heard about this she decided to have her marriage to Hervey registered in the parish church at Lainston. She was looking for an insurance policy in case Kingston deserted her, a decision she would regret bitterly.

Hervey, having exhausted himself on a tour of Europe's port brothels, returned home seeking a divorce so that he could be free to marry. Elizabeth, fearing her new boyfriend wouldn't want to marry a divorcee, swore an oath in an ecclesiastical court denying that any marriage to Hervey had taken place – therefore, they could not be divorced. The court ruled in her favour and within a month she became the Duchess of Kingston. She might have got away with the deception had the duke not died five years later, leaving Elizabeth everything and his sister's family nothing.

In the hope of overturning the terms of the will, the late duke's dispossessed nephew decided to dish the dirt on her marriage to Hervey and she was indicted for bigamy. Meanwhile, the Earl of Bristol died and Augustus Hervey succeeded to the title, making Miss Chudleigh a genuine countess as well as a bogus duchess. After a five-day trial in April 1776, in Westminster Hall before six hundred spectators she was found guilty of bigamy. Her age and rank saved her from the usual punishment due a bigamist

– the branding of her right hand on the block – but she was stripped of her titles, although she continued to call herself Duchess of Kingston to her death.* She was, however, allowed to keep her fortune, which she continued to enjoy for the rest of a life spent in self-imposed exile. She sloped off to Russia, where she became a friend of Catherine the Great, then to France, where she died aged sixty-eight, after receiving yet another offer of marriage from Prince Radziwiłł.

STATELY HOMOS

In 1631 the complicated domestic arrangements of Mervyn Touchet, 2nd Earl of Castlehaven, were laid bare in a sensational trial that was followed all over Europe and as far away as North America. The earl was married to Lady Anne Stanley, eldest daughter of the Earl of Derby. Castlehaven tried to liven up his wedding night by inviting his favourite servant, Henry Skipwith, to share their marital bed: at one point Lady Anne was asked to comment on which of them had the bigger penis. When she declined to take part in this threesome, her husband pinned her down while she was raped by a second servant, a butler called

---

* The downfall of Elizabeth Chudleigh had collateral damage when playwright Samuel Foote viciously satirized her as the character of Kitty Crocodile in his play *A Trip to Calais*. In the play, Foote made reference to her trial for bigamy and joked about her relationship with her male secretary, the Rev. William Jackson. The reverend retaliated by bribing the writer's former footman to bring charges of homosexual rape against Foote. He was acquitted of the trumped-up charges, but the scandal effectively ended Foote's stage career.

Giles Broadway. Afterwards the butler was in turn raped by his employer, as was a page, Laurence Fitzpatrick. The earl was also accused of encouraging sexual relations between his twelve-year-old stepdaughter and Skipwith. When Castlehaven's son James informed on him to the authorities, the earl admitted that he might have slept with his servants now and then, but only because his house was short of bed space.

Convicted of rape and sodomy by a jury of his aristocratic peers, Castlehaven was beheaded on Tower Hill on 14 May 1631. The butler Broadway and the page Fitzpatrick were also hanged the same day (which seems rather harsh on Fitzpatrick). The earl went to his death protesting that he was the victim of a plot orchestrated by his wife and son to have him judicially murdered so they could inherit his estate. He may have had a point: there were conflicts in the accounts given in evidence against him and all of his accusers stood to gain from his death. Whether he was set up or not, Castlehaven's trial was an important legal landmark because it was not only the first time a peer of the realm had been found guilty of being a practising homosexual; it also established the right of a wife to testify against her husband in cases of marital cruelty and rape.*

Aristocrats were not expected to be faithful to their wives, or pay their tradesmen on time, or bother about

---

* The only documented example of aristocratic homosexuality in the following century (technically bisexuality, since he was also notorious for his escapades with women) was that involving the Salopian squire and MP Richard 'Black Dick' Cresswell, who in 1716 was arrested in Genoa on thirty-eight counts of buggery with a local boy whom he had 'dressed up'.

money at all, except about ways of getting rid of it. There were only two sins: cheating at cards and buggery. Although it was illegal, the British authorities turned a blind eye to homosexuality until it suited them not to.

In April 1870 London police arrested two male transvestites, Ernest Boulton and Frederick Park, known to their friends as 'Fanny and Stella', outside the Strand theatre. The 'girls' were hauled before Bow Street magistrates court the next morning still in their evening gowns, charged with 'the abominable crime of buggery'. It was desperately worrying news for Lord Arthur Pelham-Clinton, Conservative MP and son of the Duke of Newcastle, who was living with Boulton as man and wife. Lord Arthur's escape route from a long term of imprisonment was death: he was said to have died of scarlet fever on the day he received his subpoena, but it was more likely that he committed suicide to escape the stigma of a trial for sodomy. At the time many people thought his death had been faked and that he was in fact living abroad; there was a suggestion that he had broadcast news of his own demise and even arranged a funeral for himself. In the event, the jury took less than an hour to acquit Fanny and Stella; simply dressing up as a woman and parading around the West End flirting with men was not actually a crime, however much the authorities might have wished it to be. It also helped that the father of one of the accused was a judge.

Ten years before Oscar Wilde's name became synonymous with homosexual scandal, another case involving buggery and the aristocracy was being played out in the London press – an 'indescribably loathsome scandal', one newspaper called it – involving a number of upper-class patrons of a male brothel in Cleveland Street, London, which was home to several young male prostitutes.

In 1889 a policeman apprehended a fifteen-year-old telegraph boy called Charles Swinscow, who was found carrying eighteen shillings – the equivalent of about two months' wages. Swinscow was immediately suspected of theft but protested that he had earned the money by 'going to bed with gentlemen' at the rate of four shillings a time. Scotland Yard put 19 Cleveland Street under watch and confirmed that 'a number of men of superior bearing and apparently good position' were frequent visitors. One of these gentlemen, it was widely speculated, was the heir to the British throne, Prince Albert Victor, known in the family as Eddy. Although his name was never mentioned in the British press, in America and France the newspapers reported on his alleged involvement quite openly.

There were no doubts, however, about the identity of one regular aristocratic visitor to the brothel – Lord Arthur Somerset, younger son of the Duke of Beaufort, known to his friends as 'Podge'. There was ample evidence of Lord Arthur's involvement, including letters and several statements from various rent boys, but the government was reluctant to prosecute and 'Podge' was allowed to escape to Vienna, subject to his resignation from the Royal Horse Guards and the royal household.

Two months later the editor of the *North London Press*, Ernest Parke, wrote an article naming another well-known member of the London gay community, the Earl of Euston, eldest son of the Duke of Grafton, as a regular at the Cleveland Street brothel. According to Parke, Lord Euston had already fled to Peru. On this point, Parke was wrong: on the contrary, his lordship was very much still in England

and was busy instructing a leading barrister Sir Charles Russell QC to sue for libel.

During Parke's libel trial, Euston admitted visiting the brothel but said he was expecting to see some female strippers and had left as soon as he realised what was going on. There was compelling evidence to suggest otherwise, including the graphic testimonies of six witnesses who had seen Lord Euston in the club, but the jury chose to believe the word of the middle-aged peer and he was exonerated. Ernest Parke was sent down for twelve months with hard labour.

The spectre of homosexuality continued to haunt the late Victorian and Edwardian aristocracy. There was a scurrilous rumour doing the rounds that Princess Louise, fourth daughter of the queen, had been forced to brick up the garden door that led from their London apartment onto Hyde Park, to prevent her husband, the Marquess of Lorne, later the 9th Duke of Argyll, from escaping at night to pick up soliciting guardsmen from the nearby barracks. In 1907 Argyll was implicated in another scandal concerning the robbery of the Irish Crown Jewels from Dublin Castle. Police enquiries revealed that Argyll was a close friend of one of their chief suspects, Frank Shackleton, disreputable younger brother of the great Antarctic explorer Ernest, and one of a number of homosexual employees at the castle who were said to have taken part in drunken parties on the premises involving 'unnatural vice'. The investigation into the heist was closed down – probably at the instigation of King Edward VII who didn't want the lid lifted on a sex scandal so close to home – and the jewels remain unrecovered.

Although Queen Victoria herself was said to be unaware of such matters, there was also avid speculation about the sexuality of some members of the aristocratic sisterhood. In 1864, Admiral Sir Henry Codrington found himself at the heart of a first-class scandal when he sued his wife for divorce, accusing her of misbehaviour with several men, mostly with an officer in the Guards, a bewhiskered cad called Anderson. Lady Codrington meanwhile counter-claimed that Sir Henry had misbehaved while in Malta with a Mrs Watson. The admiral was also suspicious of his wife's friend, a Miss Emily Faithfull. He had become aware that during his absences at sea, Emily and Lady Codrington had shared a bed. This practice, his wife explained, was helping with her asthma. One evening, when the two ladies were in bed together, the admiral entered the room and attempted to rape Emily. He offered the explanation that he'd only come in to look for a poker.

Since homosexual acts between men were illegal (and until 1861, actually punishable by death) it is hardly surprising that many gay men were so carefully closeted that their wives and children had no inkling about their sexual preference.

In 1902 the 7th Earl Beauchamp, a rising star in the Liberal Party, married Lady Lattice Grosvenor, sister of the immensely rich and extremely reactionary 2nd Duke of Westminster, known to his circle as Bendor.* It was, to all outward appearances, a happy and successful marriage, attested by their seven children. According to

---

* Although christened Hugh Richard Arthur Grosvenor, he was known as Bendor or Benny after his father's famous racehorse Bend Or.

informed gossip, however, Lord Beauchamp's preference was for footmen and grooms, several of whom liked to show off expensive diamond rings, presents for granting sexual favours to their aristocratic master. Beauchamp's 'weakness', as it was referred to, was well known in the parliamentary and social circles in which he moved, but it was never used as a political weapon against him. To have done so was considered improper and ungentlemanly. He was able to go happily about his business, confident that he wouldn't be outed by his political enemies, and that his double life would not be discovered by his exceptionally naive wife. His political career prospered and over the next three decades he accepted a catalogue of official appointments and titles including Lord Lieutenant of Gloucestershire, Lord Steward of the Household, Lord President of the Council, Lord Warden of the Cinque Ports and a Knight of the Order of the Garter, the oldest and grandest of all the chivalric orders. He might have carried on collecting honours for several decades more had it not been for his spectacularly vindictive brother-in-law Bendor, who decided to destroy Beauchamp's life and career by exposing his homosexuality.

The 2nd Duke of Westminster was a singularly unpleasant character. He was one of a significant group of British peers who supported efforts to appease Hitler through the 1930s. The Duke of Westminster gave money to Link, an extreme right-wing group whose most prominent members were interned on security grounds in 1940. Rabidly anti-Semitic, he believed countless conspiracy theories concerning British Jews supposedly aiming to subvert the country, and made a number of speeches to that effect. What made his ramblings even more odious was that he continued to air his views long after Hitler's persecution of Germany's Jews had become public knowledge.*

It isn't clear why Bendor chose to wait so long to vent his homophobia. Perhaps he had only just found out about his brother-in-law's double life, although it had been fairly common knowledge in London's clubland for years. Or it may have been jealousy because Beauchamp's marriage to his sister had produced three male heirs, while Bendor's sole male heir had died aged four. Whatever his motive, he went about exposing Beauchamp with a vengeance. When King George V was informed that he had conferred the Knight of the Garter on a practising homosexual, the king was astonished and could only splutter, 'I thought chaps like that shot themselves!' Lady Beauchamp was even more amazed, professing some confusion as to what homosexuality actually was. Broken and ruined, deserted by all but his children and a few friends, the disgraced Beauchamp went into exile abroad, where the vindictive Bendor wrote to him, triumphantly, 'Dear Bugger-in-Law, you got what you deserved.'

---

* Also prominent among these fascist aristocrats was Lord Brocket, said to be 'a fundamentally nice but stupid man', who attended the celebrations for Hitler's fiftieth birthday and was said to have lit fires on his estates to guide German bombers on their way to London. Another was Winston Churchill's cousin Lord Londonderry, who formed a close relationship with the Nazi leadership and often entertained Joachim von Ribbentrop, Hitler's ambassador in London. A string of British dukes at that time were also quite openly enthusiastic about the dictators – Wellington, Buccleuch, Bedford, Marlborough and Hamilton, to name just the highest ranking.

Rather less convincing than Lord Beauchamp's marriage of convenience was that of Henry Paget, 5th Marquess of Anglesey, known as the 'dancing marquess' for his habit of performing 'sinuous, sexy, snake-like dances'. In 1898, age twenty-three, he inherited his title and the family estates with about thirty thousand acres, providing an annual income of £110,000 (around fifty-five million pounds today) which he mostly spent on jewels, outlandish clothes and such bizarre fripperies as a Rolls-Royce with Louis XV-style decorations and a perfumed exhaust. In 1898 he married his cousin Lillian, presumably to keep their aggregate fortune in the family. He was particularly fond of using his beautiful young wife to showcase his vast collection of gems, often all of it simultaneously. On their honeymoon he bought the entire window display of the jewellers Van Cleef & Arpels, then made her wear all of it to the races. Marital relations were further strained when he woke her in the middle of the night, ordered her to strip naked, then covered her with gems. Lillian filed for annulment two years later on the grounds of non-consummation. The 'dancing marquess' died childless.

VICTORIAN FAMILY VALUES

In the mid-nineteenth century most respectable British people took their cue from the court, where the queen and her dutiful and priggish German husband Albert set almost impossibly high standards of decency and sobriety. The aristocracy, however, continued to behave exactly as they pleased.

Chief among the offenders was a travelling circus of wealthy revellers known collectively as the Marlborough

House Set, after the Prince of Wales's London dwelling, which became a by-word for moral laxity. This notorious clique included the Duke of Sutherland, Lord Randolph Churchill, various Rothschild brothers and cousins, and many other prominent young aristocrats. The louche behaviour was not confined to the men. Lady Harriet Sarah Moncreiffe was just eighteen years old when she became married to thirty-year-old Sir Charles Mordaunt, 10th Baronet, a stolid country squire with few interests beyond hunting and shooting. He was oblivious to the antics of his giddy young wife, who was entertaining numerous lovers, including the Prince of Wales and several of his aristocratic pals, until one sweltering summer's day in 1868. Sir Charles returned home unexpectedly to find the prince eyeing Lady Mordaunt covetously while she gave a demonstration of her carriage-driving skills in front of the house with a pair of white ponies. Sir Charles, mindful of Bertie's reputation as a philanderer, asked him to leave, then ordered his groom to bring the ponies down on to the lawn below the conservatory, then dragged his wife from the house and made her watch as they were shot. If Sir Charles thought that this shock tactic would cure his young wife's inattentiveness, he was mistaken.

The lid was sensationally blown off Lady Mordaunt's sex life eighteen months later. Harriet gave birth to a daughter, Violet, born prematurely with a sight-threatening eye infection. Fearing she had passed a case of gonorrhoea on to the child, Harriett panicked and confessed all to her husband. 'Charlie,' she sobbed, 'I have been very wicked. I have done very wrong. With Lord Cole, Sir Frederic Johnstone, and the Prince of Wales and with others, often, and in open day.'

Sir Charles filed for divorce and Lady Mordaunt's

multiple infidelities were raked over in the newspapers and in the law courts. The scandal snowballed when flirtatious letters from the Prince of Wales to Mordaunt's wife were unearthed as evidence and Bertie was called up as witness for her defence. Bertie took the stand and flatly denied any impropriety. Harriet's family, loath to lose her two-thousand-pounds-a-year allowance from Charles (the equivalent of about £150,000 today), did their best to thwart his divorce attempts by having her declared insane and her confessions of promiscuity passed off as the ravings of a madwoman. Eventually, Lord Cole of Enniskillen, in exchange for a compensatory sum, gallantly claimed paternity of Violet in order to save the prince from further disrepute. Charles was then granted his divorce, while poor Harriet, disgraced and divorced at twenty-eight, languished in the lunatic asylum, where she'd remain for the rest of her days.*

The Mordaunt affair gave the public a rare and shocking glimpse into what went on in Britain's elite bedrooms and introduced them to an event that was now the epicentre of the late Victorian social scene, the country house party, where shooting came a poor second to free love, or 'corridor creeping'. These house parties went on for days on end and offered ideal conditions for a spot of adultery – husbands and wives among the upper classes rarely

---

* Her daughter Violet's fate was better than may have been expected. With eyesight restored, she rose above the scandal to marry a viscount. Her grandson, the current Marquess of Bath, has enjoyed the company of seventy-five mistresses – 'wifelets' – many of whom lived with him in an English aristo version of Hugh Hefner's Playboy Mansion.

occupied the same bedroom, unless by mutual arrangement. Negotiating one's way around a large mansion at
night in order to carry out an assignation, however, could
be tricky. To avoid confusion, guests at Wentworth
Woodhouse, seat of the earls Fitzwilliam, were given silver
boxes containing confetti so they could sprinkle a trail to
help them find their way between rooms. On the opera-
tional side, codes might be devised to avoid embarrassment. One lady arranged to leave a plate of sandwiches
outside her door to indicate that the coast was clear, only to
have them eaten by a passing guest; the disappointed lover
decided it was wise to stay away. If only Lord Charles
Beresford, a notorious philanderer, had done the same. In
the 1880s he burst into a bedroom supposedly occupied by
his latest mistress and gleefully flung himself onto the bed
crying 'Cock-a-doodle-doo', only to find it occupied by the
Bishop of Chester and his wife.* To make sure that everyone was back in his right place when it mattered, gongs
were beaten, once in the evening to announce the arrival of
servants to help with dressing for dinner, and again in the
morning for breakfast.

Absolute discretion was the code governing the idle
gentry's adulterous liaisons, and by and large that code
was scrupulously observed, making public scandals rare,
and divorce, which was expensive and highly stigmatising,
very much a last resort. Jealous husbands dealt with the
discovery of affairs in their own ways. In 1884 the
Marchioness of Londonderry had the misfortune of having

* The story was such a good one that it has been recycled several
times with different participants. The second most popular
protagonists are the Bishop of Leicester and his wife.

her letters to her lover Harry Cust intercepted by her rival for his affections, Lady Gladys de Grey. After amusing herself by reading the letters aloud to all of her friends, Lady Gladys tied them up with a ribbon and sent them to Lord Londonderry. He read the letters, carefully tied the ribbon back around the envelopes and placed them on his wife's boudoir table, with a note which read: 'Henceforth, we do not speak'. He was as good as his word. From that day on for the next fifty years they only ever communicated through a third party, meanwhile continuing to live in the same houses, eat at the same tables and stand shoulder to shoulder to receive guests every time they held a reception. Even as the marquess lay on his deathbed, he refused his wife's note begging to see him.*

One of the Marlborough House Set's most high-profile members was the 7th Earl of Aylesford, known as 'Sporting Joe'. A famous inebriate and practical joker, he amused himself by standing on the roof of his moving carriage and tossing bags of flour at London pedestrians. In 1876 Aylesford was in India on a seventeen-week hunting trip, shooting tigers from the back of an elephant with the Prince of Wales, when he received a Dear Joe letter from wife Edith, signalling her intention to elope with Lord Blandford, eldest son of the Duke of Marlborough. The duke was separated from his wife and had been all but living with Lady Aylesford in her husband's absence. When

* These house parties continued to be places of courtship for the upper crust throughout the twentieth century. Most famously, it was at a house party that the romance of Sarah Ferguson and Prince Andrew, later Duke of York, began when they flirted by flinging profiteroles at each another.

Aylesford told the prince about his spot of bother, the prince professed outrage, declaring that Blandford was 'the greatest blackguard alive' – hypocritically, as Bertie was also having an affair with the lively Lady Edith, but Aylesford was either too loyal or too stupid to make a fuss about it.

Aylesford cut short his trip and swiftly returned to England, where he petitioned for divorce, citing Blandford as co-respondent. Blandford's younger brother, Lord Randolph Churchill, jumped to the defence of his sibling, brandishing a large stack of love letters the prince himself had written to Lady Aylesford. Randolph threatened that the contents of the letters were so incendiary they would ensure that 'the prince will never sit on the throne of England'. Bertie was infuriated and offered to meet Lord Randolph on the duelling grounds of northern France, a challenge Randolph dismissed as 'absurd'. The affair caused uproar: Prime Minister Disraeli was called in to sort it out; the prince's letters were retrieved and burned.

The heartbroken Aylesford took himself off to America, eventually fetching up in Big Spring, Texas, where, unable to find any other suitable lodging, he simply bought the town's only hotel. At first the local Texans weren't sure what to make of him or his title, which they mysteriously changed to Judge Aylesford. He in turn insisted on referring to his new neighbours as 'cow servants', which didn't win him many friends. In time, however, his generosity, especially his habit of picking up the tab in the local saloon, won them over.

Aylesford bought a thirty-seven-thousand-acre ranch and stocked it with forty thousand dollars worth of cattle, along with thirty-odd horses, thirteen dogs and five servants. Unfortunately, he brought with him few transferable skills that would come in useful for running a ranch, but no one could say that he wasn't an incredibly accommodating host. His regular all-night drinking parties, according to witnesses, resulted in a pile of empty bottles outside his home 'as big as a haystack'. Within two years he drank himself to death. When the local doctor prepared the earl's body for shipment back to England, he described the liver as being not unlike a rock. At the time of his death he was thirty-six years old.

America's got talent

In the final decades of the nineteenth century, the upper-crust families of Europe received a much-needed transfusion of new blood and new cash when hard-up peers, who had seen a depression in agriculture and their fortunes halved, chased the affections of American heiresses to shore up their ailing finances. From 1870 to 1914 around 350 US heiresses married into the British aristocracy, bringing with them the equivalent of one billion pounds of New World cash. Fans of *Downton Abbey* will recognise the fictional Countess of Grantham as part of this traffic. In the TV series, Lord Grantham marries his American heiress for her money before he eventually falls in love with her, but the reality was often very different for the so-called Dollar Princesses.

There was no shortage of pushy American mothers hoping that an exchange of dollars could buy their daughters a titled, if unhappy, marriage, perhaps none more desperate than Alva Vanderbilt, mother of Consuelo, heiress to the legendary Vanderbilt millions.

The Spencer-Churchill Dukes of Marlborough were particularly partial to the money of rich American brides. The 8th duke, after being divorced by his first wife, the respectable Lady Alberta Hamilton, married Lillian Price, a wealthy American widow, in 1888 and used her money to put electric lighting and central heating in Blenheim Palace. The 8th duke's brother, Lord Randolph Churchill, married the American heiress Jennie Jerome in 1874. When Alva Vanderbilt discovered that the freshly divorced 9th Duke of Marlborough, known as 'Sunny', was also in the market for an heiress, she placed her eighteen-year-old daughter, who was already in love with someone else, under virtual house arrest and intercepted all her mail to make sure that she had no contact with anyone who might scupper her chances of becoming the next Marlborough duchess. The duke was also in love with someone else, but needed the money for more improvements to Blenheim, and so the deal was struck and they were wed in 1896. From a financial point of view, the marriage was a success. It came with a massive dowry worth three million pounds (about a hundred million pounds today) and a twenty-thousand-pounds-a-year income from the Vanderbilt wealth. From a personal point of view, however, it was a disaster. Sunny made no effort to hide his reasons for marrying and, during the carriage ride after the ceremony, coldly informed his new wife that his mistress was waiting for him in England. When that marriage ended in divorce in 1921, Sunny married another wealthy American, Gladys Deacon.

Despite their potential for marital misery, transatlantic matches became so much the rage that a whole industry sprang up to serve their needs, including a quarterly publication *The Titled American* which contained a register of all the eligible titled European bachelors, with a handy description of their age, accomplishments and prospects – for example, this in March 1890:

> The Marquess of Winchester is the fifteenth Marquess and Premier Marquess in the Peerage of Great Britain. He is also the Hereditary Bearer of the Cap of Maintenance. The entailed estates amount to 4,700 acres, yielding an income of $22,000. He is 32 years of age, and a captain of the Coldstream Guards. Family seat: Amport House, Hampshire.

Many of the new imports came from New York families who were desperate to stand out in a famously snobbish society where money was no guarantee of social acceptance. Despite her great wealth, Winaretta Singer, the sewing machine heiress, was snubbed by Nancy Astor, the most powerful woman in New York society, on account of her perceived lack of 'good breeding'. But when Winaretta went to Europe and married the French Prince de Polignac, she was very quickly admitted to Lady Astor's inner sanctum.

Among the most successful of the 'Dollar Princesses' was May Goelet, an American heiress who, after flirting with almost all of the British aristocrats listed in *Burke's Peerage*, settled on the Duke of Roxburghe in 1903. The duke was keen to play down any suggestion that he was a fortune hunter: he reassured an assembly of US news reporters, 'I am merely an Englishman who believes in American institutions.' No one was rude enough to ask if this belief had been shaped by the bride's vast dowry. After ten childless years, the duke and duchess went to see a specialist in Vienna, offering £1,000 if he could help them conceive – double that if the child was a boy. The doctor earned his fee by advising the duchess to give up sugar: a boy, the Marquess of Bowmont, was born a year later, in 1913.

The new American imports found that, on the subject of providing heirs, the British aristocracy could be remarkably blunt. On being introduced to her husband's grandmother for the first time, the new 9th Duchess of Marlborough was informed: 'Your first duty is to have a child, and it must be a son, because it would be intolerable to have that little upstart Winston become Duke. Are you in the family way?'* It was standard procedure for a new bride to become pregnant as promptly as possible. The American heiress Florence Garner had a shock on her wedding night when her new husband Sir William Gordon-Cumming told her, 'I won't come in to say goodnight unless you want me to.' She replied innocently, 'Oh, that would be nice.' Poor Florence was astounded by what followed.

One of the more desperate toffs to try his luck with an American heiress was Winston Churchill's uncle, Moreton Frewen, a charmingly incompetent adventurer who had such a knack for mismanaging his affairs that he became known as 'Mortal Ruin'.† He was born in Sussex in 1853 into one of England's very oldest landed families, the

---

* The pressure was always on to produce a boy; the 9th Duke of Buccleuch, on hearing that his daughter-in-law, the future duchess, had had a girl, immediately cancelled the planned celebrations.
† His descendants, however, refer to him to this day not as Mortal Ruin but as 'Immortal Ruin', as he got through two family fortunes.

Frewens being Saxon nobility at the time of the Norman Conquest. By the age of twenty-five Moreton had blown all of his inheritance on the turf and cards, but in 1879 he persuaded his brother Richard to put up sixteen thousand pounds so he could start a cattle ranch in America. Frewen built himself a home in Wyoming just north of Cheyenne, a huge Jacobean-style black-and-white mansion known to the local cowboys as 'the Castle', replete with a solid walnut staircase and huge dining room with a balcony at one end from where musicians played. His extravagance was an unending source of astonishment to his neighbours. He ordered fresh cut flowers from Denver, crates of champagne from Chicago and oysters from the Atlantic coast. They found it particularly amusing when the cattle trader Tim Foley managed to sell him the same herd of cattle twice in one afternoon; legend has it that Foley drove the herd past Moreton to count, then around a hill and past him again.

Frewen had to borrow heavily to keep his ambitious enterprise going. Fortunately he had a knack for convincing members of the English nobility to invest in Wyoming cattle. Part of his strategy was to invite potential investors to stay with him at his ranch, where he entertained titled guests with lavish hunting parties. One who took up the invitation to hunt buffalo with Frewen was the diplomat Sir Maurice de Bunsen. Early one morning, Bunsen spotted what he took to be an undersized buffalo grazing at some distance from the camp. After stalking the beast for several hours he shot it, only to discover that it was in fact the dairy cow on which the party depended for its supplies of fresh milk.

Another of Frewen's guests, the future Lord

Desborough, took a bet that he would shoot an animal before breakfast the next morning. Within minutes of setting out he became lost and was found, dishevelled and dehydrated, two days later, by a trapper. He fared much better, however, than his friend 'Gilly' Leigh, eldest son of the cricketer Lord Leigh. One evening Leigh left the campfire to empty his bladder behind what he took to be a line of brush, but which turned out to be the tops of pine trees growing at the bottom of a sheer-walled canyon a hundred feet below. His body was discovered at the bottom of the cliff a couple of days later.

Another of those entertained was the Earl of Mayo, who made himself unpopular by bringing with him six dogs. One of Frewen's neighbours complained. 'That crazy ass Mayo has been spoiling everyone's sport with a lot of curs ... he has succeeded in scaring all the elks off the mountain.'

Despite all of this aristocratic patronage, Frewen's cattle enterprise struggled. Two bad winters brought losses, while rustlers, raiding Indians, wolves, grasshoppers and prairie fires all took their toll. His financial prospects, however, were about to take an upturn. In 1881 Frewen went to New York, where it was open season for Europeans in pursuit of heiresses. There he met Clara Jerome, the daughter of the speculator and New York millionaire Leonard Jerome, known as 'the King of Wall Street'. His other daughter, Jennie, had recently married young Lord Randolph Churchill. The Jerome family was wealthy enough and certainly snobbish enough to turn up their noses at a penniless English baron, but Clara fell for Frewen's good looks and charm and the couple were married. Soon afterwards, however, Leonard Jerome went bankrupt, leaving Frewen with little else but a pretty wife and the honour of becoming uncle to a future British prime minister.

Within three years Frewen's cattle business collapsed. He returned shamefaced to England, where he was dubbed by the press, without a trace of irony, the 'Wyoming Cattle King'. He tried to raise more funds, but this time his powers of persuasion failed him. He returned to Wyoming one more time to sell up. Even then he missed out on making a fortune, because he sold for a song the land on which West Superior City now stands.

In the years that followed, Frewen got involved in various mad business ventures in places raging from Canada to Australia, India and Africa. He tried supplying axle grease for locomotives, making artificial ice, extracting gold from refuse ore, separating tin from zinc, shipping timber from Siberia to Europe via the Northwest Passage, using bat guano from Mexico for fertiliser (when he gave some to friends for use in their gardens, the plants died), creating a disinfectant made from seawater and putting forward a proposal to capture German zeppelins and use them to carry the Royal Mail. He borrowed heavily and lost money on them all. He also speculated unsuccessfully in shares in De Beers Consolidated. It is difficult to see how anyone could lose money on South African gold and diamonds, but Frewen managed it somehow.

Mysteriously, given Frewen's doubtful business acumen, his brother-in-law Randolph Churchill got him a job as financial adviser to Sir Salar Jung, prime minister of the Indian state of Hyderabad. In the end the only deal struck by Frewen was a bargain in a Turkish harem for a bride for his new employee. In 1897 Moreton's nephew, Winston Churchill, wrote his first book and entrusted the correction of his proofs to his Uncle Frewen. Unfortunately he was almost as useless a proofreader as he was a businessman and the first edition appeared, according to Churchill, with 'many scores of shocking misprints and with no attempt to organise punctuation'.

For the rest of his life Frewen continued to spend beyond his means, meanwhile neglecting to pay his servants, arguing that they preferred it like this because 'it made them feel more part of the family'. When he died in 1924 his estate was worth less than fifty pounds; his financial adventures had cost his friends millions. Rudyard Kipling noted, 'he lived in every sense except what is called common'.

Some of the noblemen who followed Frewen in the hunt for an American bride were even more hopeless. Alice Thaw, heiress to a Pittsburgh railroad fortune, married the Earl of Yarmouth in 1903. On the morning of the wedding, the groom was arrested for failure to pay outstanding debts and the bride was kept waiting at the church while her intended and her father renegotiated her dowry. During the wedding ceremony the mood turned even sourer when Alice's favourite dog jumped on Yarmouth, who then flung the dog violently against a wall. The only grounds for annulment of an English marriage were insanity prior to marriage, an already-existing marriage or non-consummation: on the last point the marriage was annulled and Lord Yarmouth received no money at all. The Thaws, suspecting that an English aristocrat's marriage proposal was less a compliment than a calculation, had taken the precaution of tying up their daughter's money in trusts. After 1895, a year that saw many Anglo-American matches, the practice tapered off. The American nouveau riche began to doubt the wisdom, or the necessity, of having an impoverished aristocrat in the family.

HIGHLAND FLINGS

When it came to aristocratic dirty linen aired in public, there were few piles of soiled laundry quite as smelly or heaped quite as high as that exposed in the Argyll divorce case of 1963. Neither the press nor the public were strangers to tales of upper-class adultery and the occasional unnatural practice (see the Ampthill baby case) but nothing would have prepared them for what was about to emerge.

The parties to the divorce were Ian Douglas Campbell, 11th Duke of Argyll, and his third wife Margaret, who was thought of as a great society beauty. The duke instigated proceedings after reading his wife's diary, in which she had carefully detailed the physical attributes of her many lovers, according to her *Daily Telegraph* obituary, 'as if she was running them at Newmarket'.

When it came to possible co-respondents the duke was spoilt for choice. He eventually whittled them down to eighty-eight men, including two politicians, three royals and an American businessman whose activities the judge likened to a tomcat, as well as two unidentifiable men shown in a series of thirteen Polaroid photographs. The photos shed light on two episodes; in the first, the duchess, naked except for three strings of pearls, is fellating an unknown male, known to posterity as 'the Headless Man'. The second set of pictures captured another unidentifiable man masturbating, one captioned, 'Thinking of you', and another, unnecessarily, 'Finished'.

Seventeen-year-old Michael Thornton described the duchess's seduction technique. While wandering near the Argyll estate on a hot day in 1958 he was approached by her ladyship and offered a drink and a hot bath. No sooner had he started to soap himself in the castle's pink tub than the naked duchess stepped into the bathroom to offer more hospitality. Her friends ascribed her nymphomania to injuries sustained in a fall down a lift shaft in 1943. It was all too much for the judge, Lord Wheatley, who denounced the duchess as 'a completely promiscuous woman' who 'indulged in what I can only describe as disgusting sexual acts'. Speculation over the identity of 'the Headless Man' – or rather headless men – continued to entertain the public. Among the frontrunners were Winston Churchill's son-in-law Duncan Sandys (aka 'Shrunken Glands'), on the basis that he was one of the only people in the country with a Polaroid camera.*

The duchess lost the case and had to pay seven thousand pounds in damages but it was the victorious duke who suffered most from the fallout. His attempts to publish his ex-wife's private medical notes, including observations from her doctors on her fragile psychological state, in a series of Sunday newspaper articles led to accusations of ungentlemanly behaviour and he was forced to resign his membership of his London club White's.

As for the duchess, within a year or two of the divorce, her name was back on the invitation lists of all the London embassies, but as her life spiralled into decline she remained a firm favourite of gossip columnists who tracked her various feuds with her family, landlords, bankers and servants. She was forced to open up her Mayfair house to

---

* It is now generally understood that the first "headless man" was probably Duncan Sandys, while his masturbating rival was the actor Douglas Fairbanks Jr.

paying visitors until, in 1978, she was obliged to sell it and move into an apartment in the Grosvenor House hotel. In the 1980s she fell out with a recalcitrant maid, Mrs Edith Springett, after the servant was found unconscious on the floor of the duchess's bedroom with an empty bottle of her whisky lying nearby. The duchess dispatched solicitor's letters instructing Springett to desist from calling her a 'Mayfair whore' and a 'silly old bitch' in front of her guests. By 1990 her fortune, left to her by her millionaire father, had gone, swallowed up by litigation and general extravagance, and she was evicted from her hotel for unpaid rent and placed in a nursing home. Three years later, penniless and alone, she suffered a fall in her bathroom that broke her neck, instantly killing her.

7

Sporting Grandees

The gaming rooms of White's and Brooks's were not the only means by which the aristocracy could divest themselves of their family fortunes with spectacular rapidity.

Over a period of roughly 150 years between the middle of the eighteenth century and the end of the nineteenth, the British upper classes more or less invented organised sport. They didn't invent every sport, of course, and many types developed elsewhere in the world, but they did invent the rules for major sports such as boxing, cricket, horse-racing, football, golf and tennis, to name but a few.

209

Why was the British aristocracy in particular so enthusiastic about games? You might think that it was something to do with their innate love of sport as a builder of manly character; teamwork and moral fortitude, qualities that made a gentleman good at war – 'the playing fields of Eton' and all that. Admittedly, some of that came into it, but not until much later when the Victorians invented the idea of the 'noble amateur'.

In the beginning, it was all about the gambling.

In the eighteenth century most of the money in Britain belonged to the landed classes and what they loved doing with their money more than anything else was having a flutter. But in order to make a sporting bet you need competition, and for competition you need rules. The aristocracy wanted to know exactly what they were betting on, so they regulated sport. Put another way, much of global sport as we recognise it today would not exist were it not for the British aristocracy's addiction to hard-core gambling.

PAY UP AND PLAY THE GAME

The real purpose of organised cricket was an excuse to gamble. Despite the best efforts of historians we don't know exactly when cricket began, but the British aristocracy's love of the game dates at least as far back as 1677 when Thomas Dacre, Earl of Sussex, drew three pounds from his treasurer to go 'to the crekitt match at ye Dicker' (although it seems his sixteen-year-old wife was much less enthralled with the game than he was). It only started to emerge as an organised sport when the nobility realised the game offered more betting opportunities than any sport yet devised by man.

In cricket's early days the amounts bet were enormous. In 1731 there was a 'great match' between the Duke of Richmond's XI and an XI of Mr Chambers in Surrey for a stake of two hunred guineas. For major matches, stakes could be as high as one thousand guineas – the equivalent of around one hundred thousand pounds in today's money. They were not sedate affairs, as *Fog's Weekly Journal* recorded: 'The same night the Duke of Richmond and his cricket players were greatly insulted by the mob at Richmond's, some of them having their shirts torn off their backs: and it was said a lawsuit would commence about the play.'

Cricket was also attracting strange bets from its earliest days. The 4th Earl of Tankerville once bet one hundred pounds that his gardener, the bowler 'Lumpy' Stevens, would land his ball on a feather placed at a certain distance. Lumpy won the bet for his employer.

Organised cricket may have arisen from the aristocracy's love of gambling, but that's not to say that they didn't also enjoy the game for what it was. It has a tradition of nothing much happening for a long time, which made it the perfect sport for a gentleman with lots of leisure time to spare. Among the prominent Georgian cricketing aristocrats were the 4th Earl of Sandwich, who was often pictured with a cricket bat, Lord Mountfort, Lord Temple and the Duke of Bedford, all of whom organised their own teams. The most important development in upper-class patronage of cricket was probably the arrival on the scene of Frederick Louis, Prince of Wales – 'Poor Fred' in his famous epitaph – who was so taken with the game that he had cricket bats shipped out to Hanover where he was schooled. By all accounts Poor Fred wasn't a gifted player but he was a very enthusiastic spectator. In 1744, he and his brother Augustus, Duke of

Cumberland, and the Duke of Richmond went to watch 'the greatest cricket match ever known' between the county of Kent, led by Lord John Sackville, and 'All England'. The most memorable feature of this encounter, once again, was crowd trouble, and ropes had to be used to separate gentleman spectators from the riff-raff. Prince Frederick left the crease for the last time in 1751, killed, according to one account, by the delayed effects of a blow on the head from a cricket ball.

As a popular song of the Georgian era put it, cricket was 'the game for the low and the great'; the Duke of Richmond, for example, was quite happy to play in a team captained by his gardener. Despite the sporting mixture of patrons and plebeians during matches, however, the game was run strictly along class lines. There was no social mixing outside of the match and strict codes of deference were imposed on the pitch. No one thought it strange that during play, gentlemen always wore top hats while the lower orders were obliged to wear caps. In one game, a bowling shepherd called George Lamborn repeatedly beat the Duke of Dorset's bat. One unplayable ball missed leg stump by a whisker and Lamborn shouted: 'It was tedious near you, sir!' There were gasps all round, not because Lamborn's skill had made Dorset look silly, but because he had addressed him incorrectly as 'sir' rather than 'your Grace'.

John Sackville, 3rd Duke of Dorset, was a cricket fanatic whose patronage of the game was legendary. He was one of the original members of the MCC who drew up the laws of the game, and he maintained his own team of cricketers at great expense by giving them spurious jobs around his country estate at Knole in Kent. Dorset was also a notorious gambler who spent considerable sums in the gentlemen's clubs of St James's. He was involved in a number of allegedly crooked cricket matches. In 1783 high odds were laid on a game in which the duke, playing for Kent, missed a couple of suspiciously easy catches.

Dorset was also a cricketing evangelist. In 1784 he was appointed as ambassador to France, although he spent most of the summer hopping back to England to catch up with the cricket. While he was in Paris he hatched an ambitious plan to turn the French into a nation of cricket enthusiasts by assembling the first ever international touring side. On 10 August 1789, just as his team was about to leave Dover for Paris, they were surprised to encounter the duke fleeing in the opposite direction from the French Revolution. He never forgave the French for wrecking his tour, describing them as 'a nation of intriguing, low, artful and cretinous people'.

Another famous cricketing toff, Lionel, Lord Tennyson, grandson of the poet Alfred, was a veteran of the Somme and Ypres where he was wounded three times and reported dead twice. Off the field he was chiefly famous for his play-boy lifestyle and running up substantial gambling losses – twelve thousand pounds in a week (about three hundred thousand pounds today). Tennyson earned his place in sporting history with his brief but brilliant spell as captain of the England cricket team midway through the home series against the Australians in 1921. England had just been defeated inside two days at Trent Bridge and were facing humiliation with their worst ever run of Ashes defeats. Tennyson, a hard-hitting batsman, was thirty-two and had played in only a handful of Test matches with only moderate success when the selectors took their gamble on him. He often went for days without sleep, especially when

Hampshire were playing in London, and received news of his appointment for the game, which was starting later that day, by telegram well past midnight while 'relaxing' with friends at the Embassy Club in London. He said later that if he had only heard the news earlier he would have 'knocked off a cigar or two'. He then confidently struck a fifty-pound wager that he would crack a half-century.

Tennyson went on to hit a swashbuckling 74 not out, returning to the pavilion 'black-and-blue all over'. He only played in one more match and his batting heroics were thereafter confined to his captaincy of Hampshire. He was distrusted by the MCC for his autocratic behaviour, not least of which was his insistence on using his butler, Walter Livsey, as wicketkeeper; he had instructions to keep several bottles of champagne handy for his lordship to celebrate victory or drown the disappointment of defeat. Tennyson also had an idiosyncratic method of keeping in touch with his players from the pavilion. One struggling Hampshire batsman was surprised when a boy in a blue post office uniform approached him at the crease bearing an orange envelope. Inside was a note from Tennyson, which read: 'For pity's sake, what do you think your bat's for?' Despite his breeding, he often resembled 'an unmade bed' in the words of cricketing author Jeremy Malies. He once arrived at the crease the worse for wear, wearing his protective box outside his trousers. He died a virtually penniless alcoholic in 1951 but, according to his biographer, 'in the manner of an English gentleman, sitting up in bed smoking and reading *The Times*'.

Cricket gambling scandals are almost as old as the game itself. In 1744 the *Morning Chronicle* complained about 'the excessive gaming and dissipation' and that 'cricket matches are now degenerated into business of importance'. In 1817 the MCC player William Lambert achieved a curious double when he became the first player to score two centuries in the same match. It turned out to be his farewell appearance, because soon afterwards he became the first cricketer to be banned for life, following match-fixing allegations in an earlier game. The legendary all-rounder 'Silver Billy' Beldham* recalled a match played at Lord's in which both sides had been got at. The bowler refused to bowl straight and the batsman refused to try to hit the ball: the game ground to a halt. By the late nineteenth century, cricket was institutionally corrupt on a worldwide basis. In 1879 there were riots at the Sydney cricket ground when England played Australia because gamblers were unhappy when the heavily backed local hero, Billy Murdoch, had been given run out.

By the early 1800s, traditional village cricket organised by aristocratic patronage was all but dead and professionalism came to the fore, but class divisions within the sport remained as strong as ever. From 1803 the MCC insisted on a distinction between Gentlemen – cricketers who didn't play for money – and Players – those who did. A gentleman amateur was much worthier of admiration than the professional who trained hard and may have absorbed some nasty and ungentlemanly techniques such as 'gamesmanship'. The 7th Lord Hawke, who captained Yorkshire from 1880 to 1910 and led teams on several world tours, once noted it would be a 'black day' for national prestige if a

---

* Clearly a splendid sporting specimen, he is reputed to have fathered thirty-nine children.

professional ever captained a touring team. For much of the twentieth century cricket was still riddled with class distinction. Hawke and his ilk must have been spinning in their graves when the MCC finally abolished the distinction between Gentlemen and Players in 1963.

PUGILIST PEERS

Aristocratic patronage of boxing, or prize fighting as it was properly called, helped it emerge as a fashionable spectator sport during the Regency period. The first recorded modern prize fight, however, took place much earlier, in January 1681. This is a description of the event written up in *The London Protestant Mercury*: 'Yesterday a match of boxing was performed before his Grace, the Duke of Albemarle, between the duke's footman and a butcher. The latter won the prize, as he hath done many others before, being accounted, though but a little man, the best at that exercise in England.'

The 'noble science' reached a peak in the nineteenth century, a golden age of pugilism when 'heroes of the fist' were revered as gods and were courted and feted by the upper classes. The sport attracted the likes of Lord Byron, who wrote about boxing and often put on gloves himself. The Dukes of York and Clarence, the Earl of Barrymore and the 'half-mad Lord' Camelford were all boxing patrons and regularly attended fights.

Like cricket, boxing was a magnet for high-stakes gamblers and riddled with corruption. In 1750 the Duke of Cumberland lost a staggering ten thousand pounds on the disputed 'fight of the century' when hot favourite Jack Broughton was defeated by Jack Slack. The victor later confessed to earning more by losing fights than winning them. The fact that these contests were illegal added to the excitement. In 1842 the 6th Viscount Chetwynd was charged with organising a prize fight in rural Bedfordshire and obstructing the local magistrate who tried to stop it. One of the viscount's twelve co-defendants was a former champion of England, 'Blind Burke'; each was fined forty pounds.

England's public schools also played an important role in the development of boxing. Conditions in the schools were appalling and brutality was rife (in the 1840s Lord Salisbury, a future prime minister, described how a boy called Troughton Major drank ten pints of beer then held a burning candle in a fellow Etonian's mouth) so it was always a good idea to be able to defend yourself. Organised fist-fighting became popular among public school boys because it was evidence of physical courage and 'bottom'. These contests were highly dangerous and sometimes fatal. At Eton in 1825, following a classroom squabble, Francis Cooper, the thirteen-year-old son of the Earl of Shaftesbury, fought Charles Wood, who was a year older and much bigger. After a brutal fistfight lasting more than two and a half hours both boys collapsed. Cooper fell unconscious and died later that evening.

To begin with, boxing was an exclusively British sport.* Foreign visitors to England were completely baffled by the idea that you could get enjoyment out of watching grown men giving and receiving hard blows about the head. Henri Misson de Valbourg, a Huguenot refugee in London,

---

* America didn't catch on to the fight scene until well into the nineteenth century and even then it was mostly under the influence of immigrants from England and Ireland.

recalled in 1685 that even if two little boys started a street fight, crowds would gather, 'not only of other boys, porters and rabble, but all sorts of "men of fashion" pushing to the front and hiring seats if they could'. It also came in useful when dealing with coachmen who overcharged. Misson recalled seeing the Duke of Grafton 'at fisticuffs in the open street with such a fellow whom he lambed most horribly'. It would never have happened in France, Misson noted.

The history of organised boxing is generally linked with the names of two sporting peers in particular: John Sholto Douglas, 9th Marquess of Queensberry, and Hugh Lowther, 5th Earl of Lonsdale. The first is remembered eponymously as the sporting gentleman who turned the barbarous activity of bare-knuckle fighting into a civilised contest by formulating a set of rules governing professional boxing, thereafter known as the 'Queensberry Rules'. The second gave his name to the much-prized accessory sought after by every British boxer, the Lonsdale belt. Appropriately, both men were handy with their fists. Oddly enough, they seem to have enjoyed rather more credit for their respective contributions to boxing than they actually merited.

FIGHTING MAD

John Sholto Douglas, 9th Marquess of Queensberry, was a mean-tempered, aggressive bigot who was ready to slap anyone who gave him so much as a sideways look. His background goes some way towards explaining his bad behaviour. The Queensberry family history was a series of farcical personal disasters interspersed with the odd catastrophe.

His ancestor, the 3rd Marquess, James Douglas, is referred to in some peerage records as having 'died young', beyond which there is very little mention of him at all. Other accounts describe him as an 'imbecile' and 'violently insane'. From childhood he was kept under lock and key in a ground-floor room of the family home in Edinburgh with the windows boarded up in permanent darkness. One evening in 1707 he escaped then killed and ate a kitchen boy. It was some time before his escape was discovered, by which time Douglas was standing over what was left of his victim, roasting on a spit.

The continuing family line was riven with suicide and sadness, if not actual cannibalism. The fourth marquess was a sex pest with a taste for opera girls and teenage ballerinas. His wife Catherine and their son were also afflicted by the family madness: the son shot himself dead in 1754 while on a coach journey to London with his mother. Another heir drowned when he tried to jump a wide river with his horse and both fell in. Other holders of the title drank themselves into early graves.

The early and often violent deaths that had plagued the family were not only confined to its heirs. Several male Douglases were killed in hunting accidents, usually when guns were discharged as they crawled through hedges. The seventh marquess died on 6 August 1858 while out shooting rabbits from the 'accidental explosion of his gun', although some suspected gambling debts were to blame; the *Evening Herald* reported, 'in sporting circles a belief is expressed that the death was not accidental; he had recently sustained severe losses'. Also worthy of a special mention was the 10th Marquess, Percy Douglas, who hated cars so much that he tried to get a court permit that would allow him to shoot drivers dead on sight. In 1900 he was left three hundred thousand pounds but within eighteen months somehow managed to become bankrupt three times. You could describe the Douglas family as gloriously dysfunctional.

And so to our boxing patron, the 9th Marquess of Queensberry. His education, if you can call it that, was harsh. As a naval cadet at Portsmouth he was expected to scrub the decks at 5 a.m. The on-board entertainment was a game called 'sling the monkey', in which a cadet would be swung from a bowline while his messmates would hit him with knotted ropes. When Queensberry was fourteen his father Archibald committed suicide, having lost all his money in one mad bet on a horse called Saunterer. As a young man Queensberry was a derring-do sportsman who spent his time on long, death-defying swims in the open sea or falling off his horse and breaking limbs, injuries he dismissed as 'temporary inconveniences'. Short and stockily built, he excelled at boxing; contemporaries described him as 'absolutely fearless'. He lost his Christian faith following a tragic accident shortly before his twenty-first birthday in 1865, when his eighteen-year-old brother went missing while climbing the Matterhorn mountain in Switzerland. Queensberry led an exhibition to locate the body, but found only a belt, one boot and a pair of gloves. His atheism hardened as the years passed.

He had a difficult relationship with his mother, who seemed to pick causes just to annoy him. She was anti-blood sports and a rabid Irish nationalist, despite only visiting Ireland once, at the age of two. She infuriated her eldest son by sending money to the families of Fenians who had murdered policemen. Many people suspected that

Queensberry's entire immediate family were unhinged. One of his sisters married a baker's boy more than twenty years her junior. Another sister concocted a stunt involving a forged letter from the king of the Zulu people, then hoaxed newspapers with a claim that assassins had tried to stab her. Another brother, James, was an alcoholic who was once imprisoned for sending insulting Christmas cards. In 1891 he was found in the Euston Station Hotel, having slit his own throat.

John Sholto Douglas was meanwhile steadily acquiring a reputation as a side-whiskered psychopath. On a luxury steamboat in Brazil he got into a row with a fellow passenger over the difference between emus and ostriches and knocked him out cold. He was once arrested for giving his second son, Percy, a black eye during an altercation on the corner of Old Bond Street. His reputation as a violent crank was sealed when he challenged the Liberal Foreign Secretary Lord Rosebery to 'fisticuffs' for elevating his eldest son to the peerage behind his back. In 1880 Queensberry was ejected from the House of Lords for refusing to take the oath and openly mocking Christianity as 'mumbo-jumbo'. He wasn't too popular in the House of Commons, either, after describing the prime minister, Gladstone, as a 'Christian whoremonger and hypocrite' and his successor the Earl of Rosebery as an 'underbred disgusting Jew pimp'. His Tourette's-like outbursts regularly disrupted theatrical events. He was thrown out of the Lyceum Theatre in London for threatening and abusive behaviour when he objected to a scene mocking 'free-thinkers' in Tennyson's play *The Promise of May*.

Queensberry married at the age of twenty-one and fathered five children in seven years, but his first marriage ended in divorce when his wife sued for adultery. At the age of forty-nine he married again, this time to a girl from Eastbourne a few days after her twenty-first birthday. She left him more or less immediately because he was unable to consummate the marriage. Divorce papers were served within months and he underwent humiliating examinations to discover if he could manage an erection. It turned out he was afflicted with Peyronie's disease – 'the formation of lesions resulting in a distortion of the erect penis' – possibly caused, it was believed, by spending too much time in the saddle astride a galloping horse; the marriage was annulled.

There was worse to come. In 1894, his eldest son Francis, at the age of twenty-six, blew his brains out in a turnip patch on the day before his engagement was to be announced in the newspapers. Francis worked for Lord Rosebery, the foreign secretary and future prime minister. Francis, it was widely gossiped, was in a homosexual relationship with his employer. The marquess followed Rosebery all the way to Bad Homburg where he was taking the waters and threatened to horsewhip him. Rosebery was saved by the intervention of the Prince of Wales and the local police. Afterwards, Rosebery wrote to Queen Victoria complaining, 'I am unhappy at being pursued by a pugilist of unsound mind.'

Only a year after public revelations of his impotence and his son's death in a homosexual scandal, Queensberry discovered that his third son, Lord Alfred, was in a relationship with Oscar Wilde. In the context of the widespread homophobia of the age, his distress was understandable; to have one gay son might be seen as unfortunate; to have two was starting to look like carelessness. Queensberry certainly seemed to believe that homosexuality was contagious. He planned to humiliate Wilde publicly by disrupting the

London premiere of *The Importance of Being Earnest* in February 1895, but was denied entrance. A few days later he went to Wilde's club and left a calling card which read: 'To Oscar Wilde, posing as a Somdomite.' (*sic*) Wilde sued for criminal libel, disastrously, and the lurid details emerging from the trial led to the media furore of 1890s. When Wilde was convicted of gross indecency and sentenced to two years' hard labour, Queensberry was jubilant: he boasted that he had received a telegram reading: 'Every man in the City is with you. Kill the bugger!' Queensberry died suddenly in January 1900 of a cerebral haemorrhage, convinced to the end that he was being stalked by 'unknown persons' seeking revenge for his persecution of Wilde. In its obituary, the *Sporting Times* noted, 'It is not for us here to inquire into the workings of his peculiar mind. It had a craving for something: it knew not what.'

What of his celebrated role as the author of the Queensberry Rules? They were written by someone else – his old Cambridge classmate, a Welsh journalist called John Graham Chambers. It was Chambers who drew up twelve guidelines, including three-minute rounds, the ten-count for a knockout and the mandatory use of gloves, which have formed the basis of boxing rules ever since. They were named in Queensberry's honour after he donated three prize cups to a boxing tournament in 1867 and Chambers shrewdly surmised that his friend's name would carry more clout.* To his credit, Queensberry never

---

* Queensberry's greatest ambition, however, was to ride in the Grand National and win, scuppered when his cousin, who owned what turned out to be the winning horse, decided that Queensberry was past his best. The marquess never forgave him.

pretended to have had a hand in their actual formulation. Honesty, no matter how brutally he expressed it, was one of his more endearing traits.

THE YELLOW EARL

The history of the aristocracy is littered with examples of people who have drunk, gambled or otherwise roistered themselves into oblivion, but few succeeded in running down the family fortune with such single-minded dedication as our second boxing peer, Hugh Lowther, 5th Earl of Lonsdale, the best known sporting patron and the most extravagant spender of his generation.

Like Queensberry, Lonsdale had a colourful family history. His ancestor James Lowther, the 1st Earl of Lonsdale, seems to have had few redeeming features judging by his various nicknames: 'Wicked Jimmy', 'The Bad Earl', 'Jemmy Grasp-all', or according to the Scottish church leader Alexander Carlyle, 'a madman too influential to lock up'.

The son of a wealthy governor of Barbados, in his teens James Lowther inherited the baronetcy of Lowther along with vast estates and mines on both sides of the Pennines. Driven by his ruthlessly ambitious, widowed mother, he became an MP before he was twenty-one and went on to control nine parliamentary seats, known as 'Lowther's Ninepins'. Thanks to the prevailing corrupt political system, neither Manchester nor Birmingham had a single MP, but the 'rotten borough' of Appleby (population 1,233) had two. Into one of these, Lowther put 'his man', the twenty-one-year-old William Pitt. When Pitt became prime minister three years later, he rewarded Lowther with an earldom. Lowther's wealth, derived mostly from Cumbrian coal, was staggering, but he was a notoriously tight-fisted employer. One of his land agents was John Wordsworth, father of the poet William. When John died, leaving William a young orphan, the earl owed him about five thousand pounds in wages. The money was never recovered in the earl's lifetime. After a pit disaster in Whitehaven one brave employee threatened to sue the earl, who responded by closing the mines, rendering 2500 jobless until the lawsuit was withdrawn.

Another employee, Daniel Bloom, managed the Lowther carpet factory, where the workers, orphans from a local foundling hospital, were paid a pittance. After years of hardship and no pay, Bloom was heavily in debt and paying his child workforce out of his own pocket. He eventually found the courage to send a begging letter to the earl for money to support his wife and family and run the factory. The letter was ignored.

Lonsdale kept a string of mistresses but he fell in love with a tenant's daughter and kept her in luxury. When she died he went from 'wicked' to just plain weird. He couldn't bear to be parted from her, so her body remained lying in bed until the smell became unbearable, at which point he had her embalmed and placed in a glass-lidded coffin, which he used as a sideboard in his dining room. That's what you call commitment.

Wicked Jimmy finally died in 1802 from 'mortification of the bowels', unloved and unregretted. Besides the wealth of his vast estates, they found sixty thousand pounds in cash stashed away at Lowther Hall.

William Lowther, the 2nd Earl of Lonsdale, was distinguishable by his vivid red wig. His two favourite pastimes were hunting and 'entertaining' actress, and, although unmarried, he fathered several illegitimate children. He died in 1872 'in the arms of', or more accurately, on top of, a well-known opera singer, succeeded by his nephew Henry Lowther, who became MP for Westmorland. Although an MP for fifty-five years, during the whole of that time he never once made a speech. A political opponent, enraged at being beaten yet again at the hustings by 'Lowther the Silent', made an impassioned speech against him from the platform. When pressured to respond, Lowther replied: 'I point, gentlemen, to the polls', then left the stage.

The best known of the Lonsdales, and in his day probably the most famous English aristocrat in the world, was the 5th Earl, Hugh Cecil Lowther, born in 1857. His tenants knew him as 'Lordy'. In the popular press he became known as the Yellow Earl. The Prince of Wales, less charitably, called him 'the greatest liar in my kingdom'.

Hugh Lowther was the second son of the earl and had little prospect of inheriting, so his education was more or less abandoned. He was sent to school in Switzerland, where he ran away to join a travelling circus. Thereafter his schooling was performed by his father's former batman from the Life Guards and then by Jem Mace, the last bare-knuckle champion in England, who taught him very little apart from how to box.

As a young man he was prone to gambling disasters. He lost eighteen thousand pounds at one session and faced social ruin because he was unable to pay, but was bailed out by a family friend. When he was twenty-two, Lowther pawned his claim to the family estates for forty thousand pounds to speculate on the cattle-ranching boom in

Wyoming with his fox-hunting friend Moreton Frewen. The venture collapsed, leaving Lowther with massive debts, but he was bailed out yet again, this time by his family trustees, who quietly bought back the young lord's squandered birthright.

In 1882 Hugh Lowther unexpectedly inherited the earldom when his elder brother George obligingly drank himself to death. From near poverty Lowther suddenly ascended to dizzying heights of wealth, including hundreds of thousands of acres, a 365-room castle, two steam yachts, two London mansions and an annual income from Cumbrian coalmines of one hundred thousand pounds (about five million pounds today). At the age of twenty-five, with seemingly unlimited funds at his disposal, he had free rein to indulge his love of the finer things in life, which he did, in very fine style indeed.

The epithet 'colourful character' has been applied to several members of the Lonsdale family tree but the fifth earl would more truthfully be described as monochromatic. He was known as 'the Yellow Earl', not because of a self-inflicted liver problem (although he did drink a large brandy and half a bottle of white wine every morning for breakfast followed by champagne for 'elevenses') but because of his insistence that his entire estate, from his servants to his cars and carriages, should be kitted out in canary yellow. Even the wheelbarrows in his gardens were yellow, as were the cardigans worn by his gardeners as they grew the yellow gardenias in the hothouses of Lowther Castle. The gundogs on his estate were yellow Labradors, naturally. Another of his extravagances was his yellow Rolls-Royce, specially adapted with a raised roof, so he could wear his top hat while sitting inside. Although some argue that they are coincidences, his yellow livery may also have found its way onto the vehicles of the AA, which he helped found, and the away shirts of Arsenal football club, of which he was briefly chairman.

It was a time when dressing up like a dandy had largely fallen out of fashion but Lonsdale set a new standard for ostentation. He changed his clothing four times a day and had his suits made from his own Lonsdale tweed. His annual cigar bill alone was three thousand pounds. These cigars, six inches long and made to order, christened Lonsdales by his grateful tobacconist, were as much of a trademark as the fresh yellow gardenias he wore in his buttonhole, sent to him daily wherever he was in the world, regardless of cost.

Much of what Lonsdale owned was covered by one of the settlements that were commonly made among aristocratic families in Victorian England, designed to prevent heirs from frittering away the family's fortunes, and he was accountable to a committee of family trustees headed by his uncle William. His expenses, however, regularly exceeded his one hundred thousand pounds a year income and his battles with the trustees over his profligate spending were bitter and lifelong.

He ran a small army of officials and servants to spare him any administrative headaches arising from his vast inheritance. His retinue, which usually numbered around a hundred people, included a private orchestra of twenty-five musicians under his Master of Music, who travelled with him whenever he moved from one of his many grand homes to another. A special train was laid on for his household with a carriage reserved for himself and another for his dogs. Lonsdale had a quick temper and no one in his household was safe from it. Insubordinate staff could find themselves flat on their backs, at the receiving end of one his lordship's uppercuts to the jaw.

He took the same reckless, highly conspicuous approach to his private life. Throughout his marriage to Lady Grace Gordon, daughter of the 10th Marquess of Huntley, his name was linked to a string of beautiful women and he was rarely out of the Victorian scandal sheets. He and Sir George Chetwynd were rivals for the attention of Lily Langtry, who was also mistress of the Prince of Wales. The two grandees went toe-to-toe in Hyde Park, shouting 'Don't meddle with my Lily!' Sir George struck Lonsdale with his riding whip, then they fought with fists, before wrestling in the dust until they were separated by the Duke of Portland.

Lonsdale's brazenly public affair with the married actress Violet Cameron made international headlines. He and the actress were living in a house in Hampstead as Mr and Mrs Thompson until her real husband sued for adultery when it became evident that Violet was carrying the earl's child. Queen Victoria took a hand in the matter and let it be known that she expected Lord Lonsdale to 'disappear' until the scandal subsided.

He took the hint. In February 1888 Lonsdale set off from Liverpool for Arctic Canada 'in search of pleasure and sport', taking with him his butler and four springer spaniels. The trip was officially termed an exploration to collect specimens on behalf of a body called the Scotch Naturalist Society, but it was mainly an extended hunting trip. He wrote home to Lady Lonsdale, 'I have found out the best hunting ground in America. You can see 50 or 60 bear a day, and deer, walrus and sea lion, etc. I also know where thousands of walrus and polar bear breed, and we could easily get at them in a yacht.'

Although the expedition, for its time, was undoubtedly remarkable and dangerous, Lonsdale's gift for telling tall tales about his travels would have given Baron Munchausen a run for his money. One of the earl's frequently told anecdotes was about how he saved the Cheyenne stagecoach from bandits. Another was his personal discovery of the Klondike gold field; he claimed he walked over it and came across a few nuggets, but nothing worth picking up, so he simply reported the matter to the governor general of Canada. Flying in the face of the polar exploration history, Lonsdale also claimed that he discovered the North Pole, twenty years before Robert Peary got there. 'People who haven't been to the North Pole always imagine that the snow there is white', his lordship explained helpfully in his memoirs. 'They are quite wrong, the snow is pink.'

Lonsdale clearly wasn't quite cut out to be a scientist but, as was the custom with aristocratic Victorian travellers, he dutifully collected artefacts and souvenirs along the way and later gave around two hundred items to the British Museum, which now form the core of its Arctic collection. He also kept a vivid journal, parts of which were an eye-watering *tour de force* of political correctness. He disliked the Athapaskans and called the Chipewyan 'dirty filthy brutes', while the Slavey were 'a funny-looking lot'. One day, after watching some Inuit driving beluga whales into the shallow waters as he was 'walking home', he sensed the threat from a man 'with a villainous countenance' and a large knife in his hand. Lonsdale wrote: 'He immediately made one spring at me, & a stab with his knife, only to find himself reclining in the corner of his house, his nose having come violently in the way of my left. I pulled out my revolver & showed it to him, sat down, lit my pipe and offered him a piece of tobacco.'

Lonsdale's forceful left hook wasn't only used to lay flat recalcitrant Inuits, or for that matter employees. He also claimed he defeated the reigning world heavyweight boxing champion John L. Sullivan in a 'secret' boxing match in New York. Lonsdale gave a detailed account of this heroic bout, explaining how he wore down then knocked out the champ:

'Though I was certainly hard-pressed, I knew quite well that Sullivan was in a much worse plight. I had shaken him up time after time, and he was breathing hard, and finding it difficult to time his punches. As he came at me in the opening of the sixth, I decided it was now or never. I let fly with my right and caught him solid in the solar plexus, and he went down without a sound, apart from a faint grunt. He lay there for several minutes after the final count, and when I went over and put out my hand to shake his, his face wore a dazed sort of smile as he accepted my grip.'

A remarkable triumph for the plucky English gentleman amateur. The only problem is that Lonsdale never actually met John L. Sullivan, in or out of the ring. In 1888, the year Lonsdale claimed the bout took place, Sullivan spent the first six months touring Europe, culminating with a bout in France. From June onwards he was ill and spent the rest of the year convalescing. Lonsdale continued to tell this story for the rest of his life and it was repeated in most of his obituaries in 1944. One of the more entertaining passages in his memoirs concerns his meeting with Rasputin, which is also unlikely since Lonsdale never in his life set foot in Russia.

Lonsdale re-appeared from his Arctic sojourn fifteen months later, complete with stuffed polar bear and musk ox, and was greeted at Penrith by the local band playing 'See the Conquering Hero Comes'. He distributed photographs of himself in various Arctic costumes, all of which were posed studio portraits, with suitable Arctic backgrounds added afterwards. The Violet Cameron affair was completely forgotten.

'ALMOST AN EMPEROR, NOT QUITE A GENTLEMAN'

Apart from his various scandals and the occasional whopper it was for his passion for all things sporting that Lonsdale was chiefly known. He first caught the public's attention with a couple of famously odd wagers. In 1878 he overhead a conversation in his club about an American, Edward Weston, who was touted as an exceptional road walker. Lonsdale summoned the bemused Weston and challenged him to a 'walking match'. The contest was fixed to take place from Knightsbridge Barracks in Chelsea to the Ram Jam Inn beyond Stamford, a distance of almost exactly one hundred miles. Lonsdale won, completing the course in seventeen hours and twenty-one minutes, stopping for a change of shoes and socks every five miles, averaging about six miles an hour.

He struck another, even odder wager with the American John Pierpoint Morgan. Legend has it that notorious playboy Harry Bensley overheard a conversation between Morgan and Lonsdale at the National Sporting Club in London in 1907. They were speculating whether or not a man could walk around the world without being identified (as you do). By the end of the evening, Morgan and

Lonsdale had placed a £21,000 wager – equivalent to £1.5 million today – on Bensley completing the journey. There were certain strings attached. Bensley was to walk through 169 specific British colonies in a particular order, push a baby carriage the entire way, wear an iron mask throughout and find a wife along the way (despite wearing said mask). On New Year's Day 1908 Bensley set off from Trafalgar Square wearing a four-and-a-half-pound iron helmet, pushing his pram. The details of what happened on his trip are disputed but according to most accounts he had to abandon it after six years of walking with the onset of the First World War; the bet was never collected on.

Lonsdale was also renowned as a keen, not to mention ruthless, huntsman. When he was out chasing foxes he was in the habit of lashing out at members of the 'lower orders' and even his fellow riders if they got in his way. His horses fared worse. When he spent five hundred pounds on a new hunter and it refused to jump, he ordered his groom to shoot it.

His connections within sport blossomed. He became a senior steward of the Jockey Club, first president of the International Horse Show at Olympia, and chairman and honorary president of Arsenal football club as well as a successful racehorse owner. In 1887, after shamelessly flaunting his reputation as the man who knocked out John L. Sullivan, he became chairman of the boxing committee of the Pelican Club, an aristocratic sports club in Gerard Street in Soho that had taken to hosting boxing matches in which American 'coloured gentlemen' competed with local talent. Four years later he was invited to become the first president of the National Sporting Club in Covent Garden, which was to have a worldwide influence on boxing, a job he was to hold on to for the next thirty-eight years.

He also donated the original Lonsdale Belts for the Club's first boxing trophy. No one is quite sure who originally came up with the idea, but someone put it to Lonsdale that it might be a clever marketing ploy if he agreed to put up the first belts – which he did, commissioning the jeweller Mappin & Webb to design them at a cost of £250 each. The first was won by a lightweight, Freddie Welsh, in November 1909. From that day on, winning a Lonsdale Belt would be the greatest ambition of a British boxer.

It was through his prowess as a yachtsman that Lonsdale acquired an interesting friend, Kaiser Wilhelm II. The two men met in their teens and their friendship survived the First World War. The Kaiser was a regular visitor to Lowther Castle, where he attended grouse shooting parties, fantastically expensive events that caused many anguished groans among the estate's trustees.

By the 1920s, Lonsdale's mutton-chop whiskers, nine-inch cigars, yellow gardenia buttonholes and estate check tweed suits made him look like a throwback to the Victorian era, but his omnipresent yellow livery and his almost feudal lifestyle made him one of the best-known figures in Britain, arguably second only to the king and queen. His public appearances at sporting events caused almost as much of a stir as the royals themselves. At the races, wherever the royal car was parked, you would usually find Lonsdale's yellow Daimler, a present from the Kaiser, parked right next to it.

Despite his curious and controversial connection to the Kaiser, as the years rolled by Lonsdale's popularity increased, even among his west Cumberland miners, whose living conditions he did nothing to improve.

Wherever he went he was wildly applauded by well-wishers (or possibly fans of the colour yellow). There wasn't a newspaper that didn't praise him, or a sporting event where his appearance didn't cause great excitement. The papers tagged him 'the sporting earl' and 'our foremost sporting peer'. Less charitably, Edward VII described him as 'almost an emperor, not quite a gentleman'.

The press were also willing to overlook Lonsdale's sins, which were on the same scale as his larger than life personality. In 1928, on the occasion of his golden wedding, the public contributed £250,000 so that Lonsdale could build a 'sportsmen's convalescent home' for broken jockeys and battered pugilists. The money disappeared into his bank account, no questions asked.

Lonsdale knew nothing of the day-to-day economics of living and hadn't the slightest idea about what anything cost. The only money he handled was the cash he carried to hand out tips – a quantity of pound notes and half-crown coins. The pound notes were for handing out, the half-crowns so they could be easily thrown out of his carriage or car. He received sack loads of begging letters and dealt with them generously. His staff went to great lengths to check that the letters were not from fraudsters, but when he came across a case he thought was deserving he would always help out. He gave away about five thousand pounds a year.

This largesse was paid for by the fortune he received from his Cumbrian coalmines. On 11 May 1910, 136 men and boys died following an explosion and fire at his Wellington Pit in Whitehaven. Chalked messages found afterwards showed that many of them had survived the initial explosion. One man was found cradling his teenage son and his son's friend in his arms. Another man had taken off all his clothes and neatly folded them up in a pile beside him; no one knows why. Dead fathers, brothers and sons, some from the same family, left already desperately poor families facing destitution. Eighty-five women were widowed and 260 children lost their fathers.

On 5 September 1922 another thirty-nine men and boys were blown to smithereens at Lonsdale's Haig Pit at Whitehaven. A mother identified her son by a darn in his sock. One young wife identified her husband by a patch on his trousers. A young miner called Sammy McLintock, whose outline was found blasted into the coalface, had bet a pound on the earl's horse Royal Lancer to win the St Leger, which was being run at Doncaster the day after.

The following day, Lonsdale saw his horse come in at 33/1, the first win in the Yellow Earl's racing colours. He left the royal box to lead in the winner as the crowd rose to their feet and cheered and cheered again. A British Pathé film captured the moment, Lonsdale in the winner's enclosure, beaming widely, ever-present cigar clenched firmly in teeth.

Sammy McLintock's widow paid her late husband's winnings into the distress fund.*

It didn't occur to Lonsdale to abandon the race meeting and travel to Whitehaven to console the victims' families. Once his plans were fixed, they were immutable. Besides, he didn't like to think about death or other people's misfortune and he had a phobia for funerals. According to Lonsdale's biographer Douglas Sutherland, during his whole life he never attended a funeral, apart from that of his wife and several members of the royal family. It was the

---

* Four separate explosions over the period 1922–1931 at Haig Pit together killed eighty-three people.

same with animals. If any of his beloved dogs or horses showed signs of being past their prime, he ordered them to be put down and he never mentioned them again.

Although he was childless, Lonsdale had a younger brother to continue the family line, but he was not in the least interested in preserving, let alone adding to his inheritance. Every available penny was spent on maintaining his golden image. By the 1930s his extravagance had made the financial position of his estate so dangerous that the trustees instructed him to leave England for twelve months. He and his wife spent the year on a fabulous, no-expense-spared trip around the world. When he returned, however, his public appearances were as flamboyant as ever and he continued to entertain just as lavishly. For days before the Derby, for example, an army of his staff would scour the fields around his estates to collect plover's eggs that were then served up by the bowlful to his guests in his private box.

In 1935, having finally blown his funds on liveried footmen and various other extravagances, he was forced to abandon Lowther Castle and set off in his yellow Daimler for the more modest surroundings of Stud House, Barleythorpe, where he died eight years later, aged eighty-seven. His tombstone was inscribed 'a great English sportsman' but as far as his immediate family were concerned, his legacy was debt. His selfishness, lack of foresight and bad management had wrecked the family fortune, bankrupted the coalmines in Whitehaven and ensured the eventual dereliction of his family seat. It was left to his younger brother's family to pick up the pieces. In a final letter to his niece, Lonsdale had written, typically, 'Life has been such lovely fun.'

SPORTING CHANCERS

In a world before association football and Formula 1, it was horse-racing that gripped and galvanised the British nation. In the beginning, however, the Sport of Kings was literally the preserve of the upper classes. In 1674 a tailor was punished for racing his horse, 'it being contrary to the law for a labourer to make a race, it being the sport for gentlemen'. By the eighteenth century, however, the racecourse was where dukes and dustmen bet and cursed together.

For the aristocracy, the Derby wasn't just the premier fixture on the sporting calendar, it was the single most important event of the year. After 1847 even parliament adjourned for the running of it. A British prime minister, Lord Stanley, said that he would have rather have won the Derby once than been prime minister twice.* According to racing folklore it was literally a toss-up whether the race would be called the Derby or the Bunbury. The race's founder, the 12th Earl of Derby, was rather more interested in cock fighting than horses and was fond of staging them in his drawing room (which may have been why his wife decided to elope with the Duke of Dorset). Derby won the naming rights of the inaugural race in a coin toss with Sir Charles Bunbury. The earl won, but Bunbury won the first running of the race with his horse Diomed in 1779.

Bunbury was also the first senior steward of the Jockey Club, an assortment of aristocrats, landowners and significant men-about-town who met in a central London public house, the Star and Garter, to regulate racing. It was a favoured watering hole for sporting aristocrats of the day

---

* In fact Lord Stanley was prime minister three times.

and also played an important role in the development of two other great gambling conduits, boxing and cricket.

Wherever racing went, deception and fraud followed. One of the founding members of the Jockey Club was the 4th Duke of Queensberry. He was a famous patron of the turf and no stranger to sharp practice. In 1750 his horse won a race against one owned by an Irish peer. It came to light afterwards that Queensberry's jockey had slipped some of his weights to an accomplice before the start then replaced them for the weigh-in. Queensberry refused to apologise and was challenged to a duel. The two men met at sunrise the next day and as they were preparing their guns, someone delivered a coffin with Queensberry's name on it. His lordship lost his nerve; ashen-faced, he made a grovelling apology and fled the scene.

The early nineteenth-century turf was bedevilled by various forms of race fixing, especially doping, which reached epidemic proportions. Horses were fed anything from a few pounds of lead shot to opium balls. In 1812 several horses were poisoned, for which a groom was hanged. Apart from poisoning, the other most common ploy was the substituting of horses. The Derby of 1844, which featured both, is remembered as the most crooked and corrupt major race ever run on British soil and marked an all-time low in the sport.

At that time the Jockey Club was presided over by Lord George Bentinck, a rather obsessive and humourless character known as 'the Dictator of the Turf'. Bentinck was the third son of the colossally rich 4th Duke of Portland and could afford to pursue his patronage of racing both as a gambler and horse breeder in style. In the Doncaster St Leger he once lost a spectacular twenty-seven thousand pounds (around £3.25 million today). Only the very best was good enough for his horses. For example, he became convinced they would perform better if he fed them fresh eggs and milk. His stables got through so much dairy produce that a farmer once offered to sell him his entire farm. On another occasion, Bentinck sent his valet out to scour London for giant sponges because he didn't think the ones being used were soft enough for his horses. If he set his sights on acquiring a horse he was prepared to spend any amount of money to get it. He paid Lord Jersey four thousand pounds for the bay Middleton – a colossally inflated price, it was generally agreed, especially as the horse was lame and never ran again.

Bentinck pursued racing with a ruthless, maniacal zeal and was more than ready to use skulduggery to achieve his ends. One of the most telling stories about Bentinck's underhand behaviour was his victory in the 1836 St Leger at long odds. At the time, horses travelled to race meetings on foot and everyone knew which horse was on the move and when. When the bookies discovered that Bentinck's much-fancied horse Elis was still at Goodwood just four days before the St Leger was due to be run at Doncaster, over two hundred miles away, they thought it didn't have a prayer of recovering in time from the journey, so they lengthened Elis's odds to 12/1. Bentinck, however, had ordered the construction of a prototype horsebox – unheard of at the time – to carry Elis to Doncaster in time for the race. Elis won easily and Bentinck, who had backed his horse heavily, pocketed a small fortune.

Bentinck had an infamous run-in with another colourful character in the world of racing, 'Squire' George Osbaldeston, a pint-sized powerhouse known for his fine horsemanship. If contemporary accounts are to believed, the squire was a truly remarkable all-round sportsman: he played billiards for fifty hours non-stop, won boxing matches despite giving away up to four stone to his opponents, beat the French tennis champion using his hand instead of a racket and once put in a winning performance for Sussex county cricket team despite bowling while drunk and with a broken shoulder. Osbaldeston inherited and then gambled away an eye-watering two hundred thousand pounds on racing. He could never resist a bet – the more outlandish the wager, the better. He is chiefly remembered for a famous wager made in 1831. Osbaldeston accepted a bet of one thousand guineas that he could ride two hundred miles in ten hours. His chances of collecting were slim; at forty-four years old he was long past his prime and limping badly as the result of an old hunting accident. Osbaldeston offered to make the bet more interesting by doing it in nine hours. Fortified by a lunch of partridge washed down with brandy, he completed the two-hundred-mile circuit in eight hours and forty-two minutes, an average speed of twenty-two miles per hour, then jumped on a fresh horse and galloped off to the Rutland Arms at Newmarket, where he declared himself so hungry he 'could eat an old woman'.*

Osbaldeston clashed with Lord Bentinck over a controversial race at Heaton Park in 1835 when Bentinck accused the former of cheating. Osbaldeston insisted on a duel, which was arranged to take place at Wormwood Scrubs. In

---

* Osbaldeston died a few weeks after winning his final bet: unable to walk and confined to a bath chair, he wagered a sovereign that he could sit for twenty-four hours without moving.

addition to his various other sporting accomplishments, Osbaldeston was a crack shot – capable, in his own words, of 'putting ten bullets on the ace of diamonds at thirty feet' – which gave his argument with Bentinck an added piquancy. His opponent, who had never fired a pistol in anger in his life, had every reason to be worried. It was such an obvious mismatch that great efforts were made by various go-betweens to get it called off. In the event, when the two men squared up, Bentinck fired first and missed. He was now completely at the mercy of Osbaldeston, who fired and, according to one account, neatly put a bullet a couple of inches above Bentinck's head through his hat. There was a suspicion, however, that the seconds, who didn't fancy the idea of being accomplices to what in effect would have been cold-blooded murder, had quietly agreed to supply the pistols unloaded. Osbaldeston died in celebrated poverty in 1865, having won and lost several fortunes.

In 1844 Bentinck, as senior steward of the Jockey Club, embarked on a personal crusade to rid racing of its various malpractices, an act of astonishing hypocrisy given that Bentinck himself was a notorious cheat. He got an early chance to make his mark in that year's Derby. It was won by the colt Running Rein, earning fifty thousand pounds for the horse's owner, Abraham Levi Goodman. Almost as soon as the horse crossed the winning line there were whispers around the track that something wasn't quite right. Not only had the favourite, Ratan, mysteriously dropped dead in his stable shortly before the race, but Running Rein had finished so strongly that it made the win look easy.

The Derby was run between three-year-old horses and substituting an older, stronger horse would have given Goodman a big advantage. Bentinck was certain that

Running Rein was over-age and was determined to prove it. After nearly a year of investigation, he heard a rumour that the horse's legs had been dyed another colour before the race. Following an astonishing piece of detective work, Bentinck found a London hairdresser who confirmed he had sold dye to Goodman before the race. When the case finally came to court, some even more surprising facts about Running Rein emerged. The supposed Derby winner was really a four-year-old, Maccabeus, exchanged secretly some eighteen months before the race. The horse with dyed legs was disqualified and Orlando, which had finished second, was declared the winner.

In 1846 Bentinck stunned the world of racing by suddenly selling his entire stud, the finest in England and arguably in the whole world, for the knockdown price of ten thousand pounds, so he could spend more times in politics. Having spent his whole adult life and most of his considerable fortune in pursuit of a Derby win, to his mortification, one of the horses that he had as good as given away, Surplice, romped home to win the Derby two years later. Just a week after that, Bentinck dropped dead from a heart attack at the age of forty-six.

Another outstanding figure on the racing scene around this time was James Carr-Boyle, 5th Earl of Glasgow. He was one of a group of all-powerful 'plungers' who liked to live hard and dangerously; he and his cronies the Marquess of Queensberry, Lord Kennedy, Sir James Boswell and Sir John Heron Maxwell were said to be 'as rollicking a quintet as ever drained a bottle and drank a toast'.* In every sense, Glasgow qualified for the description 'larger than life'. He

---

* *The Gentleman's Magazine.*

was a big man who favoured colourful waistcoats several sizes too big and trousers several inches too short, worn over heavy, unlaced boots. He was also a bully and known for his vile temper, which was made worse by chronic headaches and back problems. He would try to relieve the pain by draping a chloroform-soaked handkerchief over his face. One evening he dropped in late at the Doncaster Club and demanded a whisky. When told that there was no service because the steward had retired for the evening, Glasgow went upstairs and set fire to the steward's bed. He once lost his patience with a waiter and threw him out of a window, quipping that he should be added to the bill: the waiter sustained serious injury including a broken arm, for which Lord Glasgow was charged a fiver.

When he wasn't defenestrating unruly waiters, Glasgow bred racehorses. He owed the largest stable in the UK, but was arguably the worst owner and breeder in the history of the sport thanks to his dogged persistence in breeding from bloodlines everyone else knew to be useless. Adding to the problem was the earl's refusal to give any of his horses names until they had proved themselves by actually winning a race. He was oblivious to the general confusion that this caused, especially when it came to identifying which horses came from the best, or worst bloodlines. One evening before a race his trainer persuaded him to break his lifetime habit, so three of his horses ran with the names 'Give-Him-a-Name', 'He-Hasn't-Got-a-Name', and 'He-Isn't-Worth-a-Name'.

If a horse failed to show promise, Glasgow had it shot on the spot. After his daily gallop he thought nothing of executing half a dozen horses; as most of them didn't have names, it was anybody's guess if the right ones ended up at the knacker's yard. One that got away was the great Carbine, sensational winner of the Melbourne Cup carrying a record weight of ten stone and five pounds, setting a new race record time. Carbine went on to win two races on the same day at four different meetings. The earl had intended to have him shot at the age of two, despite his trainer's pleas, but fate intervened when his lordship dropped dead himself.

Addictions to betting and bloodstock could prove ruinous. The turf swallowed up some of the great fortunes of the nineteenth century, among them that of Lord Foley, noted Regency horse owner and gambler, who was forced to raise almost one million pounds (about £120 million today) by selling his Worcestershire estate to pay his racing debts. Cully, the greatest racecourse bookmaker of his day, would take a bet of ten thousand pounds from a gentleman simply on the nod of a head. He knew that default meant social ruin.

The career of Henry Weysford Charles Plantagenet Rawdon-Hastings is a cautionary tale about the inheritance of huge sums of money and the perils of the turf. He succeeded as the 4th Marquess of Hastings in 1851 when he was nine years old. His short, tragic life reads like a Barbara Cartland novel. A suicidally heavy drinker from early adulthood, he began the day with a breakfast of mackerel cooked in gin – an 'eye-opener' that he did his best to live up to for the rest of the day. In between emptying a bag of rats on the dancefloors of exclusive nightclubs for fun, he gambled recklessly. One night he lost three consecutive games of draughts for a thousand pounds a game. He then cut a pack of cards for five hundred pounds a deal and lost five thousand pounds in an hour and a half: he paid both debts before leaving the room. He spent a fortune on expensive thoroughbreds in his quest for flat racing success.

In 1864 he eloped with Lady Florence Paget, the fiancée of his one-time close friend Henry Chaplin, a landowner and horse breeder, leaving Chaplin the embarrassed victim of one of the juiciest society scandals London had seen for many years. The two rivals in love subsequently became fierce racing rivals. After his abandonment by Lady Paget, Chaplin 'bought horses as if he was drunk and betted as if he was mad'. One of his shrewder purchases was Hermit, winner of the 1867 Derby. Hermit had been written off as a no-hoper with a starting price of 66-1. Hastings lost a staggering £120,000 when he bet against Chaplin's horse, amid strong suspicions that the race had been rigged. Hastings lost another fortune in the same race the following year trying to recoup his losses. Even his one great betting coup, when his horse Lecturer won the Cesarewitch, ended in farce because Hastings was too drunk to remember his bets.

Within eighteen months Hastings' reckless 'Champagne Charlie' lifestyle devoured him. Forced to sell his Scottish estates to pay his debts, he died a broken man aged twenty-six. His obituary in *The Times* noted: 'We have to record the death of a youthful nobleman of high rank and extensive property, of whom it may unfortunately be said with some truth that he was his own worst enemy.' A much longer article the following day detailed his gambling losses under the heading 'The Turf Career of Lord Hastings'.

In defeat, however, Hastings showed he had 'bottom'. After losing his shirt on the 1867 Derby he was the first to pat the winning horse on the neck. His final words as he lay dying were, 'Hermit fairly broke my heart, but I never showed it, did I?'

Not everyone was impressed by this brand of aristocratic stoicism. The writer Henry Blyth noted bitterly, 'At a time when the poor were existing on shillings per week rather than pounds, and women could be employed at a penny an hour, Harry Hastings lost more than one hundred thousand pounds in the two-and-a-half minutes in which it took to run the Derby.'

GENTLEMEN JOCKEYS

Boxing, horse-racing and cricket were usually sports that the aristocracy paid the lower orders to play on their behalf, but many a lord enjoyed having a go at all three. In the early days of organised horse-racing, owners often rode their own horses and it wasn't unusual to see aristocrats doubling as jockeys. King Charles II rode to victory at Newmarket in 1671, receiving a prize flagon worth thirty-two pounds. A few of these so-called 'gentleman jockeys', including 'Old Q', the Duke of Queensberry, were said to be almost as good as the professionals. Over time, however, the job devolved to lighter, more agile household servants and, since then, aristocratic participation in the Sport of Kings has largely been limited to ownership and betting on races, with one very odd exception.

The Spanish aristocrat Beltrán de Osorio y Díez de Rivera, the 'Iron' 18th Duke of Alburquerque, decided to take up horse-racing after receiving a film of the Grand National as a gift for his eighth birthday. He set his sights on winning England's greatest steeplechase and almost died trying. He entered the Grand National seven times from 1952 and the outcome was nearly always the same. He would usually start with the others, jump a few fences and then wake up hospital.* On his first attempt he fell from his horse at the sixth fence and was hospitalised after almost breaking his neck. He tried again in 1963 and was unseated at the fourth, much to the satisfaction of the bookies, who were offering odds of 66-1 against him finishing. Two years later he fell and broke a leg after his horse collapsed beneath him. Over the course of his painful career he finished one race. In 1974, just after having sixteen screws removed from his leg after another nasty fall in another race, he fell again while training for the National, breaking his collarbone. He competed in a plaster cast, finishing the race for the only time in his career in eighth (and last) place, a very long way behind the winner, Red Rum. The Spanish duke was delighted, but conceded after the race that he had 'sat like a sack of potatoes and gave the horse no help'. At one point his horse collided with that of Ron Barry at the second Canal Turn. Barry said, 'What the fuck are you doing?' to which the duke replied: 'My dear chap, I haven't a clue, I've never got this far before.'

In 1976, he sustained his worst injuries yet after falling in a race and being trampled by several horses. He received seven broken ribs, several fractured vertebrae, a broken wrist and thigh and major concussion, and he spent two days in a coma. After recovering he announced, at the age of fifty-seven, that he planned to race yet again. Grand National officials had other ideas and revoked his licence 'for his own safety', although the brave duke continued to ride competitively in Spain up until 1985 – at the age of sixty-seven. The 18th Duke of Alburquerque never

---

* The Royal Liverpool, where he always took the precaution of booking a private room before the race.

achieved his childhood dream of a Grand National title, but he did break a record, having sustained more fractures than any other jockey in the race's history.

A POSHER BECKS

Before association football was reclaimed by the northern industrial working classes, it was overwhelmingly southern and gentlemanly. The rules were invented by ex-public schoolboys, whose lordly alumni populated the successful cup-winning teams of the day, including Oxford University, Old Etonians, Wanderers and Royal Engineers. The David Beckham of the 1870s, and arguably the world's greatest player in his day, was the Old Etonian captain Lord Arthur Kinnaird, baron and later knight, owner of twelve thousand acres, homes in London and Perthshire, and a director of Barclay's Bank. Easily distinguished by his lavish red beard and long white knickerbockers, he played in nine FA Cup finals, winning five times. His astonishing versatility puts modern players to shame. In the course of his nine FA Cup finals he played in every position, from forward to goalkeeper, while simultaneously serving as treasurer and later president of the Football Association.

Kinnaird continued to turn out as a player until he was forty-seven and, despite his aristocratic breeding, was always respected as a hard-as-nails opponent. His wife confided to a friend that she was afraid that her husband would come home one day with a broken leg. The friend replied: 'Don't worry, madam. If he does, it won't be his own.'

Kinnaird's sporting accomplishments were widespread. He was a Cambridge University tennis blue, a university fives and swimming champion, and took first place in an international canoe race. He won athletics prizes as a youth and played competitive cricket past his fiftieth birthday. His life, however, was not an unburdened triumph. He lost two sons in the First World War, tragedies that eventually led to the demise of the Kinnaird title before the century was out.

SOARING AMBITIONS

Hot air ballooning was originally a sporting fad of the French aristocracy. In 1783 François Laurent, Duc d'Arlandes, was one of two men chosen to pilot the very first hot air balloon flight. The local farmers didn't much like rich people setting balloons down on their land, crushing their crops, but champagne smoothed things over and a sporting tradition was born.

Hot air ballooning also became the sporting flight of fancy of several British toffs, including the Irish peer Benjamin O'Neale Stratford, 6th Earl of Aldborough, the last of a long line of notable oddballs. His great-grandfather, the first earl, created a bogus family tree claiming descent from William the Conqueror, then took to introducing himself as the Earl of Aldborough in the Palatine of Upper Ormonde. Sharp-eyed students of heraldry noticed that there was no such place and that his family coat of arms was identical to that of Alexander the Great. Having gone to the trouble of establishing his fake pedigree, he died four months later.

The second earl liked to throw lavish house parties. He died in the middle of one of them in 1801, to which he had invited around a hundred young people with the apparent intention of marrying them off to each other. The third earl was a much less gregarious type. He anticipated the arrival of visitors by hiding all the fruit from his garden to stop them from eating it and would greet each guest with: 'What time do you leave?' The fifth earl was a hopeless spend-thrift who, when short of funds, would visit London money-lenders with a gun and threaten to shoot himself if they did not give him cash. He was also a bigamist (possibly even a trigamist); consequently on his death the eldest son from one of these marriages, Benjamin O'Neale Stratford, had considerable difficulty claiming a right to the title and what remained of the family property.

The sixth earl was a prototype Howard Hughes. He dedicated his life and his fortune to constructing the world's biggest hot air balloon. Highly reclusive and rarely seen outside his family estate, he worked on his fantasy dirigible in absolute secrecy in the grounds of Stratford Lodge in a vast hangar. He toiled for twenty years on his all-absorbing ambition, so fearful of rivals stealing his design that he kept only one trusted manservant and refused even to employ a cook; he had meals-on-wheels delivered daily by Royal Mail coach from Dublin. The earl planned to pilot the balloon himself on a grand inaugural flight across the Channel to France. In anticipation, he bought an acre of land on the banks of the Seine where he confidently expected to be greeted by swarms of cheering Frenchmen, then he hoped to extend his visit by flying across Europe to contribute to the British war effort in the Crimea by sniping at Russian troops from the air.

One Sunday morning in 1856, however, tragedy struck when Stratford Lodge went up in flames. Lord Aldborough, who was much less interested in saving his historic family home than in preserving his precious airship, ran around the blazing estate urging onlookers, 'Save the balloon house.' Although hundreds of buckets of water were flung over the great hangar, the balloon was exterminated in a sheet of flame. Aldborough was a broken man. He moved to Alicante in Spain where he lived reclusively in hotels. He had meals sent up to his room, but wouldn't allow anyone to remove the used dishes. When his suite was full of soiled crockery he would simply move to another. He died, filthy and neglected, in a hotel room littered with dirty cutlery and old crockery, the earldom expiring with him.

The seventeen-stone Irish peer Arthur Frederick Daubeney Eveleigh de Moleyns, the 7th Lord Ventry, was also a champion of hot air ballooning and airships. Ventry, known as Bunny, began work in 1949 on a sausage-shaped, 108-foot-long dirigible *The Bournemouth*, the first airship to be built in Britain for nearly two decades after the famous R101 crash in 1930. It was scheduled to make its maiden flight in July 1951 but it failed to rise, so the peer was forced to give up his place for a lighter man. At the second attempt *The Bournemouth* rose, but then got stuck on the roof of a gymnasium at RAF Cardington. Undaunted, Lord Ventry spent the rest of his life campaigning for the revival of airships on the basis that they were 'in fact more reliable than present-day aircraft and of course vastly more comfortable'. In 1981 he wrote to the Royal Navy with his suggestion for a new British airship, *Skyship 500*, pointing out that it would also be the ideal vehicle for 'monster hunting over Loch Ness'.

The Victorian baronet Sir Claude Champion de Crespigny, soldier, sportsman and adventurer, took up ballooning in 1882. Rather ambitiously, on his very first flight he tried to cross the English Channel from Dover to Calais. As the balloon was being launched the basket collided with a wall and Sir Claude broke his leg and several ribs. A year later he became the first man to cross the North Sea in a balloon.

Sir Claude's life reads like that of a fictional Victorian action hero. He was also a big-game hunter, a fearless diver, canoeist, sailor, swimmer and jockey, riding his last steeplechase at the age of sixty-seven. In 1905, as he recalled, 'I went out to East Africa for a little big-game shooting, and had the luck to arrive just in time to join the Sotik punitive expedition, so that I was able to combine a certain amount of fighting with some excellent sport.' One hobby he preferred to keep to himself was his job as volunteer hangman in Carlisle, hiding behind the *nom de noose* Charles Maldon.

Sir Claude had an unusual interview technique when taking on new staff at his home, the aptly named Champion Lodge at Heybridge in Essex. Every prospective male employee had to box a few rounds with him. Win or lose, they got the job providing they had shown sufficient spirit. Similarly, homeless people would be offered the chance to box him for a hot dinner. His eldest son, another sporting Claude, committed suicide by shooting himself in 1910, a tragedy exacerbated, his doctors believed, through an attack of madness induced by several heavy falls during polo games.*

* The one sport that the aristocracy ensured remains the domain of their own kind: in order to compete, you must own at least two polo ponies and, in order to be any good at it, you must own a big field in which to practise.

8

Out for Blood

On Boxing Day 1986 two men tried to dig up the corpse of Henry Somerset, 10th Duke of Beaufort, from where it had lain for almost two years in the family's private burial ground near Badminton. They were hoping to cut off the duke's head, parcel it up and post it to Princess Anne. They only thing that stopped them was that their shovel broke after three feet of digging.

You might suppose that the perpetrators of this macabre act of desecration had been driven to it because the grave contained a war criminal or a child murderer, but the duke was neither. He did, however, symbolise something they detested. His long and mostly happy life had been entirely devoted to the killing of foxes. In fact he was descended from a long line of similarly dedicated foxhunters. For four hundred years, for six days a week during the season, his family, the Beauforts, lived for the hunt and apparently very little else. On hearing that a future heir to the dukedom was thinking of marrying, their first question was not 'How much is she worth?'; it was 'Does she hunt?'

For most of his life the tenth duke was known as 'Master', which makes him sound like a *Dr Who* villain, but it was a nickname he'd lived with ever since he was given his first pack of hounds when just nine years old. Master is the name his wife called him by, as did his personal friends the Queen and the Queen Mother. His car registration plate was MFH1. It stood for Master of Foxhounds No. 1, signifying his position as the high priest of the hunt world.

His father, the 9th Duke of Beaumont, was also obsessed with hunting. He devoted every second of his waking life to the killing of foxes and the breeding of hounds. The ninth duke was setting off to hunt when he heard the news that his wife had given birth to a son. It didn't occur to him to interrupt his plans to visit them or even enquire after their health, but in a quiet moment during the hunt he told his followers his good news. His huntsman suggested they give three cheers. 'Certainly not,' the duke replied, 'you might frighten the hounds.'

His son succeeded him to serve as master of the hunt that bears his name for forty years, making him the longest serving in British hunting history. For most of that time, during the season, he hunted foxes six days a week. Throughout the Second World War he continued to wage his own private war against the fox. He was often described 'as tough as nails', as befits a man whose daily routine involved getting up at seven o'clock and riding round the estate before breakfast; however, in 1940 he was declared unfit for military service because of a duodenal ulcer. Sceptics pointed out the ulcer had probably been brought on by stress – not from fear of fighting, but worry over being unable to hunt. Despite his ill health he still managed to chase foxes throughout the war on average four times a week. When invasion seemed likely, he took the precaution of evacuating fifty Badminton hounds to Canada, so that if Britain fell to the Nazis, at least the precious breed would continue; he was very clear where his priorities lay.

Master was not a man to cave in to pressure of any sort. When he became Chancellor of the University of Bristol in 1966 his appointment provoked violent opposition from the students and there were clashes with the police that made the front pages of the national newspapers. Even *The Times* joined in, noting that the appointment was ill considered, but the duke rode it out.

When he wasn't hunting, he enjoyed thumbing his aristocratic nose at animal rights groups. As an unabashed and outspoken defender of his life's hobby, he wrote: 'We have fought, and won, two world wars for the right to be free. Now all we want is to be able to enjoy our field sports without interference from people who often, more's the pity, do not in the least understand what it is they are opposing.' Critics pointed out that he hadn't fought in either conflict.

The duke died of a heart attack at the age of eighty-three while following his pack of hounds in his car. In his later years, when he was too frail to ride a horse, he had taken to shooting foxes from his Land Rover. This was an extraordinary thing for someone in his position to do, because for fox-hunting purists, among whom the 10th Duke of Beaufort was top dog, shooting a fox without chasing it on horseback – i.e. 'vulpicide' – is the most terrible crime anyone can commit. He once famously said of fox hunting, 'Killing is not the important thing,' but it's hard to escape the conclusion that he got his pleasure from simply seeing a living creature made dead.

At his memorial service in 1984, attended by almost every member of the royal family, he was remembered as 'the noblest Master of them all'.

STAG PARTIES

To understand how the killing of wild animals came to be hardwired into the nobility we need to go back over a thousand years to the time of the Norman Conquest.

Although we have come to think of the hunt as quintessentially English, the killing of animals for sport, as opposed to killing for food, was arguably a French tradition. William the Conqueror found the state of British hunting too crude and disorganised for his liking and much less sophisticated than his own elaborate hunts back in Normandy, and it was he who brought to the hunt most of the pageantry and discipline that it has today. He was the first to insist that the hunters wear fancy costumes – the precursors of hunting pink – to make his hunters look like soldiers going into battle. The essential form of the hunt today – mounted riders, a trained pack of dogs, a single quarry – were all a Norman import.

The arrival of William 'the Bastard', as he was known out of earshot, also marked a significant shift in assumption regarding the ownership of wild animals. Before William, the right to kill them rested with whoever occupied the land, so a tenant could trap an animal on his land for food and no one, not even a king, could interfere with this right. William decreed that only the king and certain landowners were entitled to hunt. Almost overnight the country's wild animals became the exclusive property of one social class – the landed nobility. Anyone else who chased or killed a deer was a criminal. At a stroke, hunting became repressive and socially divisive.

At first the only people allowed to hunt with the king were his Norman barons, but over time members of the Anglo-Saxon gentry were also allowed to join in the 'chase'. It also gave them an opportunity to show off their skill at remaining in the saddle – a quality much admired by the medieval nobility. So the hunt became the occupation of the elite, a symbol of wealth and status for those whose lives were not complicated by the daily grind of earning a living.

The Tudors and Stuarts were keen hunters of deer, although from the prey's point of view the hunts were not very sporting. The deer were often chased around enclosed parks or driven past lines of ladies and gentlemen who shot at them with crossbows at point-blank range. Alternatively, they were chased by hounds, whose job was made considerably easier by slicing the tendons or cutting the hooves off their prey.* The estates of the aristocracy were often

---

* A more recent equivalent is the practice of 'bagged foxes' whereby a fox is caught the night before it is hunted. Its earth is blocked up and the trapped animal is dug out of the ground and put in a bag or kept in a darkened cellar until 'turned out', dazed

landscaped to make them more suitable for the hunt. There were masked and fancy dress hunt parties where the participants were very often drunk. Sometimes the prey was also dressed up, with stags going to their slaughter with fancy ribbons tied to their antlers.

Under Cromwell, stag and deer hunting went out of fashion and all but disappeared as a sport. After the Restoration, hunting became popular again, but by this time deer were hard to find. Starving soldiers from armies disbanded after the Civil War roamed the forests killing every animal they could find, and the deer population was decimated, so the aristocracy took to hunting hares instead.

The rise of fox hunting from obscurity to respectability was very odd. Hunting the fox was traditionally held in very low esteem because a fox didn't have the size, strength or beauty of a male deer, nor was it a powerful and dangerous quarry like the wild boar, which could turn and run at its attacker and was more than capable of killing a dog or a man. Furthermore, unlike a boar or a deer, the fox wasn't even edible. With the decline in deer and other larger mammals, however, hunters began to take an interest in whatever was available and within a space of about fifty years, the fox, long regarded as unworthy of a gentleman's attention, became fashionable hunting quarry.

According to hunt folklore it was the Master's

---

and half-blind. Occasionally a hunt servant slashes the fox's paws with a knife so that the hounds can quickly pick up the scent of the fox from its wounded feet. As the fox is generally caught within a matter of minutes, this practice was generally reserved for impressing visiting dignitaries.

ancestor, Henry Somerset, 5th Duke of Beaufort, who discovered the delights of fox hunting by accident. He was returning from an unsuccessful day out with his stag-hounds when he came across a fox and found it was fun to chase, and others soon copied him. George Villiers, 2nd Duke of Buckingham, was the sport's first human casualty. One evening he was out in the freezing cold waiting for a fox to be dug out of its hole when he caught a chill and died. Charles Paulet, the 1st Duke of Bolton,* hunted with hounds by torchlight. In fact, he lived a mostly nocturnal life, sleeping during the day and allegedly holding orgies at night. There may, however, have been some method in his madness. Some said it was a ruse devised to convince King James II that he was a harmless lunatic, whereas he was in fact a supporter of King William of Orange, who later deposed James. It was rumoured that the night hunting and orgies were actually a cover for secret military manoeuvres.

The fox-hunting craze quickly captured the imagination of landowners of all ranks. In Queen Anne's reign, fox hunting was largely a local pastime organised by local gentry who raised hounds for their friends or local farmers. By the 1760s it had become professional, with hunt clubs using selectively bred hounds and hunters patronised by hard-drinking, hard-living, risk-taking young aristocrats who could show off their fearlessness, nerve and audacious horsemanship. The fox really acquired 'status' when George IV joined in, although it's hard to say how much fox hunting he actually did himself, given that he was so fat he couldn't mount a horse without the aid of a winch

* In Wensleydale, not Lancashire.

and pulley system. For the socially ambitious, riding to hounds was now an important way of integration into aristocratic society. Many members of the old aristocracy, however, still resisted its allure. Fox hunting, Lord Chesterfield noted with disgust in 1751, was fit 'only for bumpkins and boobies'. Until the late eighteenth century in some upper-class circles 'foxhunter' was a synonym for 'clown' or 'dunce'.

Ironically, it was in the reign of Queen Victoria, a monarch who never hunted and wholly disapproved of the sport, that fox hunting had its golden age, but it had nothing to do with royal patronage. The 1830s onwards saw a collapse of agriculture, which was catastrophic for farm labourers. Their average wage fell to three shillings a week. More than half the land that had once grown crops such as wheat was put back to grass, which provided perfect conditions for foxhunters because it allowed for long, interrupted runs. At least now the English peasantry, whom the radical MP and journalist William Cobbett described as 'troops of half-starved creatures flocking from the fields', had something to occupy them – mending the fences and closing the gates behind well-to-do fox-hunters.

GAME CHANGER

The reverse side of hunting was poaching. Before the 1500s, a large proportion of Britain's countryside was public property. People were free to hunt for food and generally enjoy the space. But during the sixteenth century most public land was redistributed into private ownership and working-class people were no longer permitted to source food or 'trespass' on that land.

Wild animals became the exclusive property of the few: anyone who used his skill at poaching them was a criminal and punished accordingly. This privilege was confirmed by the 1671 Game Act, which restricted the taking of game to landowners. Unable to access this private land, many people were left with two options: break the law or starve to death. The landowner was backed by a formidable armoury of legislation, as the penalties for poaching increased in severity. The most notorious was the Black Act of 1723, which made poaching of deer, fish, rabbits and other animals a capital crime. Villagers and farmers were not even allowed to kill deer that wandered out of the reserves into their gardens without risk of the gallows. Morbid tales of hangings and murders plagued the British countryside.

One of the most ruthless persecutors of poachers was Richard Temple, the 1st Viscount Cobham. In 1748 two young men were caught while raiding his deer park. Knowing of his lordship's reputation, the wives of the men presented themselves at his house at Stowe and begged for their husbands' lives. It seemed that old Cobham, now in his eightieth year, was moved by their tears and he promised that their husbands would be returned to them forthwith. He was as good as his word; the two men were soon returned to their cottage doors in body bags. According to strong local tradition, Cobham celebrated the occasion by erecting statues of the dead men in his park, a deer across their shoulders.

Gamekeepers were entitled to shoot a poacher on sight or set man traps that would take a leg off and guarantee a lingering death from gangrene. But for many it was a risk worth taking. In the 1820s a hare fetched two shillings and a brace of pheasants three shillings and sixpence. At a time when farm labourers rarely earned more than seven shillings a week, a night's poaching could bring in the equivalent of a month's earnings.*

It wasn't until chronic agricultural recession in 1880 that the old Game Laws were overturned, permitting tenants to hunt hares and rabbits on their own land. Among those supporting the bill, the 5th Marquess of Ailesbury pointed out that it was no longer acceptable for a labourer and his family to go hungry while 'half-tamed pheasants' wandered about near his cottage. Ninety-four of his fellow peers agreed with him and voted for the bill, fifty-nine voted against.

In Georgian Britain, hunting played such an important role in upper-class life that it became an essential part of a young gentleman's education. It was not, however, yet considered a fit sport for women. John Cook, in his classic treatise *Observations on Fox Hunting*, advised that women were 'more in their element in the drawing room or in Kensington Gardens than in the field'. One very notable exception, the Marchioness of Salisbury, succeeded as Master of the Hatfield Hunt after her husband's death in 1793. The marchioness was a very grand, imperious lady often to be seen driving around the family estate in a blue-and-silver carriage, surrounded by dozens of liveried

* In 1814 a vagrant called John Bibby was sentenced to death at the Old Bailey for stealing a sheep from the Duke of Richmond's estate. Bibby ran up the ladder to the scaffold shouting, 'I am the Duke of Wellington! I am the Duke of Wellington!' When the trapdoor opened, Bibby bounced back as though he was on a trampoline, shouting, 'What did I tell you?' After a struggle, he was subdued and hanged.

footmen and pages, one of them carrying a large velvet bag of gold guineas which she could throw to any members of the deserving poor who happened to catch her eye. She was a keen sportswoman and in spite of poor eyesight and failing strength she continued to hunt well into her seventies, although she had be tied into her saddle and led by a groom.

Masters of Foxhounds enjoyed immense local prestige and many went to great lengths to put on lavish entertainments at meets. It was their job to ensure that nothing interferred with or disrupted the sporting pleasure of the hunt members. In 1844 the 5th Earl Fitzwilliam demanded a detour in the London–Edinburgh line near Peterborough so that trains wouldn't disturb the foxes in one of his best coverts. A hunt Master was also obliged to ensure that there were enough foxes to go round. The hunt had become so popular that the British fox population stood on the brink of extinction. They were so scarce in fact that, by the mid-1800s a thousand foxes a year were being imported from Holland, Germany and France and a booming commercial trade in continental foxes was established at Leadenhall Market in London. Fox trafficking was subsequently replaced by an intensive breeding programme. It wasn't until the mid-twentieth century that it became expedient for the hunting fraternity to pretend that foxes were occurring naturally in the wild and that they were performing a useful pest control service.

In the Victorian era, for sheer snob value, deer-stalking was the thing, the very height of gentlemanly sophistication.* Typical of its more excitable enthusiasts was

* As the Victorian dramatist W.S. Gilbert observed, 'Deerstalking would be very fine sport if only the deer had guns.'

Grantley Berkeley, son of the Earl of Berkeley. Rigid, arrogant and heavily bewhiskered, he favoured an attention-grabbing mode of dress, wearing two or three different-coloured satin waistcoats at the same time and round his throat three or four silk neckerchiefs held together with a gold ring.

He wrote a couple of novels. When a reviewer from *Fraser's Magazine* described one of them as 'about the stupidest it has ever been our misfortune to read', Berkeley went round and thrashed him with his horsewhip. He also had a reputation as one of the most rapacious huntsmen of his generation. There were occasions when his passion blurred the divisions between the city and countryside. This from his book *Reminiscences of a Huntsman*, written in 1854:

On one occasion we ran up to the entrance of a gentleman's kitchen, in the rear of his premises, and the hounds bayed at the closed door. Heads of domestics through the pantry window informed me that the stag was in the house, and that they would admit me 'if I would keep the dogs out, as the children were afraid of them'. The door being opened and closed carefully behind me, I went in, ushered by a butler, and peeped at by many maids; and, on asking where the stag was, the butler replied that he had been in all the lower offices, and when he last saw him he was going up the drawing-room stairs . . . The butler introduced me to the drawing room, but neither master nor stag were in it, when at that moment a door at the other end opened, and the owner of the house came in, under visible though suppressed excitement. I began all sorts of apologies, as usual, and for a moment the gentleman was civil enough. But on my asking where the stag was, all restraint gave way, and in a fury he replied, 'Your stag, sir, not content with walking through every office, has been here, sir, here in my drawing-room, sir, whence he proceeded upstairs to the nursery, and, damn me, sir, he's now in Mrs. ——'s boudoir!'

Eventually the aristocrat secured the stag with the help of some butcher boys and a metal tray.

If you want to see a member of the aristocracy become emotional, talk to them about dogs. Here's Berkeley on the subject of one of his favourite hounds.

Old Stamford's soft and prolonged note, when he found a fox, sweeps by my ear now: and often and often had I to cheer the young ones to him throughout my first fox-hunting season. What he must have been in his youth . . . I can easily guess; and if these pages meet the eye of the gentleman who bred him, he will accept this tribute to the memory of as gallant, as sensible, and as attached and faithful a hound as ever killed a fox . . . I shall never forget how proud that old hound was when he found I petted him, and that he was still to be treated with all the ceremony and usages of a well-ordered foxhound kennel. And when we began cub-hunting, his alert dignity and industry was so great that he still more won my heart.

You wouldn't guess straight away from this sentimental prose that Stamford's job was to rip the throat of a fox cub. The Victorian hunting fields were also a dangerous place for humans. The range of opportunities for accidents was enormous and the English shires echoed with the dull crack of breaking legs, ribs and collarbones. In 1859 the 3rd Marquess of Waterford became the third British peer that year to die while hunting. Lord Charles Beresford was so obsessed with fox hunting that he had his entire back tattooed with a hunting scene (depicting the fox disappearing up his anus). Beresford's uncle was killed in a riding accident, his brother was crippled in another and Lord Charles himself managed ten broken bones. One Victorian hunting parson bequeathed his skeleton to the Royal College of Surgeons because every bone had been broken at different times. The sporting novelist Major George Whyte-Melville, keenly alive to the dangers of his favourite sport, even expressed a wish that his death might take place in the hunting-field – which it did, while galloping across a ploughed field in 1878.

THE WAR EFFORT

When the First World War broke out in 1914 *Country Life* magazine lectured its readers sternly: 'The rich ought to live more sparingly, so that they may not consume food that might otherwise be available for the poor. Let it be fully understood that indulgence in luxury is not only a foolishness but a crime.' The magazine also tried to shame aristocrats who employed servants fit enough to fight. 'Have you a Butler, Groom, Chauffeur, Gardener or Gamekeeper serving you, who at this moment should be serving your King and Country? Will you sacrifice your personal convenience for your Country's need? Ask your men to enlist TODAY!'

At Blenheim the Duke of Marlborough did his bit for the war effort by replacing the mowers in his gardens with sheep and planting cabbages in the flowerbeds. His austerity measures were not lost on *The Times*, which observed drily, 'the national food problem may not have been greatly lessened by these practices, but it was a patriotic gesture'.

Generally, however, the social elite was determined to defy the Hun by keeping up appearances, which meant attending house parties, consuming copious amounts of alcohol, dancing and gambling. The hunting, by and large, also continued uninterrupted. The 5th Earl of Lonsdale poured a great deal of his money and energy into keeping the Cottesmore Hunt going. When critics pointed out that the maintenance of hunting was not wholly essential to the war effort, Lonsdale was mystified and demanded to know: 'What on earth are officers home from the front going to do with their time if there is no hunting for them?' It was beyond the earl's comprehension that some British officers had never even seen a fox.* It's hard for us to imagine able-bodied people riding horses and hunting foxes while their fellow countrymen were laying down their lives on the Western Front, but that's exactly what happened.

For some fox-hunting aristocrats, the Second World War was also an annoying interruption to their routine and they responded by carrying on as though nothing had happened. In 1939 the British government requisitioned all of the nation's hunting horses, which you might think was an odd

---

* Before the Battle of Waterloo, the locals had great fun watching British officers trying in vain to introduce fox hunting into Belgium, but according to the French historian Jean-Claude Damamme, the foxes refused to join in.

thing to do, given what happened to the cavalry in the First World War. It led to some very strange situations, because some members of the hunt fraternity simply hid their mounts wherever they could. Horses were hidden in billiard rooms and wine cellars, where they remained for the duration of the war, which for some animals must have been an altogether more surreal kind of War Horse experience.

TRIGGER-HAPPY

In the second half of the nineteenth century the aristocracy discovered a new diversion, the shooting party. It was an entire social system organised around the sporting gun, involving groups of friends and relatives moving from house party to house party through the season. No expense was spared and the scale of the major shoots was staggering, involving armies of gamekeepers and estate workers.

It wasn't everyone's bag. Dame Edith Sitwell was repulsed by her family's obsession with shooting, and memories of gamekeepers releasing rabbits from sacks to be shot or beaten with sticks made her a lifelong campaigner against blood sports. Gladys, wife of the 9th Duke of Marlborough, was also a well-known animal lover who hated the regular autumn shooting parties. But for many aristocrats like Cromartie Sutherland-Leveson-Gower, 4th Duke of Sutherland, shooting was their greatest joy in life. In his autobiography *Looking Back*, for the most part a chronicle of the idle slaughter of wildlife, the duke boasts that he shot his first stag when he was ten years old and killed well over a thousand over his lifetime. He enjoyed visiting his estate at Lilleshall, because 'what I enjoyed best . . . were the pheasant shoots when, with seven to nine guns, we would bring down anything from eight hundred to a thousand birds in the day'. Abroad, he found the shooting of elephants, from a safe distance, 'exciting' and was very pleased when he 'got a bison and several tigers'. When a man in his party, Montague Guest, fell dead during the shoot, the duke noted, 'Personally, I can imagine no pleasanter way to die.'

In its traditional form, shooting was both a sport and a suitable form of exercise to alleviate gout. A landowner would walk his estate with a shotgun and a couple of dogs and considered himself lucky if he shot half a dozen birds in a day. Around the 1860s, however, the sport changed completely. Now it was the estate workers who did the walking, driving fat pheasants that could barely get off the ground towards the gentlemen who stood at the other end. The invention of the breech-loading shotgun and the systematic raising of birds made the killing even easier. The aristocracy could now spend their time knocking thousands of virtually domesticated birds out of the sky without raising a sweat.

As well as the social life, statistics mattered greatly. The 2nd Marquess of Ripon, a close friend of King George V, was a shooting monomaniac. Instead of sending Christmas cards he would send lists of the game he had killed that year. Over his lifetime he killed 556,813 head of game (he was very precise about the figure). Pheasants were his prime targets. He slaughtered 229,976 at his Yorkshire estate Studley Royal and once downed twenty-eight pheasants in sixty seconds at a shooting party at Sandringham. He also bagged 97,503 grouse, 11,258 partridge, 2,454 woodcock, 2,882 snipe, 3,452 wild duck, 30,280 hares, 34,118 rabbits and 382 red deer.

Lord Ripon kept meticulous notes. An entry for 1886 during a tour of Spain, records, 'Green woodpecker, hard to kill.' Another, made during an 1876 visit to Egypt, recalls, 'brought back 44 varieties for stuffing'. In Lancashire in 1883, he claimed a world record of 2,105 game from 2,800 shots over three days, and at Lambton he bagged his best ever pheasant haul, 894. On 30 August 1887 he wrote: '328 grouse; next highest 79. Wind puzzled others.' Lord Ripon maintained his appetite for killing wildlife to the end. He dropped dead in the heather, gun in hand, while grouse shooting in 1923, having killed fifty-two birds that morning.

Second only to Ripon's record was that of the intellectual, mutton-chop-whiskered Thomas de Grey, 6th Baron Walsingham. Even by the standards of late-Victorian shooting his record was extraordinary. On a single day, 28 August 1888, he killed 1,070 grouse on Blubberhouses Moor at a rate of more than two birds a minute. He employed forty beaters, shooting from dawn till dusk, with four guns and two loaders. What prompted this apparently senseless orgy of slaughter? He had invited the Prince of Wales to a shoot, but had been snubbed because the prince didn't think there were enough grouse on the moor to make his journey worthwhile – Walsingham just wanted to make a point.*

Walsingham was also a noted entomologist. In breaks between shooting he capered about with a butterfly net, hoping to capture rare specimens. He would disappear into

---

* The biggest day's shooting of all occurred on Count Louis Károlyi's estate at Totmeyer, Hungary, when 6,125 pheasants were shot, together with 150 hares and fifty partridges.

the Cambridgeshire fens at night looking for moths, dressed in a moleskin coat, snakeskin waistcoat and a hat made out of a whole hedgehog, complete with spikes, head and artificial eyes. He amassed a huge collection of stuffed birds – all shot by him, naturally. He also brought down the hummingbirds now in the Natural History Museum in London, using special shot that had been ground to a fine dust so that it wouldn't damage the feathers.

Walsingham's obsession with his sport was so all consuming that he worked his way through the family fortune and had to sell almost everything they owned, including the site on which the Ritz was built. He spent the last few years of his life abroad and died in 1919 virtually bankrupt. Shooting parties contributed to more than a few bankruptcies, including that of the anglophile Indian Prince Victor Duleep Singh, who shot through his fortune on his father's Suffolk estate Elveden Hall with the Prince of Wales.

Shooting accidents were commonplace. In 1895 the 10th Baron Beaumont killed himself accidentally with a shotgun when crossing a stile at the family seat, Carlton Towers in Yorkshire. Minor shooting mishaps were never allowed to interfere with the day's sport. In 1848 the Duke of Gloucester, who was a very erratic shot, deprived his equerry of an eye, then complained when the injured man 'made such a fuss about it'. When the Duke of Newcastle shot himself in the foot he delivered a stern rebuke to the loaders who rushed to his aid; he could learn to hop as well as the next man. Which is exactly what he did after they amputated his foot.

The Duke of Devonshire was one of the worst shots in England. Consistently hopeless, in 1884 with one blast he hit a pheasant, the dog that was chasing it, the owner's dog and his own chef. He apologised to his guests that, as his chef was incapacitated, lunch might not be quite up to its usual standard.*

Shooting etiquette dictated that killing a fellow shooter dead was an unfortunate accident but winging a beater – worse still, a keeper – was unforgivable. The Duke of Wellington was said to be more lethal on the moor than on the battlefield. While visiting Lord Granville in 1823 he accidentally shot his host in the face. Shooting at Lady Shelley's, he hit one of her tenants while she was hanging out her washing. When the victim complained, 'My lady, I've been hit!' Lady Shelley reassured her: 'You have endured a great honour today, Mary, you have the distinction of being shot by the Duke of Wellington.'

Arguably the most important shooting accident was significant because it was non-fatal. The Gothic castle of Konopiště in central Bohemia was once a much-favoured weekend holiday retreat for the Nazi SS. The castle, said to be the most tasteless residence in Europe, contains a massive collection of game trophies, comprising thousands upon thousands of animal heads, bodies, teeth and antlers, mounted on walls and stored in glass display cabinets. Incredibly, the immense haul of trophies represented a

---

* His descendant, the eleventh duke, anomalous as owner of one of the country's finest grouse moors, did not enjoy shooting and was also a terrible shot. While serving with the Coldstream Guards in Italy, he spotted a German soldier sitting under a tree, eating a sandwich. In his autobiography he recalled: 'I drew my revolver and fired at him several times. I'm no Wyatt Earp but some of the shots must have gone fairly close. He showed not the slightest reaction.' In disgust the aristocrat hurled the gun at the squaddie and walked off. He regretted that later: 'Before leaving the army I had to pay 30 shillings for losing that revolver.'

small fraction of the handiwork of one man, the former resident of Konopiště Castle. His preferred hunting weapon was the machine gun. Animals were driven into his line of fire so that he could mow them down in large numbers. According to his own diaries, in his relatively brief lifetime he exterminated nearly one-third of a million head of game, including six thousand stags. He hunted kangaroos and emus in Australia and on one of his trips to Poland he killed so many European bison that he personally brought the species close to extinction. He had another, much more extraordinary claim to fame. His name was Archduke Franz Ferdinand d'Este.

In 1913 the archduke's passion for killing wild animals took him to Welbeck Abbey in Wiltshire, where he was a guest at a shoot hosted by the Duke of Portland. While the party was out shooting pheasants, one of the loaders slipped and dropped his gun. It hit the ground, discharging both barrels, the shot passing within inches of the archduke's head. The following year, on 28 June 1914, during an official visit to the Bosnian capital, the archduke and his wife Sophie were shot dead by the Serbian nationalist Gavrilo Princip, setting in train a series of events that led to the outbreak of the First World War. Later, the Duke of Portland mused in his memoirs, *Men, Women and Things*: 'I have often wondered whether the Great War might not have been averted, or at least postponed, had the archduke met his death then, and not at Sarajevo the following year.'

At home the British aristocracy shot small birds, abroad they killed large animals. In 1882 the Duke of Portland went to Nepal with some friends, accompanied by seven hundred elephants. In six weeks they killed fourteen tigers, eight rhinoceros and a crocodile, which his lordship declared 'good fun'. He followed up with another shot arranged by the Maharaja of Durbangah, at which they killed three tigers, twenty-eight buffalo and 273 pigs. In 1913 the 18th Lord Dunsany went to Kenya, where he embarked on a killing spree that would freeze the blood of any animal lover: fifty-five beasts including four warthogs, six zebras, three jackals, eight impalas, a lion and a rhinoceros. Lord Lonsdale decorated his staircase with stuffed crocodiles shot in Africa, while Lord Egerton built a new wing at Tatton to show off his trophies. The Duke of Sutherland built a museum in the grounds of Dunrobin Castle to display his, including hundreds of disembodied animals' heads and horns alongside other more macabre trophies, from elephants toes to rhinos tails. Occasionally, the animals bit back. Sir Edward Grey, British Foreign Secretary at the beginning of the First World War, had one brother eaten by a lion and another killed by a wild buffalo while on safari in Africa.

CAMP STEWART

In the early 1800s most of the people who crossed the Atlantic to North America were poor emigrants escaping from extreme poverty, or skilled workers hoping for a better life, but by the early 1830s a new type of traveller was going west: blue-blooded Europeans in pursuit of adventure and sport.

The key draw was one of the strange new animals that the aristocracy had heard about from traveller's tales: the buffalo. It was the lifeblood of the American West. Native Americans depended on it for their basics; food, clothing, bedding, skins to make tepees, sinews for bow strings, bones for tools and needles. They used buffalo to carry water and burned buffalo dung for fuel. To white Americans it was an essential source of food during long overland journeys. For the professional hunter it was a living; a hide was a valuable commodity to be sold to fur companies. For a small group of wealthy travellers the American buffalo offered the ultimate sporting experience. There were buffalo (or bison) in Europe and Asia but they were much smaller and there were fewer of them. The American version was considerably heavier and much more powerful and there were millions of them to shoot at.

The first British aristocrat to venture from St Louis across the Great Plains was the Battle of Waterloo veteran Sir William Drummond Stewart, soon to become the 19th Laird of Grandtully. Ostensibly, Stewart took inspiration for his epic trip from reading James Fenimore Cooper's 1827 novel *The Prairie* and its descriptions of vast herds of buffalo,* although it has more recently been suggested that he had a pressing reason for going west. His lordship was probably on the run from the British authorities, having fallen victim to a campaign instigated by the London Metropolitan Police whereby young plain-clothes officers were being used to entrap homosexual men.†

Stewart was so taken by the landscape and abundant

---

* Although, ironically, Cooper never laid eyes on them, having trekked no further west than Buffalo, the terminus of the recently opened Erie Canal in western New York state.

† Stewart also acknowledged an illegitimate son, who had an illustrious career in the army and was awarded the Victoria Cross for his actions in relieving the Siege of Lucknow during the Indian Mutiny. He died during a drunken attempt to show off his skills at sword swallowing.

game that he spent nearly seven years in North America. The archetypal British eccentric, he could be seen striding through the Rockies dressed in tartan trousers and a white leather jacket, meanwhile fending off marauding bears and Indians with his umbrella. Stewart didn't just shoot buffalo; he captured live specimens and shipped them back to Scotland, hoping he could breed them in the glens. In 1843 he returned with thirty friends on a farewell tour, littering the prairies with buffalo carcasses. One of Stewart's travelling companions was his cousin, Charles Murray, a younger son of the Earl of Dunmore, who lived for several months with Pawnee Indians. The Old Etonian was somewhat taken aback when his hosts ate his dog, but was able to impress them with his rock-throwing skills, honed during the Highland Games.

Stewart also resurrected the abandoned tradition of the annual trapper 'rendezvous' camp, where men in the fur trade sell their catches then hang out together, spend all their money on gambling, prostitutes and alcohol and wake up hungover and in debt weeks later to start another year's trek. Stewart's rendezvous, however, had a different kind of camp. Instead of trappers' costumes, his companions wore medieval pageant velvet, silk and lace costumes made in Europe, and the entertainment was of a generally more homoerotic nature.

BLOOD AND GORE

Most of the aristocrats who travelled west to hunt buffalo went on the journey in the spirit of an extended picnic outing. Some took their valets with them to ease the daily bother of washing, dressing and looking after their baggage. Chief among these blood-sport tourists was the Anglo-Irish aristocrat St George Gore.* Brighton-born and Oxford-educated, Gore inherited his title in 1842 when he was thirty-one. His family estates in Ireland amounted to over seven thousand acres in County Galway, as well as other lands in Donegal, Limerick and Offaly. In the classic manner of the absentee landlord, he left management of his estates to his agent so he could lead the life of a wealthy sporting bachelor. His income, based on unfeasibly high rents demanded from thousands of Irish peasants, was mostly spent on field sports. He spent his winters fishing and duck-shooting in Scotland and his summers grouse-shooting and deer-stalking: he once shot eleven stags in a week, four of them in a day.

Gore's expensive obsession was threatened in 1847 and 1848 by the Great Irish Famine. While his tenants starved as their crops failed, Gore's agent Charles Cage evicted those unable to pay their rents, cleared their land, then handed out small amounts of cash to persuade the dispossessed to join emigrant ships to America. Others were simply herded off the estate to join the thousands of other famished souls roaming the countryside. In 1849 Gore's despised agent, Cage, was shot dead on his way to church. Overcoming his annoyance at having to interrupt his hare-coursing season to attend Cage's funeral – a rare visit to his Irish lands and probably his last – Gore planned himself another hunting trip, as far away from Ireland as he could possibly get. He had hunted in Africa and Asia, but now he had in mind something more ambitious and more

* Today Sir George's best-known kinsman is former US Vice-President Al Gore.

extravagant than anything he had ever done before. In 1854 he set off to try his luck in North America.

If the sight of a genuine British baronet, complete with deerstalker hat, Norfolk jacket and carefully combed and perfumed ginger side-whiskers, was a rarity in the Wild West, Gore's entourage was something else. The bare essentials he thought necessary for his trip amounted to forty men, including his personal retainers, cook, gunsmith and a man whose only job was to tie flies to the baronet's fishing rod. He also took fifty hounds from his Bedfordshire kennels, 112 horses, eighteen oxen and three cows to provide milk for the baronial breakfast, six heavy wagons and twenty-one two-wheeled carts. One wagon carried his armoury of seventy-five guns including rifles, shotguns, revolvers and pistols. Another carried three tons of ammunition; a third was full of fishing rods, lines, nets, flies and hooks. Gore saw no reason to rough it in the wilderness. He took with him a green-and-white-striped tent equipped with French carpets, a brass bedstead complete with canopy, a steel bathtub, a fur-lined commode, solid silver drinking cups, a converted wagon for rainy weather, a violin, and a small library of classic novels, guide books and journals. It looked more like an invasion force than a hunting party.

For the next three years Gore and his retinue wheeled through the Rockies laying waste to anything that moved. He hunted nearly every day, setting off after a late breakfast with a small group of servants to carry his guns. A gun bearer stood close by, feeding him a continuous circle of fully loaded shotguns so he could blaze away without distraction. This unbridled killing spree would generally continue until 10 o'clock at night. The carcasses were left to rot where they dropped.

Gore was an aloof, arrogant nobleman, not given to small talk with his servants, but along the way he struck up a rapport with his American scout, Jim Bridger. Known as 'Old Gabe', Bridger was a famous frontiersman, but not a complete stranger to British aristocracy, due to an earlier encounter with Sir William Drummond Stewart, who surprised Bridger by presenting him with a suit of full armour. Gore and Bridger often dined together and Bridger later told how, after a couple of glasses of French wine, Gore would treat his bemused and illiterate guest by reading him some passages from Shakespeare.

Gore spent thirty-seven months in North America dispatching every living creature that came into his sights. According to his own logbooks, this included two thousand buffalo, 1,600 deer and elk, 1,500 antelope and 105 grizzly bears, as well as thousands of mountain sheep, coyotes and timber wolves and sundry smaller animals and birds. Described as 'a good shot from a rest, but rather indifferent offhand', he probably wounded more animals than he killed outright.

In 1857 Gore got his comeuppance when he decided to explore the Black Hills on his way to St Louis. The area was marked 'unexplored' on Gore's map for good reason: the Sioux didn't take kindly to white men trespassing onto their hunting grounds. Gore's party found themselves surrounded by a war party of 180 Lakota Sioux. They gave him a choice – give up your possessions, including your clothes, and start walking, or die fighting. Gore stripped and ran. The naked aristocrat spent the next five weeks plodding three hundred miles back to base, living on plants and a few animals they managed to trap along the way. This time there were no fur-lined commodes available and he was reduced to squatting in the bushes.

After cutting a path of blood-letting across the American West and spending around half a million dollars – the equivalent of three years' income from his Irish estates – Gore decided it was time to go home, just in time for the Scottish stag-hunting season. He was planning on one more trip to America, this time to shoot alligators in Florida, but to the eternal gratitude of the sunshine state's wildlife, he died before he could make good on his promise, aged sixty-seven.

9

Officers and Gentlemen

They might have been mad, bad and dangerous to know, but these were also the very qualities that made the aristocracy quite useful in times of war.

For several centuries the great armies of Europe were largely run as a private club for the sons of the nobility. In Britain, serving in the army was one of the few respectable careers available for a gentleman and the ideal occupation for those second and younger sons who wouldn't inherit the family estate. For many officers, the battlefield was a form of aristocratic sport; serving as a soldier on horseback was little different to a day's hunting.*

An influential position in the army, just like a title or an estate, was something that could be handed down the generations. For a long time this sort of patronage seemed to work well. The grateful public loved their aristocratic military heroes and the newspapers were full of stirring reports of the exploits of well-born young officers who set their men examples of selfless courage. Victorious commanders like Wellington and Kitchener had statues erected to them and were rewarded with titles and stately homes.† The likes of the Marquess of Granby, a dashing, eighteenth-century cavalry general, had inns named after them by hundreds of patriotic landlords.‡

There was one military leader above all who was said to embody all the very finest qualities that the nobility

---

* Throughout the Spanish campaign the Duke of Wellington himself dressed in the light blue coat of the Hatfield Hunt (although he drew the line at officers carrying umbrellas on the battlefield).

† The Duke of York, commander of the British forces against Napoleon, had his statue paid for by deducting one day's pay from every soldier in the army.

‡ They were also immortalised in more creative ways. Despite his fighting in several campaigns, the career of the grandly named Sir James Charlemagne Dormer wasn't especially memorable, although his death was. Known in the officer's mess as 'Cesspool Dormer' because he had to hide in one to escape from rebels during the Indian Mutiny, he met an even less illustrious end when he was eaten by a Bengal tiger while commander-in-chief in Madras. Uniquely among the Victorian aristocracy, Dormer has a bat named after him: Dormer's Pipistrelle, *Pipistrellus dormeri*.

had to offer. John Churchill, Duke of Marlborough, whose career spanned five British monarchs, was arguably his country's greatest ever general. According to his biographer, Richard Holmes, in his book *Marlborough: Britain's Greatest General*, 'of him alone could it be said that he never besieged a town he did not take, or fought a battle he did not win'. Marlborough was a military genius and a brilliant strategist with a cool capacity for bold and quick decision. As commander-in-chief he looked after the welfare of his men and in return was so loved by them that they gave him the affectionate nickname Corporal John. He was an aristocratic superman; clever, affable, incredibly brave and so handsome, according to Lord Chesterfield, that he was as 'irresistible to either man or woman'. Even King Charles II must have fancied him a bit, because he didn't seem to mind too much when Marlborough slept with his favourite mistress. OK, the duke might have abused his position as captain-general of British forces by accepting backhanders for army contracts and creaming off a percentage of the money paid to foreign troops, but this was par for the course at the time; nobody's perfect.

Unfortunately, there were in truth very few aristocrats serving in the armed forces of the calibre of the Duke of Marlborough. Running a modern professional army based on patronage and trusting your military leadership to an elite of gentlemen amateurs, as it turns out, was not a very good idea, because, as we will see shortly, for every Marlborough there was a Buller, for every Granby a Lucan, for every Wellington an Elphinstone.

OLD SOLDIERS NEVER DIE

By the mid-nineteenth century the British army was essentially an old boys' club. 'Old' was the operative word. The Horse Guards, who controlled the army in the same way they had commanded for two hundred years, promoted solely on the basis of seniority. As the army had no official retirement age the high command became filled with very elderly officers. Sir Francis Compton, lieutenant colonel of the prestigious Royal Horse Guards, was still serving at the age of seventy (although clearly a man of exceptional physical stamina, having just married a girl of seventeen). His colonel, the Earl of Oxford, was seventy-three. The cavalry commander Lieutenant Colonel Alexander Pope was so decrepit that he needed the assistance of two soldiers to mount his horse and so near-sighted that at Chillianwala in 1849 he faced his cavalry in the wrong direction and led them in a charge away from the battlefield.

Like Marlborough, the Duke of Wellington was that rare nobleman: a man of remarkable intellect and energy and a brilliant strategist who had mastered the mechanisms of war, but the aristocratic principle didn't serve him well. Wellington is regularly quoted as having remarked of his men, 'I don't know what effect they will have upon the enemy, but by God, they frighten me.' What he actually said, or rather wrote, was a borrowed quote first attributed to Lord Chesterfield about the quality of his generals of the day: 'I only hope that when the enemy reads the list of their names, he trembles as I do.'

During the Peninsular War, Wellington was saddled with so many elderly and incompetent generals that he must have wondered at times which was the greater threat, Napoleon or the War Office. One of his senior commanders, Sir William Erskine, 2nd Baronet, was promoted to major-general despite being twice confined to a lunatic asylum. Wellington received news of his appointment with disbelief and wrote to the Military Secretary in London for an explanation. The secretary replied, breezily, 'No doubt he is a little mad at intervals, but in his lucid intervals he is an uncommonly clever fellow, and I trust he will have no fit during the campaign, although I must say he looked a little wild as he embarked.'

During one of Erskine's less lucid intervals he was found at dinner when he should have been defending a strategically important bridge. He eventually sent five men to defend it. When a fellow officer queried his decision Erskine changed his mind and decided to send a whole regiment, but pocketed the instruction and forgot all about it. He found the order in his trouser pocket much later when he was getting into bed and passed it a junior officer, who arrived at the bridge too late to stop the French and ended up taking the blame. Erskine was also said to be 'blind as a beetle' and had to ask someone to point him in the general direction of the battlefield. His military service ended in 1812 when he was declared insane and cashiered. A few months later he jumped out of a hotel window in Lisbon. Found dying on the pavement, his last words were, 'Why on earth did I do that?'

The proliferation of old, unfit and incompetent leaders wasn't just a problem for the British military. The great armies of Europe were dominated by elderly aristocratic generals. During the Peninsular War the Spanish army was led by the cantankerous, xenophobic seventy-year-old

Spanish general Gregorio de la Cuesta. He and Wellington were allies but they took an instant dislike to each other, Wellington regarding Cuesta as an elderly idiot, the Spaniard refusing to cooperate with Wellington because he was a British upstart. At one point during the campaign, when the British and Spanish armies were supposed to be taking part in a joint attack. Wellington found Cuesta sound asleep. When aroused, Cuesta complained that he was too tired to fight that day and went back to bed.

In the Austrian army it was commonplace to find commanders in their seventies. A quarter of all the regimental and battalion commanders of the Prussia army were over sixty and many were in their eighties, including their legendary cavalry commander General von Pennavair, eighty years old at the Battle of Colin in 1757, having acquired the nickname 'anvil' because he had been beaten so often. Wellington's ally at Waterloo, the seventy-three-year-old Prussian field marshal Leberecht von Blücher, was said to be in the early stages of senile dementia.

BATTLE OF THE MOSELLE

The class-defined status quo of the British military remained unchanged for centuries, largely because of the purchase system, by which an army commission could be bought all the way up to the rank of lieutenant colonel. For example, if a major retired, the senior captain would be offered the chance to buy his commission, which in turn would create a vacant captaincy, and so on down the ranks. In practice, however, the system could be short-circuited by a rich officer. The official going rate for the rank of lieutenant colonel in the 1820s was £6,175, but the laws of supply and demand often drove up prices far beyond the official limits – the smarter the regiment, the higher the price. The third Lord Lucan was said to have paid £25,000 for the lieutenant-colonelcy of the 17th Lancers, nearly four times the regulation price.

A cavalry officer also had to provide his own horse and uniforms and was expected to lead a social life consistent with his standing as an officer and a gentleman – hunting, yachting at Cowes, attending dinners and balls, and paying one's huge mess bill and so on. The only people who could possibly afford it necessarily came from the very highest rungs of society. Most officers bought commissions and swapped regiments on a whim. For many the motivating factor for choosing one regiment over another was fashion. A gentleman's regiment was as much a style statement as his carriage or his tailor.

As owner of one of the biggest fortunes in the kingdom, a young British officer like James Brudenell, 7th Earl of Cardigan, could afford to move swiftly up the ladder of seniority.* Cardigan embodied all of the worst qualities of the stereotypical Victorian aristocrat. He was a spoilt, pompous bully and, according to his biographer, Cecil Woodham-Smith, 'unusually stupid'. He was thought by some to be actually mad, possibly the result of a near-fatal blow on the head when he was thrown from his horse while chasing a fox. He is chiefly remembered today for his part in twenty minutes of hell known as 'the charge of the Light

---

* In politics also it was money rather than policies that mattered. Cardigan bought his parliamentary seat, the 'rotten' borough of Fowey in Cornwall, which was thought to have cost him around five thousand pounds.

Brigade', which has gone down in history as an example of great heroism, but should be remembered as one of the very worst examples of snobbery and military ineptness.

Cardigan appears as the villain in many of George MacDonald Fraser's *Flashman* novels, but in many respects his life was stranger than fiction. He was a magnet for scandal, usually involving the wives of his friends. In 1823 he eloped with Elizabeth Johnstone, the beautiful but fiery-tempered wife of his close friend since childhood, Captain Frederick Johnstone. The captain sued for damages and was awarded one thousand pounds. After the trial, Cardigan sent a messenger to Johnstone offering to 'give him satisfaction' in a duel. Johnstone was a much more experienced military marksman and must have been tempted to put Cardigan (who at the time had the courtesy title Lord Brudenell) in his place. Instead, he sent the withering reply: 'Tell Lord Brudenell that he has already given me satisfaction – the satisfaction of having removed the most damned bad-tempered and extravagant bitch in the kingdom.'

Almost twenty years later Cardigan was sued for adultery again, this time by his friend Lord William Paget. Paget's capacity for scandal rivalled Cardigan's. Formerly an MP, he'd fallen into debt, fled to Jamaica, survived a court martial and returned to London when his father bailed him out. Suspecting that his wife Frances had begun an affair with Cardigan while he was away, Paget hired a private detective called Frederick Winter to spy on them by hiding under a couch during one of their trysts. Paget sued Cardigan for 'criminal conversation', but stuck for choice between a cad and bounder, the jury found for Cardigan.

He began his career as he intended to go on, by buying positions, first in the army and then as an MP. There was huge resentment among his fellow officers when Cardigan got his first command of the 15th King's Hussars at the age of thirty-four – younger than many of his captains, many of whom had fought at Waterloo. Cardigan was a stickler for drill and discipline and quickly made himself even more unpopular as a military martinet. His tenure with the 15th was brief. Soon after taking command he arrested Lieutenant Henry Wathen over a petty dispute concerning a clothing debt. Two courts martial exposed Cardigan as an unprincipled bully and led to his transfer to the 11th Hussars, a command for which he was said to have paid ten thousand pounds. The 11th suffered equally under Cardigan, subjected to strict drills and routine floggings for minor offences. He was fanatical about the smart appearance of his men to the point of absurdity, re-equipping his regiment with blue-and-gold jackets and red trousers, earning them the nickname 'Cherrybums'.

Cardigan was also known for his petty and quite bone-headed insistence on what he regarded as 'proper form'. He even fought a duel over an extraordinary officers' mess dispute known as the Black Bottle Affair – a difference of opinion over the correct receptacle for decanting wine. In 1840 Cardigan had a fellow officer, Captain Reynolds, arrested because he had placed Moselle on the mess table in a black bottle instead of a decanter. When an account of the incident was leaked to the *Morning Chronicle*, Cardigan challenged its author, Captain Harvey Tuckett, to a duel on Wimbledon Common. Cardigan shot Tuckett through the spine, leaving him severely wounded.

When placed under arrest Cardigan, however, denied

any part in the shooting, replying: 'Do you suppose that I would fight with one of my own officers?' He was tried in the House of Lords for attempted murder but sensationally acquitted on a technicality. Despite being caught with a smoking gun in his hand, it seemed that Cardigan had a licence to break the law. The Black Bottle Affair exploded into a national scandal and there was a near riot when he was spotted in a box at the theatre in Drury Lane – not that he gave a damn.

INTO THE VALLEY OF DEATH

In 1854 the fifty-seven-year-old earl finally got his chance for military glory when Britain's ongoing power struggle with Russia erupted into war in the Crimea, a small peninsula in the Black Sea. By this time, the British army hadn't fought a continental enemy for forty years. The tactics they were using were basically still the same as those used by Wellington at Waterloo and hadn't kept pace with the new technology. The supply system meanwhile was criminally negligent in failing to provide for the troops. The Crimean campaign got off on the wrong foot, literally, when the army was sent five thousand left boots. The British high command had arrogantly presumed that the war would be over by Christmas so didn't bother equipping their men with adequate clothing for the Russian winter. Soldiers had to keep warm by pulling woollen socks over their heads and cutting eyeholes in them. When badly needed winter coats were eventually sent, thanks to bureaucratic red tape, they sat in the harbour while soldiers froze to death in the lines.

While British officers dined in their tents (or in

Cardigan's case, on board his private yacht) on chicken and champagne, the men lived on half rations or no food at all. Without sufficient food, warm clothes or shelter to survive the freezing winter, thousands perished from cold, exhaustion and disease. Meanwhile, gentlemen officers amused themselves by going duck shooting, even at the risk of getting killed by Russian snipers, or attending race meetings, one of which was mistaken for a Russian cavalry charge.

Amid this chaos, there was also some fighting to be done, and this is where they faced their biggest problem: leadership.

Unlike fine wines, generals don't necessarily improve with age, a point that was seemingly lost on the British army. At the outbreak of the Crimean War there were thirteen British generals with more than seventy years' service and 163 with between fifty and sixty years. The British commander FitzRoy James Henry Somerset, Lord Raglan, hadn't seen combat since losing an arm at Waterloo more than forty years earlier where he served as Wellington's military secretary. He had never commanded so much as a company in the field before, let alone an army. An indecisive sixty-seven-year-old with little charisma, he was appointed because he spoke French fluently and was next in line for a command. It also didn't help that he kept referring to the French as 'the enemy'; his senior officers had to remind him quietly that this time the French were on his side – the Russians were the enemy.

The combined British and French forces were advancing towards the Russian port of Sebastopol when they met the defending Russian army near Balaclava. The British had a large number of cavalry but the Russians countered with an impressive array of guns and artillery. The defenders also had control of the valley. The one-armed Raglan peered across the landscape from his high vantage point on a hill, observing the entire battlefield laid out before him. At the far end of the valley he could see Russians trying to drag away some captured British cannons. This troubled him, as he knew his old mentor Wellington had never lost a gun. Raglan sent down an order to his lieutenant-general, George Charles Bingham, the 3rd Earl of Lucan,* to recapture the guns.

Lucan had command of the British cavalry in the Crimea, including the Light Brigade ('light' because they were lightly armed, as opposed to the Heavy Brigade). He was a model peacetime commander with little knowledge of strategy or concern for the business of actually waging war. Like Cardigan, he was considerably more interested in military smartness and was said to spend as much as eleven thousand pounds a year on new uniforms – more than the actual wage bill for the men who wore them. During the Battle of Alma he played such a nominal role that he was nicknamed 'Lord Look-on'.

Lucan more than matched Cardigan in both temper and ruthlessness. His callousness in enforcing thousands of evictions on his Irish estates earned him the nickname 'the exterminator'. Although so alike in age, background and character, Lucan and Cardigan detested each other. Lucan was married to Cardigan's sister Anne, a lady of imperious ways who hated Ireland and rarely left London society, often complaining of her husband's meanness and neglect.

* Lucan's twentieth-century descendant disappeared in November 1974 after the murder of his family's nanny.

Cardigan certainly believed that Lucan had badly mistreated his sister. The animosity between the two officers was well known; they often came close to trading blows in front of their own troops. Raglan should have done something about it and sent one of them home. Instead, he simply tried to keep the two men apart – some hope, considering Lucan was Cardigan's direct superior.

The fate of the Light Brigade would hinge on the confused Raglan's ability to articulate a clear order. He handed his instructions to attack to Captain Lewis Edward Nolan for delivery to Lucan. The order read: 'Lord Raglan wishes the Cavalry to advance rapidly to the front, follow the enemy, and try to prevent the enemy carrying away the guns. Troop Horse Artillery may accompany. French Cavalry is on your left. Immediate.'

Now this made perfect sense if you were on top of the hill and could see everything that was going on. But Lucan was in a position six hundred feet lower than Raglan and didn't have the same view. When he read the order from Nolan, he was baffled. Which guns was he supposed to attack? He asked Nolan for clarification. Like Lord Raglan, Nolan had seen the location of the guns that were obscured from Lucan's view, but instead of pointing directly to where they were, he gestured in the general direction of the Russians and said: 'There, my Lord, is your enemy. There are your guns.' Nolan repeated that the order was to attack immediately then trotted off. Lucan didn't see eye to eye with the arrogant Nolan, who was a 'merit' officer with barely disguised contempt for his elderly aristocratic superiors, and so didn't bother to ask for further clarification.

The essentially dim Lucan faced a dilemma, but he wasn't one to solve anything by his own initiative. He stuck to Queen's Regulations, and these were quite explicit. Orders sent by aides-de-camp were to be obeyed as if they had been delivered personally by the commanding officer himself. The only guns Lucan could actually see were at the far end of the valley, where masses of Russian cavalry were concentrated. He assumed that these were the guns he was supposed to attack.

Lucan rode over to Cardigan, commander of the Light Brigade. There was no small talk or discussion about tactics between the two feuding brothers-in-law. Lucan simply pointed down the valley and ordered Cardigan to attack. When Cardigan mentioned the obvious flaw in Lucan's plan – the valley was heavily defended by Russian guns – Lucan simply repeated the instruction, adding only that Cardigan should ride at moderate speed so as not to exhaust the horses; Lucan would follow up with the Heavy Brigade. Both men knew that the order was suicidal, but neither wanted to lose face. So instead of ignoring an absurd order to attack from their elderly, incompetent and quite possibly senile commander-in-chief, they simply got on with it.

Leading the charge, Cardigan followed his orders with his customary parade-ground formality and discipline. He was taking his 673 men into a narrow valley a mile and a quarter long, with Russian gunners at the end and lining both sides, to their almost certain deaths. To the Russians, the manoeuvre appeared to be of such unfathomable lunacy that they assumed the British cavalry were all drunk. Unable to believe their eyes, they simply loaded their guns and waited for the slaughter to commence. The commander of the French cavalry General Bosquet summed up the unfolding disaster: *'C'est magnifique, mais ce n'est pas la guerre.'*

Of the 673 men who charged into the Russian crossfire, only 195 returned, many of whom would die of their wounds owing to lack of proper medical care. Lord Cardigan, first into the attack and first out, was one of the few to emerge unscathed. Once he saw that his brigade was lost, he simply rode off without a backward glance. In a matter of minutes, three incompetent aristocratic British officers had managed between them to destroy arguably the best cavalry regiment in the world.

Cardigan returned home from the Crimea as an unlikely hero and had the great satisfaction of seeing his hated brother-in-law Lucan receive the blame for the misdirected charge. Cardigan loved to recount the story of his heroism during the Charge, his exploits growing more glorious with each retelling. Within a few weeks of his rapturous reception, however, it became clear that all was not quite as it seemed. It was rumoured that he had galloped back to his own lines while the attack was still in progress. By and large, however, the press were more concerned with the Crimea's disastrous sanitary conditions than aristocratic ego squabbles and Cardigan was allowed to remain in his post as colonel-in-chief until his retirement. He died fourteen years later after falling off his horse while taking his regular morning ride.

WHAT'S IT ALL ABOUT, ELPHY?

The British aristocratic officer caste was shown up time and again as a collection of elderly incompetents, but there was nothing quite as astonishing as the appointment of Major-General William Keith Elphinstone as commander of the garrison in Kabul during the First Afghan War.

Elphinstone has been described, with some justification, as the most useless general in the history of the British army, but you might argue that he was also a victim of military incompetence, because it was obvious to almost everyone that he was totally unfit for command in the first place.

In the 1830s Britain was preoccupied with protecting India and its role as 'the jewel in the crown' from imperial Russian expansion. The British Governor-General of India, Lord Auckland, decided to eliminate India's troublesome Afghan neighbour the Emir of Kabul by force. In 1838 British troops invaded Afghanistan with the intention of deposing the Emir and installing an unpopular former ruler, Shah Shuja. The first round of the conflict was an easy win for Britain as they routed the Emir and captured Kabul, but the British soon learned that beating the Afghans was not quite the same as controlling them.

The Afghans refused to submit to the infidel-loving new regime and, after a succession of uprisings, the British army found themselves under siege, essentially prisoners in their own compound in Kabul. The nearest support was the British garrison in Jalalabad ninety miles away. In far-off London, the government assessed the situation and called on a flatulent, incontinent and possible senile sixty-year-old Waterloo veteran to sort the Afghan rebels out.

William George Keith Elphinstone, grandson of the 10th Lord Elphinstone, began life with certain advantages. He was born into a family noted for its distinguished public and military service. His uncle was the popular naval hero Viscount Keith; his first cousin was Mountstuart Elphinstone, governor of Bombay; his second cousin, the 13th Lord Elphinstone, was governor of Bombay. The young William Elphinstone's military career started off promisingly enough. He commanded the 33rd Foot through the Napoleonic Wars and was awarded a knighthood for his services. There followed, however, twenty-five years of military inactivity during which he saw no action at all, a large part of which was spent serving as aide-de-camp to King George IV. In 1839, in his late fifties and suffering ill health, Elphinstone was sent to take command of a division in India because his friends in high places thought the climate might be good for his gout.

In 1841 he was appointed commander of the British garrison in Kabul, numbering around sixteen thousand troops and support staff. Lord Auckland thought he was the right man for the job because 'he was of good repute, gentlemanly manners and aristocratic connections'.* He had overlooked the fact that Elphinstone was now almost sixty and so stricken with gout, rheumatoid arthritis and heart disease that he could barely move. The appointment was even more bizarre when you consider that the British had a perfectly competent officer they could have turned to nearby. The commander of the garrison at Kandahar, Major-General William Nott, was a much younger, battle-hardened officer with experience in Afghanistan. Nott, however, was lacking 'aristocratic connections'. Even poor old 'Elphy Bey', as the new Kabul appointee was known, recognised that he wasn't up to the job and pleaded to be allowed to stay put in India, but Lord Auckland would hear none of it, fatuously insisting that 'the bracing hills of

* By a quirk of fate, Lord Raglan also had a hand in appointing Elphinstone, thereby distinguishing himself by his involvement in arguably the two most disastrous decisions ever made by British military authorities.

Kabul' would prove more healthy than 'the hot plains of India'.

The strategic positioning of the British garrison in Kabul was a military blunder in its own right. It was built with little consideration for defence in a low, swampy area surrounded by hills. The stores were situated some four hundred metres outside the garrison perimeter – an open invitation to the enemy to seize their supplies and starve the population inside – which is exactly what happened. Before long, bandits were looting the British stores and killing at will any Britons who strayed out of camp. As soon as Elphinstone arrived in Kabul the situation started to go downhill rapidly. As autumn turned to winter the fighting intensified and the British camp came under daily attack from snipers on the heights above them, an area Elphinstone had failed to secure. The British formed squares to repel Afghan light cavalry whose sharpshooters found the obligingly bright red uniforms impossible to miss even at a distance.

By this point Elphinstone was permanently bedridden and had to be carried everywhere on a litter. He was also fatally indecisive. With no previous experience of Afghanistan or its people he was inclined to consult widely with men of all ranks, then agree with whoever he spoke with last, everyone that is except his second-in-command Brigadier John Shelton, a brave but widely disliked and tyrannical officer with whom he shared a mutual hatred. Shelton didn't bother to disguise his contempt for Elphinstone and would take his army bedroll into meetings with his superior and pretend to fall asleep.

With supplies gone and casualties mounting, Elphinstone continued to vacillate. The British envoy in Kabul, Sir

William Macnaghten, needled by Elphinstone's numbing indecision, took it upon himself to try to negotiate some kind of truce and organised a meeting with the Afghan leader outside the British camp. Macnaghten was promptly hacked to pieces where he stood, then his dismembered body parts were paraded victoriously through the streets of Kabul; his head was placed in a horse's nosebag and displayed in the local bazaar. Elphinstone, who had no stomach for a fight, refused to order reprisals, much to the disgust of his junior officers.

The situation descended into farce when Elphinstone got himself shot in the buttocks. This seems to have spurred him to make a decision, even though it turned out to be a terrible one. He agreed that his garrison should quit Afghanistan altogether, in exchange for safe conduct. Not only was this a shameful capitulation; it was also a tactically disastrous decision. He was abandoning a fortified position to march 4,500 troops and 12,500 civilian non-combatants in the dead of winter across mountain ranges infested with hostile tribesmen.

On the day they set off Elphinstone seems to have realised that he was signing everyone's death warrant and tried to halt the march, but half the force were already on their way and his order was ignored. No sooner had they left Kabul than the Afghan tribesman fell on the column, killing at will. The sick and injured, left behind as arranged, were massacred within minutes of the last British soldier leaving the garrison.

As Elphinstone's column staggered on through the snow, their trail was marked by a trail of slaughtered stragglers, picked off by Afghan raiders. After three days, around three thousand had died, frozen to death or shot, or in some cases having committed suicide. On the fifth day the Afghans attacked in force near Gandamak and the rest of the party were massacred, many with their throats cut as they lay defenceless in the snow. Within a week of leaving Kabul the entire column had been wiped out, apart from a dozen high-ranking prisoners, including Elphinstone and his second-in-command, Brigadier Shelton.

The loss of 16,500 people was a shocking and humiliating defeat for the British. On hearing the news, Lord Auckland collapsed with a paralytic stroke. Elphinstone did not survive to face a court martial or the furious indignation of Victorian Britain. While in captivity he died of dysentery, no doubt tormented by the agonising certainty that he was mostly to blame for the disaster, having failed to convince his superiors that he was not the right man for the job. Perhaps Elphinstone was more deserving of pity than censure.

ISANDLWANA

The Crimean War had revealed glaring defects in the British military system, not least that it could throw up aristocratic buffoons like Lords Lucan and Cardigan, but the army was still terrified of trying anything new that might challenge the supremacy of the gentleman officer. This was in no small measure thanks to the efforts of its notoriously inept commander-in-chief, the Duke of Cambridge. The duke's meteoric rise to the very top of the military establishment was accounted for by the fact that he was Queen Victoria's cousin. He vigorously resisted army reform and was particularly hostile to 'clever soldiers' who studied warfare; he once complimented one of his generals: 'Brains? I don't believe in brains. You haven't any, I know, sir.'

When William Gladstone became prime minister in 1868 the elderly duke reluctantly gave way to a series of changes, including the abolition of the purchase system, but the aristocratic tone of the British army survived intact. As army pay was barely enough to provide living expenses, let alone support the necessary equipment and expenses required for polo, hunting and fine dining, an officer's worth was still determined by his ability to maintain a sporting and gentlemanly lifestyle.

Unfortunately, Britain's army officers of the late Victorian era were infected by a dangerous mixture of aristocratic arrogance and a fatal inclination to underestimate the enemy. The most glaring example of this was Frederic Augustus Thesiger, Lord Chelmsford, commander of the British force in the Anglo-Zulu war of 1879.

In the 1870s Sir Henry Bartle Frere, the British government's top man in Cape Town, was tasked with turning South Africa's patchwork of British colonies, Boer republics and independent black states into a united Confederation of South Africa. Frere came to believe that the job he'd been sent to do was impossible unless King Cetewayo's forty-thousand-strong army of Zulu warriors – the most formidable native army in Africa – was suppressed. He decided that the only course of action was to destroy the Zulu forces as soon as possible.

In fact, Frere had misread the situation completely; the Zulus were more than keen to maintain friendly relations with the British. The queen's High Commissioner was determined to go to war anyway.

Ignoring the instructions of his own government to keep the peace in South Africa, and the advice of those who knew the Zulus well and recognised that the threat was exaggerated, Frere cynically engineered a confrontation by sending Cetewayo an ultimatum, the terms of which he knew were unacceptable. Britain went to war against the Zulu nation, the last pre-emptive war launched by the British army prior to the twenty-first-century campaign in Iraq.

The man chosen to lead the British invasion force, Frederic Thesiger, 2nd Baron Chelmsford, was the perfect Victorian gentleman: tall, handsome, amiable, softly spoken and impeccably mannered. Although he had served in the Crimea and in India he had little experience of command in the field, having served mostly on the Staff as aide-de-map and quartermaster. He was completely out of his depth when it came to fighting the Zulus. He didn't believe they would stand and fight, even though head-on pitched battle had been their classic mode of warfare ever since Shaka created the Zulu kingdom. 'If I am called upon to conduct operations against them,' he wrote in July 1878, 'I shall strive to be in a position to show them how hopelessly inferior they are to us in fighting power, although numerically stronger.' His misjudgement came to rebound on him badly.

On 11 January 1879 Chelmsford led a five-thousand-strong main British column into Zululand. Nine days later, hampered by minor skirmishes and poor tracks, Chelmsford's column had only advanced eleven miles to the rocky lower slopes of a hill called Isandlwana, where it set up camp. It was there that Chelmsford made the first of a series of blunders. He took two-thirds of his force off to pursue what he believed was the main Zulu army to the south-west. He didn't see any need for detailed reconnaissance; otherwise he would have discovered that just five miles away to the north-east, twenty thousand Zulu warriors were lying in wait. When Chelmsford received a report that large numbers of Zulus were advancing towards his camp, he simply ignored it and stuck to his original plan.

Chelmsford set off on a wild goose chase, unaware that the main Zulu army was sitting concealed close to the British camp. Four hours later, while the British defenders were fighting for their lives, a small group of Chelmsford's force at Mangeni Falls received word that the camp was being overrun. On his own initiative, a junior officer, Colonel Harness, ordered his small force of artillery and infantry to return to camp. It had only progressed half a mile when a staff officer rode up with express orders from Lord Chelmsford to resume its original march because the message was a false alarm. The last chance to save Isandlwana had been thrown away. Of 922 white troops and 840 black auxiliaries, only fifty-five of the former and 350 of the latter survived.

Isandlwana was followed immediately by the heroic defence of Rorke's Drift (the subject of the film *Zulu**) in

---

* The 1964 film was far from historically accurate. Lieutenants Chard and Bromhead, played heroically by Stanley Baker and Michael Caine, were reckoned by their superiors to be lazy, stupid and incompetent. The defence was in fact organised by the commissariat officer James Dalton, who was passed over when medals were first handed out. The action attributed to Chard and Bromhead was invented later by Lord Chelmsford's staff officer Major Francis Clery, who wasn't even present at Rorke's Drift.

which 140 British troops of the 2/24 Warwickshire Regiment defied a Zulu army of around four thousand for ten hours in which eleven Victoria Crosses were won. The award of so many medals was partly intended to distract attention from the previous day's disaster and partly to salvage Chelmsford's reputation.

Word of the disaster at Isandlwana, arguably the worst ever defeat to befall a British army in open battle, was received by the Victorian public with disbelief. The hunt was on for a scapegoat and Chelmsford was the obvious candidate. But he had powerful friends, including Queen Victoria. Chelmsford denied all responsibility for the massacre at Isandlwana, propagating the myth that the defeat was caused by a shortage of ammunition. He claimed he had nothing to do with the choice of camp, the decision to split his forces or the tactics employed in the battle, shifting the blame for the disaster to two officers, one of whom, Colonel Durnford, was conveniently dead. His cover-up convinced the queen, who invited him to Balmoral for tea and sympathy. Chelmsford gave her a large Zulu shield, saying, 'I cannot attack dead men' – then went on to do precisely that, claiming that Durnford had deliberately disobeyed orders to defend the camp.

The incompetent Chelmsford had another ace up his sleeve, the defence of Rorke's Drift, the importance of which was deliberately exaggerated to diminish the impact of Isandlwana. Thanks to Rorke's Drift, Chelmsford somehow survived the debacle of the Zulu war with his reputation more or less intact, at least in his own lifetime. The queen showered honours on him, promoted him to full general, awarded him the Gold Stick at Court and appointed him Lieutenant of the Tower of London. He died in 1905, at the age of seventy-eight, playing billiards at his gentleman's club.

REVERSE BULLER

Apart from the odd setback the British army had grown accustomed to winning small wars by vanquishing ill-armed and ill-trained foes. So when Britain sent an army of seventy thousand men to South Africa to fight the Boers in 1899, most people thought the war would be won within a matter of weeks. They had not reckoned on the incompetence of General Sir Redvers Buller.*

He was the scion of one of Devonshire's oldest and wealthiest landed families. Three generations of Bullers before him had represented Exeter in parliament and his great uncle was the Duke of Norfolk. Buller joined the King's Royal Rifles when he was nineteen and went on to serve with distinction in five campaigns, including the Zulu War of 1879, in which he was awarded the Victoria Cross for bravery. A contemporary noted, 'There is no stronger commander in the British army than this remote, almost grimly resolute, completely independent, utterly steadfast and always vigorous man.'

The announcement of Buller's appointment as head of the expeditionary force to tackle the Boers was hailed in

---

* In the latter part of his career he was known to his troops as 'Reverse Buller' because of his record of defeats. After one spectacularly embarrassing retreat, Buller boasted to his superiors in London that he had accomplished his withdrawal without losing a man, a flag or a cannon. When the artist James Whistler heard about this, he added, 'or a minute'.

the British press as a masterstroke. Even those who disliked his brusque and overbearing manner thought that he was the best man for the job. Lord Esher noted: 'Buller is said to be the best man – take him all round – in the British Army. Not a very pleasant fellow.'

Buller proved to be the classic example of a gifted soldier promoted hopelessly beyond his capacity. To begin with, the former man of action was no longer as vigorous as some might have imagined. He was now a vastly over-weight sixty-year-old with an appetite for rich food and fine wines. He insisted on going on campaigns with a specially made, cast-iron kitchen, which his men were expected to drag wherever his duties took him, along with wagons of champagne. It was rumoured that he was an alcoholic.

Perhaps more worryingly, although Buller had proved himself a brave and inspirational regimental officer he turned out to be a fairly useless strategist. His preparation before embarking to South Africa was comically inept. He returned intelligence briefings unopened because he knew 'as much about South Africa as there is to know'. During training exercises he told his men not to dig trenches or foxholes in case they damaged the countryside or to take cover in case they got their uniforms dirty. Fighting could only take place between 9 a.m. and 5 p.m. so as not to inter-fere with his officers' social arrangements. Senior officer and future Field Marshal Herbert Kitchener noted that Buller waged war 'like a game of polo, with intervals for afternoon tea'.

Buller assumed that as the Boers were descended from Europeans, they would also fight like a European army; in other words, he fully expected them to stand in the open to be shot at with British rifles. Inconveniently, the Boers refused to play by Buller's rules of engagement. They dressed in khaki clothes that blended into the landscape. They were also excellent marksmen and were happy to snipe at the British from concealed places. This, Buller complained, was very unsporting behaviour. All the same, it simply hadn't occurred to him that his regular army could be defeated by a group of scruffy locals.

Buller's inadequacies as a field commander were cruelly exposed with days of his arrival in South Africa. He was supposed to relieve the besieged towns of Ladysmith, Kimberley and Mafeking. Instead, his forces suffered three disastrous defeats within a week against an enemy who were mostly untrained farmers and farm boys. At the Battle of Colenso he launched a suicidal frontal assault against well-entrenched Boer troops. At one point his army charged straight into a swollen river and dozens of British soldiers were drowned. The rest were dragged out by the Boers and made prisoner.

Unlike the Teflon-coated Lord Chelmsford, the mistakes made by Buller that resulted in the loss of hundreds of British soldiers cost him his job and his reputation. He was relieved of his command and retired on half pay, his name remembered thereafter as that of a classically incompetent British general.

TEMPORARY GENTLEMEN

When the First World War began in 1914, some of the ruling class preferred to stay at home and keep the local hunt going and let their gamekeepers do the dying. Many aristocrats welcomed it as an opportunity to lead bravely from the front, just as many of their ancestors had done.

The war was disastrous for the British ruling classes. The public school boys who went from the rugby pitch almost straight to the front and were first in the German machine-gunners' sights could expect to last an average of of six weeks. While one in eight British soldiers perished during the four-year conflict, the ratio was one in five for the nobility. About two hundred direct heirs to titles or major landed estates were killed between 1914 and 1918 – the greatest cull of the male British aristocracy since the Wars of the Roses four centuries previously.

In August 1914 the officer class in the British army comprised a small and privileged elite numbering only fifteen thousand men, but a pressing need for more officers meant that a further 235,000 men from 'non-traditional backgrounds' were given commissions to become 'temporary gentlemen' – a sneering term of reference for those who were not from the 'quality' classes. There was less concern among the military hierarchy about military competence of these officers than there were fears that their social accomplishments might not be up to the demands of the officers' mess. Consequently many of the new officers were based in Oxford and Cambridge colleges, where the candidates received advice on 'gentlemanly behaviour'. Many of these new officers, however, struggled to finance the lifestyle expected of an 'officer and a gentleman' because they were still expected to buy their own uniforms from selected military tailors mostly based in London's fashionable Jermyn Street, which was by no means a cheap affair.

They were elevated to officer status out of necessity,

because the British army had no other choice, but no one doubted their effectiveness in the field. In that sense the First World War was a great social leveller, because class ceased to be the measure of an officer. By 1918 it seemed that the aristocracy was spent. A political observer wrote at the time, 'The Feudal System vanished in blood and fire, and the landed classes were consumed.'

THE HOLY TRINITY

Not quite consumed. There were still many aristocrats who fought bravely in the Second World War and once again it took a heavy toll on the British aristocracy. The Duke of Northumberland died in active service in 1940. The Duke of Devonshire's son and heir was killed in 1944. Sir Robert Peel, 6th Baronet, was killed on active service, bringing the senior line of his family to an end. Lords Halifax and Swinton each lost a son. Lords Zetland, Lytton, Gort and Bessborough were all similarly bereaved.

One of the most heroic losses in the Second World War was that of Charles Howard, 20th Earl of Suffolk, 13th Earl of Berkshire, known affectionately by all who made his acquaintance as 'Wild Jack'. Since the early seventeenth century the various Earls of Suffolk courted danger and controversy wherever they happened to be. The father of the first earl was beheaded by Queen Elizabeth for treason. Some of his descendants only escaped a similar fate by fleeing abroad. Another Suffolk became a pirate on the Spanish Main and yet another spent seven years wandering through the unexplored regions of South America in search of adventure. Queen Victoria called them 'the mad Howards'.

The 20th Earl, Charles Howard, was cast from the same buccaneering mould as his ancestors. He inherited his title in 1917 at the age of eleven when his father was killed fighting against the Turks. His tutors at the exclusive Radley College found him 'unteachable'. When he was eighteen, without a word to his family, he went to Liverpool where he signed on as a deckhand on a windjammer, then spent the next few years working at a sawmill, cow punching and sheep farming, eventually ending up as a part owner of a sheep ranch. When life in the Australian outback began to bore him he packed up and returned to England to manage the Howard family's ten-thousand-acre estate in Wiltshire. In 1934, at the age of twenty-eight, he decided that he wanted to be a scientist and enrolled at Edinburgh University, graduating three years later with a first-class honours degree in chemistry. It was this expertise that led him in early 1940 to be sent to Paris at the age of thirty-three as the government's liaison officer with France's armaments ministry.

As Germany started to overrun France, Howard was sent to rescue thirty-three French nuclear scientists and the world's entire supply of 'heavy water' – about fifty tons – that Norway had shipped there. He was also tasked with recovering millions of pounds' worth of industrial diamonds from a French bank. The bank manager refused to cooperate since his only authorisation was a hastily handwritten note from a French minister. At this point the earl opened his trench coat to display 'Guinevier' and 'Josephine' – the two revolvers he carried in a dual shoulder holster. He walked out of the bank with the diamonds shortly afterwards.

After his return from Paris, Howard served as part of an unexploded bomb disposal detachment in London during the Blitz, immersing himself in his new work with typical enthusiasm. A scientist who visited him at his office later described the scene: 'I found the Earl of Suffolk dressed in a most extraordinary outfit, consisting of riding boots, corduroy trousers, a striped sweater and a white aviation helmet. He was pacing up and down and raging in a frightful manner at the War Office for not giving him more bombs to play with.'

The earl's team, calling themselves 'the Holy Trinity', comprised himself, his secretary Eileen Morden and his chauffeur, Fred Hards. They detected and successfully disarmed unexploded bombs with remarkable efficiency. Their working style was honed down to a ritual: the earl would light up a cigarette, examine the bomb from all angles, then tap it and listen to it with a stethoscope while his secretary stood by his side taking notes. The earl was a fatalist and often said: 'If my name is on a bomb, that's it.'

Howard's name *was* on the thirty-fifth bomb he attempted to defuse. On 12 May 1941, as he was removing the fuse on a 500-pound booby-trapped device, it exploded, killing all three of his team and eleven other people who were standing nearby. The earl was wearing his white flying helmet and fur gloves at the time.

10

The Gentlemen Amateurs

For those noblemen who had no wish to play a part in the running of the country or in the armed forces there was the usual dilemma: apart from the drinking and the gambling, how was one supposed to pass one's time? Some kept themselves busy improving their mansions or landscaping their gardens. Others spent their time killing wild animals. The more intellectually curious travelled, or dabbled in science.

Before it became a career option funded by governments and private companies, science was largely the plaything of gentlemen (and women) who had the leisure time and the

313

money to indulge their hobby. It tended to attract extraordinary characters. The first bone fide aristocrat scientist was an imperious, hard-drinking and highly volatile Danish astronomer called Tycho Brahe. Before Brahe, astronomers made the odd celestial observation of their own, then added their findings to whatever else had been handed down to them by the stargazers of antiquity. Brahe realised that proper understanding of the universe required long and painstaking observations made with pinpoint accuracy. He is remembered today as much for his brilliant scientific career as his talent for getting involved in bizarre scrapes.

Brahe was born in 1546 into the upper crust of Danish nobility at their ancestral seat in Knudstrup, now in Sweden but then part of Denmark. He was groomed for a career in law but, to the disgust of his family, when he was a teenager he decided to become an astronomer after watching a partial eclipse of the sun. His big career break, however, came not as an astronomer, but as an astrologer.

On 28 October 1566 there was an eclipse of the moon and on the basis of a horoscope he had cast, Brahe announced that the eclipse foretold the death of the Ottoman Sultan, Suleiman 'the Magnificent'. Brahe's prediction was very popular because the Muslim Suleiman was hated by Christian western Europe. When news broke that the Sultan had indeed expired, Brahe's reputation as a fortune-teller was sealed. Some of the gloss was taken off his prediction when it turned out that Suleiman was eighty years old and had in fact already been dead for several weeks before the eclipse, but no one seems to have made too much of it.

Brahe was now internationally famous and able to hob-nob with the crowned heads of Europe. One of his biggest fans was King James VI of Scotland, the future King James I of England, who had come to Scandinavia to marry one of the Danish king's sisters. The two hit it off, and James granted Tycho a thirty-year copyright for all his writings published in Scotland.

Brahe was planning to move to Basel in Switzerland where he could be closer to the centres of European culture, but in 1576 the Danish King Frederick II, basking in the reflected glory of his new home-grown hero and desperate not to lose him permanently, made him an offer he couldn't refuse. Frederick gifted his celebrity astronomer the island of Hven, along with substantial treasury funding to set up a permanent observatory. In return, Tycho promised to make his king famous throughout Europe as a patron of the sciences.

Brahe set about building a fantastic new castle on Hven with the help of the islanders' labour, as was his due under his feudal rights. Uraniborg, as he called his new home, was equipped with a range of instruments of remarkable size and precision, the likes of which the world had never seen. As well as his observatory, it had a chemical laboratory, a paper mill, a printing press and a dungeon for imprisoning recalcitrant tenants.

Uraniborg cost the equivalent of 30 per cent of the annual revenues of the Danish crown, about three billion pounds today's currency, but in scientific terms it was money well spent. Although he didn't have the benefit of a telescope, armed with just his naked eye and a quadrant Brahe made a vast number of astonishingly accurate astronomical measurements, including a comprehensive study of the solar system, pinpointing the positions of hundreds of stars.

As well as his scientific duties he was also contractually obliged to provide annual astrological predictions for the royal court, although by now Brahe wasn't entirely convinced of its usefulness. He drew up a list of days in the year when it was considered advantageous to stay in bed, because unfortunate events were bound to occur. Even today in parts of Scandinavia, a day when everything goes wrong is called a 'Tycho Day'.

Brahe's future seemed secure, but not everyone who came into his orbit was a fan of the king's favourite. In between mapping the skies, the aristocrat astronomer ruled his island kingdom in a grand style and with a thoroughly autocratic hand. In addition to his common-law wife and their eight children, Uraniborg was home to a huge retinue of servants, including a psychic dwarf called Jepp and several scientific assistants. Every night he entertained at least two dozen visitors in grand style. The islanders, meanwhile, were expected to work for nothing while his assistants, many of them students from the University of Copenhagen, received no greater payment than breakfast and bed and the privilege of Brahe's conversation at dinner. Anyone who rejected his terms of employment had a choice between sampling the hospitality of his dungeon, or escaping – easier said than done, as Uraniborg was surrounded by six-metre-high, five-metre-thick walls and guarded by man-eating dogs.

The Danish astronomer royal was not the sort of man you would want to get into an argument with. Arrogant and hot-tempered, Brahe drank heavily, fought duels and generally tyrannised the local peasantry. Then there was some unfortunate business concerning Brahe's pet elk, which apparently got drunk during the night, fell down some stairs, broke a leg and had to be shot. What it was doing upstairs drunk in the first place was of course, nobody's business but Brahe's.

There was something else that set Brahe apart. As a twenty-year-old student at Rostock he got into a quarrel at a party with a fellow academic Manderup Parsbjerg over a mathematical formula. They decided to take it outside in the form of a duel, conducted in pitch darkness, with rapiers.* Parsbjerg got the upper hand and sliced off a large portion of Brahe's nose. The astronomer concealed the loss of face as best he could with an artificial bridge made of gold, silver and copper and carried a small pot of glue with him at all times to keep his precious metal proboscis firmly in place.

Brahe's bad behaviour was tolerated so long as his friend King Frederick was alive. His son King Christian, however, was less forgiving of the high-maintenance astronomer and promptly cut off Brahe's pension.

Brahe left Denmark in a huff. A less temperamental man might well have been able to reach an agreement with the king, but then a more even-tempered man might not have had a silver nose, or kept an elk in his bedroom, or have become such a great astronomer in the first place. Brahe went to Prague seeking employment with the Holy Roman Emperor Rudolf II. They got along famously: the emperor was considerably more interested

---

* Duels were fairly commonplace among the Danish nobility but especially frequent in Brahe's family. Two years later one of his cousins killed a man in a sword fight, then in 1581 one of Brahe's uncles slew a second cousin the same way. Brahe's first cousin was killed in a duel in 1584, as was another uncle in 1592.

in science than politics and had a number of odd interests, including a 'cabinet of curiosities' and a menagerie of wild animals, among them a pet lion and a tiger that were allowed to roam the castle and randomly attack people: there are account books recording the compensation he paid to survivors of attacks and to family members of victims. Rudolf was thought by some historians to have been insane.

Brahe was appointed Imperial Mathematician, although the job description also required him to keep the emperor up to speed on any other general insights he had about the mysteries of the universe, and, of course, he was also expected to cast the odd horoscope.

It was probably drink that did for Brahe in the end.* In October 1601 he was invited to a banquet at the Prague palace of the nobleman Peter Vok Ursinus Rozmberk. The astronomer enjoyed the generous amount of food and drink on offer, but being a nobleman with good table manners, etiquette prevented him from leaving his seat to empty his full bladder before his host left. Brahe's bladder burst; intestinal fever and delirium followed and he died in agony five days later.

In Prague people still say, 'I don't want to die like Tycho Brahe.' It means, 'I have to take a piss.' In this way, the memory of one of the world's greatest astronomers is refreshed daily.

* More recent medical experts discount this and say some kind of underlying kidney problem was the more likely cause. There is also an unproven theory that Brahe was poisoned by a jealous assistant.

BOYLE'S FLAW

Science took off in Britain with the return from exile of King Charles II in 1660. Although his court is usually more associated with debauchery than curiosity, were it not for Charles's interest in the 'new natural philosophy', modern science might have turned out very differently. The king himself dabbled in chemistry, while his friend the Duke of Buckingham was one of the original members of the new Royal Society, formed in 1662, and kept a handsomely appointed laboratory in his house.* Even the 2nd Earl of Rochester, in the intervals between seducing women and boys, was a student both of chemistry and medicine.

The first British full-time scientist, and one of the founding members of the Royal Society, was the aristocrat Robert Boyle. He was born in 1627 the seventh son (and fourteenth child) of the spectacularly procreative 1st Earl of Cork, one of the richest men in the British Isles at that time; Boyle was once introduced, to Samuel Pepys' great amusement, as 'son of the Earl of Cork and father of modern chemistry', in that order.

As a young man Boyle wanted to be a writer and wrote a series of highly moralistic musings with titles such as: 'Upon the sighting of a fair milkmaid singing to her cow'; and 'Upon my spaniel's carefulness not to lose me in a

---

* During one meeting Buckingham produced what he promised was the horn of a unicorn. Reputedly, a circle drawn with a unicorn horn would trap a spider until it died. True to the Society's motto '*Nullius in verba*' ('Take nobody's word for it'), his claim had to be tested: a circle was made with powder of a unicorn's horn and a spider set in the middle of it, but it ran off.

strange place'. Fortunately for literature, Boyle opted for a career in science instead.

His huge income meant that he could afford to employ assistants and run what amounted to a private research institute that would be the envy of many scientists today. Unlike many of his contemporaries, he could get his own books published at his own expense, ensuring that they appeared promptly, in properly printed editions; as Boyle could always be relied on to pay his bills on time, the printers took extra care with his work. His book *The Sceptical Chymist* published in 1662 set out his eponymous law, once known to all schoolchildren, relating pressure to the volume of gas.

Some of the experiments Boyle carried out at the Royal Society on animals were not for the faint-hearted. Chickens were 'choked', fish were 'gagged', dogs were strangled and live cats dissected, but Boyle and other fellows refused to allow what he called 'effeminate squeamishness' to hold them back. He was also ambitious; here is his bucket list, compiled three hundred years ago, of twenty-four scientific projects he hoped to see achieved:

1. The Prolongation of Life.
2. The Recovery of Youth, or at least some of the Marks of it, as new Teeth, new Hair colour'd as in youth.
3. The Art of Flying.
4. The Art of Continuing long under water, and exercising functions freely there.
5. The Cure of Wounds at a Distance.
6. The Cure of Diseases at a distance or at least by Transplantation.
7. The Attaining Gigantick Dimensions.

8. The Emulating of Fish without Engines by Custome and Education only.
9. The Acceleration of the Production of things out of Seed.
10. The Transmutation of Metalls.
11. The makeing of Glass Malleable.
12. The Transmutation of Species in Mineralls, Animals, and Vegetables.
13. The Liquid Alkaest and Other dissolving Menstruums.
14. The making of Parabolicall and Hyperbolicall Glasses.
15. The making Armor light and extremely hard.
16. The practicable and certain way of finding Longitudes.
17. The use of Pendulums at Sea and in Journeys, and the Application of it to watches.
18. Potent Druggs to alter or Exalt Imagination, Waking, Memory, and other functions, and appease pain, procure innocent sleep, harmless dreams, etc.
19. A Ship to saile with All Winds, and A Ship not to be Sunk.
20. Freedom from Necessity of much Sleeping exemplify'd by the Operations of Tea and what happens in Mad-Men.
21. Pleasing Dreams and physicall Exercises exemplify'd by the Egyptian Electuary and by the Fungus mentioned by the French Author.
22. Great Strength and Agility of Body exemplify'd by that of Frantick Epileptick and Hystericall persons.
23. A perpetuall Light.
24. Varnishes perfumable by Rubbing.

You may recognise some on the list as submarines (4), genetically modified crops (9), transplantation (6), psychedelic drugs (20), GPS navigation (16) and 'scratch and sniff' (24).

Boyle played a large part in turning chemistry into a rational, respectable science, but he never quite shook off his fascination with alchemy and the philosopher's stone, the magical substance that would transmute base metals into gold. He also believed that scientific experimentation was God's work and should only take place on the Sabbath. He became deeply religious after being half frightened out of his wits by a violent thunderstorm when he was on the Grand Tour. One of his lesser-known fields of research was interviewing miners to find out how many of them had encountered demons down the pit.

Although extremely rich, Boyle was a shy, reclusive bachelor and lodged for the last twenty-five years of his life with his sister, Lady Ranelagh, in Pall Mall. He was also a raging hypochondriac and commissioned a range of cloaks in various materials to cope with any possible variation in the weather, deciding which one to wear before he went out by consulting the recently invented thermometer. Boyle died on 30 December 1691, a month short of his sixty-fifth birthday. After his funeral, Robert Evelyn wrote in his diary: 'It is certainly not only England, but all the learned world suffered a public losse in this greate & good man, & my particular worthy friend.'

THE SHY GENIUS

By the eighteenth century science was becoming increasingly professional but there was still a handful of independently wealthy people working on their own. One English gentleman scientist who stood head and shoulders above all others was the singularly peculiar Henry Cavendish. He was without doubt the most productive scientist of his generation and arguably one of the greatest who ever lived, but most of his ground-breaking achievements lay hidden in notebooks read by no one but Cavendish during his lifetime. Morbidly fearful of human contact and pathologically reclusive, he was too shy to accept public acclaim or share his genius with the world.

Cavendish was born in 1731 into one of England's wealthiest and most distinguished families. Both of his grandfathers were dukes, respectively of Devonshire and of Kent. When his father Lord Charles Cavendish died in 1783, soon followed by the death of a wealthy, childless aunt, he became one of the richest men in England, but instead of enjoying his wealth he chose to live a solitary, frugal existence, working in obscure solitude in his laboratory in Clapham, his only luxuries books and laboratory equipment.

Cavendish gave little thought to the value of money in the way that only the super-rich can. At a christening, when told that it was customary to give the nurse a tip on the way out, he dipped into his pocket and gave her a handful of gold sovereigns. When invited to make a contribution for a sick employee he chipped in with a staggering ten thousand pounds. He gave short shrift to anyone who tried to discuss his finances with anyone, as a well-meaning bank employee discovered when he made the mistake of asking him what he planned to do with his fortune: Cavendish threatened to close all his accounts if it ever happened again. The only thing Cavendish cared about was the fact that vast inherited wealth gave him free time to pursue his scientific interests.

His private research spanned chemistry, mechanics, magnetism, optics and geology. He made a series of astonishing discoveries, including the chemical composition of air and water. He invented several astronomical instruments and anticipated Einstein by 120 years by calculating the effect of gravitation on light rays. He pioneered work with condensers and measured the strength of electrical currents, discovering the rules of electrical resistance more than half a century before the German scientist Ohm quantified them. But Cavendish only ever published a fraction of the experimental evidence he had available to support his theories, to the confusion of fellow scientists, who often found him referring in his papers to experiments he had yet to tell anyone about.

His most remarkable achievement was made when he was sixty-seven, the age at which most scientists were either past their prime or retired. Working from an outbuilding of his home, using primitive equipment that wouldn't have looked out of place in a torture chamber, including counterweights, pendulums, shafts and torsion wires, Cavendish weighed the Earth. He estimated that the planet weighed a little over six billion trillion metric tons. This calculation was astonishingly accurate. Two hundred and fifty years later, modern scientists armed with the most advanced technology available estimate the Earth to weigh around 5.9725 billion trillion metric tons – within 1 per cent of Cavendish's figure.

Cavendish rarely left his house and it was only when he was tempted out to attend Royal Society meetings that his eccentricities became apparent to the world. He never sat for a portrait; the only existing likeness of him, sketched secretly from a distance at a Royal Society dinner, shows a tall figure wearing an old-fashioned, faded, violet velvet frock-coat and a three-cornered cocked hat, items of clothing that had been out of date for at least half a century. He owned one suit at a time and wore it continuously until it fell apart, then he would send out for an identical one.

He was terrified of any kind of social interaction and was described by a colleague as 'shy and bashful to a degree bordering on disease'. When he spoke, if he spoke at all, it was with a shrill, high-pitched voice and a slight stammer. All his fellow scientists were ever able to squeeze out of him were a few words on technical matters if they were lucky; according to Sir Joseph Banks, the President of the Royal Society at the time, 'he probably uttered fewer words in the course of his life than any man who ever lived to four score years, not at all excepting Trappist monks'.

If a stranger came near Cavendish he would emit a high-pitched squeak and flee like a frightened animal. New Royal Society members were advised never to make eye contact with him and to introduce themselves by casually wandering into his proximity and then to 'speak as it were into vacancy'. If he found your thoughts on the matter of any significance he might mumble a reply, although more often than not you would be greeted with the sight of Cavendish's backside vanishing to a quieter corner of the room. An Austrian visitor once broke the rule and introduced himself; he had travelled all the way from Vienna, he informed the mortified scientist, in the hope of conversing with 'one of the most illustrious philosophers of the age'. Cavendish fled ashen-faced and squeaking from the building and jumped into a cab.

His favoured means of communicating with his household staff was by writing letters to them, a system he facilitated by equipping his two London houses with a complicated system of internal mailboxes and double doors. It was contact with women that troubled him most. He couldn't bring himself to talk to or even look at a female. His maids were only tolerated so long as they followed his written instructions to keep completely out of his sight on pain of dismissal. At mealtimes he communicated with female staff by leaving notes on the hall table; as he nearly always only ate leg of mutton, the notes were brief. He once accidentally bumped into a housemaid on the stairs and was so unnerved by the experience that he ordered the construction of a rear servants-only staircase so it could never happen again.

Cavendish died aged seventy-eight. Even on his death-bed he couldn't bear the idea of company and told his manservant that he had something to think about and didn't want to be disturbed; when he came back Cavendish was dead. The bulk of his estate went to his nephew George, who had no idea how much his inheritance was worth, having only ever been granted an annual audience of half an hour with his uncle in his entire life. He was staggered to find that he was now the owner of a neglected fortune that had grown, unattended, to a value of £1.75 million. It was many years later that the true value of Cavendish's contribution to science became known, when other scientists went through his papers, by which time much of his research had been wrongly attributed to others.

THE CURIOUS COUNT

The eighteenth-century French aristocrat Georges-Louis Leclerc, Comte de Buffon, better known in history simply as Buffon, was the polar opposite of Henry Cavendish. He was extrovert, vain, incredibly pompous and overbearing, but he also had a brilliant mind and, although few people may have heard of him today, he was one the most widely read authors of popular science books of his age.

Buffon acquired his estate when he was twenty-five, after getting himself expelled from university for fighting in a duel. With his vast inheritance of about eighty thousand livres a year (at a time when the minimum required for a French gentleman to maintain himself in style was about ten thousand livres a year) he could have lived his life in idle luxury, but he developed an interest in natural history and threw himself into his work with extraordinary dedication. For the next fifty years he hired a peasant to drag him physically out of bed at 5 a.m. each morning so he could start work.

Buffon's wide-ranging interests led him to study an astonishing breadth of subjects, from the possible causes of being cross-eyed (a condition scientifically known as strabismus) to the body structure of bats. He wrote up his findings in a thirty-six-volume encyclopaedia called *Natural History, General and Particular*, a project of stunning ambition, which aimed to include everything known about the natural world up until that date. In it, he anticipated some of the ideas of Charles Darwin and considered the similarities between humans and apes and the possibility of a common ancestry.

Buffon was at his most eccentric during creative spurts. Before he did any work he had to dress up in his finest clothing, from braided wig to purple silk waistcoat, lacy high-collared shirt down to polished leather boots. As he didn't like to get his famous lace cuffs dirty with messy experiments he left the bench work to his assistants while he did the thinking. It was the same with his writing; he left the bulk of it to assistants, himself contributing only the most striking and rhetorical passages. Buffon wasn't shy about declaring his genius. He was fond of telling people that there were only five truly great men: Isaac Newton, Francis Bacon, Gottfried Leibniz, Montesquieu and himself. He never responded to criticism, of which there was a great deal, because to do so was beneath his dignity as a gentleman.

Buffon's primary field of study was the Earth. A major question in his day was whether or not our planet was really only a few thousand years old, as most biblical scholars claimed. Buffon suspected it was much older and addressed the question directly. He worked on the assumption that the Earth had formed in conjunction with the much hotter Sun and had started in a molten state. To test his theory on a summer's day in 1741 he used the foundry on his estate to conduct a strange, not to mention ethically dubious experiment. He ordered the casting of two dozen small, solid iron globes. As the globes were removed from the furnaces at white-hot heat, the curious aristocrat held a watch and observed the glowing spheres carefully while they cooled to the temperature at which they could first be touched with bare fingers. He did this by rounding up several young women from his village, whose soft skin he thought would show the highest level of sensitivity to extreme heat, then instructed them to touch the spheres while he recorded their reactions. If he could measure how long it took his solid globes to cool and also show how the cooling time depended on the size of the globe, he could then figure out the cooling time for a much larger globe the size of Earth. He repeated his experiment many times to get more reliable numbers and measured the cooling time for spheres of different materials, such as glass and stone.

In 1778, Buffon published his conclusion that the planet was 74,832 years old – radically older than believed in the current thinking and a directly contradiction of biblical calculations. We know today that the real age of the Earth is vastly greater (about 4.55 billion years old) but Buffon was correct in concluding that the Earth is much older than the few-thousand-year estimate popular in those days. Despite his wild underestimation his notion was too radical for the Church, which threatened to excommunicate him. He quickly apologised, although he continued to repeat his heretical theory many times in his later workings.

Regardless of his achievements, Buffon wasn't greatly admired during his lifetime and he had to put up with attacks from mathematicians, chemists and astronomers, while others mocked him for his pompous attitude and his overblown style of writing, but there is no doubt that he was one of the greatest scientists of his era. For a while it looked as though Buffon's son, nicknamed Buffonet, might have a brilliant future in science as well, but the boy proved a sad disappointment and ended up just floating through life on his father's money. Buffon senior died one year before the storming of the Bastille; a kindness, as it turned out, because his son was to lose his head to the edge of a Revolutionary guillotine.

The first weatherman

Most people, given a few minutes to think, could probably come up with a respectable list of scientists who worked in the Victorian era: Charles Darwin, Joseph Lister, John Snow, Louis Pasteur, Charles Babbage and Michael Faraday, to name but a few. It's unlikely that very many of us would have included the name of Robert FitzRoy on our lists. As the founding father of weather forecasting and modern meteorology he should be regarded today as a national hero, but to most people he is remembered, if at all, as a footnote in the story of evolutionary theory.

Robert FitzRoy was connected to the upper echelons of the British aristocracy on both sides of his family. His father, Lord Charles FitzRoy, was a son of the 3rd Duke of Grafton, a great-grandchild of Charles II. His mother, Lady Frances Anne Stewart, was the eldest daughter of the first Marquess of Londonderry and the half-sister of the Foreign Secretary Viscount Castlereagh.

Robert was a brilliant student and at the age of fourteen graduated with distinction from the Royal Naval College in Portsmouth. By 1824, at the age of nineteen, he was a lieutenant in the Royal Navy having passed the examination with 'full numbers' (100 per cent), a result never before achieved. There was an early test of his impressive seamanship during one of his very first postings on HMS *Beagle*, under the command of Captain Pringle Stokes, who was charting the South American coastline. On 2 August 1828, while off Tierra del Fuego, Stokes came to the despairing conclusion that he had botched the surveys: he locked himself in his cabin, put a pistol to his head and pulled the trigger. He proved to be as useless a marksman as he was a mariner and it took twelve days for him to die. FitzRoy took over and steered the ship back to Rio, where he assumed full-time command of the *Beagle* at the age of twenty-three.

He returned home to great acclaim with an unexpected cargo. In Tierra del Fuego he abducted (or as FitzRoy put it, 'rescued') four natives. His plan was to take them back to England and give them the benefit of a 'proper' English education, and then return them to Tierra del Fuego as missionaries. FitzRoy pursued his bizarre social experiment with evangelical zeal. The four Fuegians were dressed in contemporary clothes and sent to a school in Walthamstow where they were taught English, arithmetic and 'the basic truths of Christianity'. Tragically, one of the Fuegians died following a smallpox vaccination, but with FitzRoy as their escort, the remaining three became a welcome novelty on the London social scene and enjoyed an audience with King William IV and Queen Adelaide, making FitzRoy famous in the process. It all went badly wrong when the senior male of the three remaining Fuegians, a hulking twenty-seven-year-old, was caught having sex with its youngest member, a twelve-year-old girl. FitzRoy, fearing ruin and disgrace, swiftly removed his charges from the school, and then using his powerful family connections, persuaded the Admiralty to send him on another expedition so he could return his Fuegians to their homeland.

In 1831 FitzRoy was appointed to captain the *Beagle* on a three-year survey of South America. By now he was widely regarded as the most able seaman of his generation, but he was uncomfortably aware of the loneliness that an extended command at sea could bring and still haunted by the suicide of the unfortunate Captain Stokes. He knew that there was a history of depression and suicide in his own family – his uncle Lord Castlereagh had taken his life by cutting his throat in 1822. FitzRoy was also a terrible snob and considered it socially unacceptable for him to fraternise with men of lower classes and ranks aboard ship, so he panicked at the thought of spending months at sea with no one to talk to. The solution, FitzRoy decided, was to take with him some 'gentleman company', someone who could share the captain's table and engage him in intellectual discourse.

The young naturalist Charles Darwin fitted the bill. Only four years apart in age (Darwin was twenty-two, FitzRoy twenty-six), both had a yearning for adventure and an interest in 'natural philosophy'. At their first meeting, however, FitzRoy had doubts, on account of Darwin's nose. FitzRoy's studies of physiognomy told him that 'people with a broad, squat nose like his don't have the character'. Not that Darwin was otherwise particularly qualified for a journey halfway round the world; the longest field trip he had been on up until then was three weeks spent in North Wales collecting insects.

FitzRoy's initial reservations about nose shape, however, were outweighed by the fact that the young amateur naturalist had also studied divinity. FitzRoy was deeply religious and a very firm believer in the literal truth of the biblical account of Creation. Darwin, FitzRoy thought, would be useful in helping him find data that would reveal God's work. Seldom in history has an appointment misfired so spectacularly.

The *Beagle* was a ten-gun brig of the type known in the Royal Navy as a 'coffin' because it had a habit of capsizing in heavy weather. Fortunately, FitzRoy was a brilliant navigator. Despite having to negotiate some of the most dangerous waters of the world, surviving storms, earthquakes, disease and encounters with hostile natives, the aristocratic young sea captain returned home with his ship and most of its crew intact.

Along the way Darwin suffered terrible seasickness – the least of his problems, as it turned out. He soon found out that the man he had to share his meals with three times a day in a tiny cabin had a very short fuse and was capable of wild mood swings. The two men had frank exchanges, later described by Darwin as quarrels 'bordering on insanity'. Darwin wrote home: 'Some part of his [FitzRoy's] brain needs mending.' At one point FitzRoy stopped eating and shut himself away for several weeks. He eventually emerged, thin and haggard, and offered his resignation. He told the crew he thought he was going the same way as his suicidal uncle and his predecessor, Captain Stokes. It seemed that the voyage would have to be cut short, but luckily for science, FitzRoy's loyal second-in-command, Lieutenant Wickham, was able to talk his captain round and continue the mission by crossing the Pacific and returning to England having concluded the circumnavigation they had set out to achieve.

In spite of their differences FitzRoy was won over by Darwin's charm and they became friends and remained in contact for many years afterwards. Darwin was very surprised therefore, shortly after they got back, at the news that FitzRoy was about to get married to a woman to whom he had been engaged for several years. Strangely, FitzRoy had never once spoken a word about his engagement, or his intended bride, Mary, throughout the five-year voyage.

The *Beagle* voyage, of course, turned out to be the defining experience of Darwin's life, providing him with the evidence for his book *On the Origin of Species* that would forever change our view of the world and our place in it, but following the *Beagle*'s return, it was the ship's captain, not Darwin, who won all the plaudits. FitzRoy wrote up his account of this voyage including masses of detailed weather observations and was awarded a gold medal by the Royal Geographical Society.

There was also a change in career direction. FitzRoy entered parliament, serving for two years as Tory MP for Durham. His unpredictable temper got the better of him and almost resulted in a duel with another Tory candidate – in the end, they settled for a fistfight in the Mall. In 1843, FitzRoy's life took another unexpected turn when he accepted the position of Governor of New Zealand. His time as governor was an unhappy one; his rigid discipline and unbending sense of religious duty made him deeply unpopular. When he sided with the local Maoris in a dispute with white settlers, he was sacked and sent home without being offered the customary knighthood. He returned to his naval duties as captain of the frigate HMS *Arrogant*, but a morbid depression, one of many, forced him into retirement in 1850. And there he would have remained, snubbed by the Establishment and forgotten, if a tragedy at sea hadn't forced the Admiralty to turn to him for help in 1859.

FitzRoy was one of a new generation of meteorologists who were trying to shed light on the secrets of the atmosphere. Until the nineteenth century no one really had a clue about how weather worked. There was no scientific explanation for storms, winds, rain or clouds. Most people believed that a storm at sea was evidence of God's great wrath. The concept of predicting the weather seemed ludicrous. When an enlightened MP suggested in the House of

Commons that someday 'we might know in this metropolis the condition of the weather twenty-four hours beforehand', the chamber erupted into laughter.

It took a disaster to make them take meteorology seriously. On 25 October 1859 the passenger ship *Royal Charter* was destroyed by a violent gale off the coast of Anglesey with the loss of 450 lives. The Admiralty sent for the recently widowed FitzRoy and asked him to investigate the effects of the weather on shipping.

FitzRoy threw himself into his role as head of the newly founded Meteorological Office with enthusiasm. He pooled data to make weather maps on which he plotted wind, barometric pressure and temperature using symbols to denote clouds, rain and snow. He made the first use of conical storm symbols – the standard gale warning still in use today. Thanks to the recently invented electric telegraph, he could plot the course of incoming storms then relay messages to key harbours, which would then hoist warnings.

He also began what he called – and what everyone still calls – the weather forecast. Before FitzRoy, the weather had only ever been presented retrospectively. *The Times*, for example, would print a report of how the weather had been across Great Britain for the period of 8 a.m. to 9 p.m. the previous day. Thanks to FitzRoy's weather maps, on 1 August 1861 *The Times* readers could actually read what the weather was likely to do over the next two days.

Although by modern standards the forecasts were very vague (the first advised: 'General weather probable during the next two days.') the nation went mad for FitzRoy's weather predictions. He was astonished one day to find one of Queen Victoria's servants at his door: her majesty was planning to make the short boat trip across the Solent to her Isle of Wight residence and she wanted to know if it was going to rain.

The popularity of his new weather forecasts and the attention that came with it were a sunny interval in FitzRoy's life. In his mind, however, dark storm clouds were gathering. His late wife Mary had been an even more uncompromisingly devout Christian than he was and marriage had marked a radicalisation of his own religious beliefs. He continued to visit his old friend Darwin at his home, Down House, but all that changed in 1859 with the publication of *On the Origin of Species*. FitzRoy, the ardent creationist, became a rabid opponent of Darwin and wrote letters to *The Times* explaining that giant animals such as the mastodon had not survived the biblical flood because they were too big to get into Noah's Ark. He was also saddened by the certainty that his old shipmate was going to hell.

On Saturday 30 June 1860, seven months after the publication of *On the Origin of Species*, science and religious dogma went head-to-head in Oxford when evolutionary theory was debated at a meeting of the British Association for the Advancement of Science. Darwin was too ill to attend, leaving the fighting to his more combative allies Joseph Hooker and T. H. Huxley, dubbed 'Darwin's Bulldog' for his staunch defence of his friend's work. More than a thousand people crowded into the chamber to hear stinging attacks from both sides. According to reports, in the ensuing commotion a member of the audience named Lady Brewster fainted and had to be carried out. Meanwhile FitzRoy, who was attending the meeting to present his own paper on weather patterns, walked around the hall brandishing a huge copy of the Bible above his head, shouting, 'The truth is in here!' He was shouted down and escorted from the building.

To the end of his days, FitzRoy was tormented over his decision to take Darwin on board the *Beagle*, blaming himself for the blasphemy of evolutionary theory. His misery was compounded by the fact that the world was becoming less appreciative of his pioneering work in meteorology. Not unlike with today's weather forecasters, the public held him to unrealistic expectations. He found himself under pressure on all sides, not only from people who were angry with inaccurate reports, but also from those who were simply irritated that he was predicting bad weather at all; fleet owners were upset about losing business when their fishermen refused to head out to sea because of an unfavourable FitzRoy forecast. He was also criticised by fellow scientists, who complained that the very idea of weather prediction was flawed; scientists should stick to the establishment of certainties, not risk their reputation on unknowable outcomes.

The unreliability of FitzRoy's forecasts was hardly surprising given that modern meteorologists with access to satellite images and computer technology still get it wrong, but it made FitzRoy a figure of public ridicule. *Punch* poked fun at the uselessness of official weather reporting with a series of badly drawn synoptic charts populated by a flurry of made-up symbols. Even *The Times*, which ran his forecasts, took to printing disclaimers, effectively disowning their author.

The temperamental, thin-skinned aristocrat took the criticisms to heart. On the morning of 30 April 1865, the world's first weatherman got up early without waking his wife, kissed his daughter, then locked himself in his dressing room and slashed his throat with a razor.

MOTHERS OF INVENTION

The inventory of recognised female scientists in the Georgian era is depressingly short. One notable exception was Ada, Lady Lovelace, daughter of the poet Lord Byron. Now considered one of the ablest mathematicians of the era, she has a very strong argument to be considered as the world's first computer programmer. She was taught maths and science at a very young age by her mother, a rarity at a time when ladies weren't supposed to be concerned with such matters. Oddly, the lessons were given primarily as a preventative method for insanity, which she feared Ada might have inherited from her mad, bad, dangerous father.

In 1833 Ada met the brilliant British mathematician Charles Babbage and they became lifelong friends. Babbage nicknamed her 'the enchantress of numbers'. She was intrigued by Babbage's idea for an 'Analytical Engine' – a mechanical calculating machine whose design predated the digital computer by over a hundred years. In 1842 the mathematician Luigi Menabrea published a memoir describing the Analytical Engine, which would subsequently be translated from French to English by Ada for Babbage. In the article she included a set of original notes that explained a method for performing calculations, which is recognised today as the very first algorithm.

Lady Lovelace also had a widely known fascination with magic. Babbage gave her taltent a second nickname, 'Lady Fairy', after she took up investigating how humans might fly. She studied the anatomy of birds and experimented with different designs before writing an illustrated book called *Flyology*.

When she was in her twenties, like many of her class, Lady Lovelace developed a serious gambling problem. This addiction was enabled by her friend Babbage, whom she had encouraged to come up with a method for mathematically predicting the outcome of handicapped horse races. Although he received hundreds of letters from racegoers who wanted to know more, Babbage turned out to be a disastrous tipster and Ada Lovelace was almost ruined by gambling debts. It got so bad that she twice had to secretly pawn her husband's family jewels. Like Lord Byron, Ada's life ended at the young age of thirty-six, her death the result of uterine cancer combined with the bloodletting that the doctors attempted to treat it with. At her request, she was buried next to the father she never met.

Another forgotten lady of science is the French aristocrat Émilie, Marquise du Châtelet, one of the few who managed to break into the male-dominated fields of mathematics and physics. She was considered to be one of the most brilliant and most beautiful women of the Enlightenment age. Voltaire, who was one of her many lovers, described her as 'a great man whose only fault was being a woman'. What's more, she enjoyed a very wild life.

Émilie was born in Paris in 1706 and grew up in a house with thirty rooms and seventeen servants overlooking the Tuileries gardens. Her father, most unusually, hired the best private tutors to teach her Latin, Greek and mathematics. She used her talent for figures to gamble at cards with considerable success – she could add up a staggering number of permutations in her head – then used the money to buy more books.

One of her tutors was France's most renowned mathematician, Pierre de Maupertuis. It was his custom to hold lessons in Gradot's coffee house in Paris, but women were banned from such establishments so the marquise arrived for lessons at Gradot's dressed as a man. She wasn't a very convincing cross-dresser but the proprietors turned a blind eye because they didn't want to lose their wealthy clientele and so she became a regular at the coffee house, always fashionably dressed as a male.

She was a very feisty lady. At the age of sixteen she was introduced to the Court at Versailles and immediately attracted the unwelcome attention of a male courtier, so she challenged him to a duel – and won. At nineteen she was married to a wealthy thirty-four-year-old army officer, the Marquis du Châtelet. It seems that she did her duty by him, bearing him three children, but while he was away on military business she took at least three lovers, including an eighteen-month affair with the Duc de Richelieu, the man who inspired the character Velmont in *Les Liaisons dangereuses*. She was the only woman who ever dumped him.

She was twenty-seven when she began her passionate, fifteen-year affair with the poet and writer Voltaire, then in his forties. They flaunted their relationship, scandalising Parisienne society by attending the opera and being seen in public places, oblivious to the outrage they caused. Her indiscretion was considered doubly scandalous because she was the wife of a respected nobleman and Voltaire was a commoner. Voltaire even moved in with the Châtelet family at their country home at Cirey-sur-Blaise in north-eastern France. Monsieur du Châtelet was happy to tolerate the arrangement and it continued for many years.

The marquise owned a huge library that ran to about twenty-one thousand volumes – a much bigger collection of books than that owned by most universities – plus a laboratory equipped with the finest scientific instruments money could buy. She and Voltaire collaborated on a succession of experiments. This was a time when it was impossible for a woman to publish a scientific paper in her own right, so it was Voltaire who got the credit, although he really wasn't much of a scientist and she was by far the better physicist and mathematician.

By 1736 they were working jointly on a translation and commentary of Isaac Newton's work *Principia Mathematica*. Again it was published under Voltaire's name although he struggled even to follow the maths. Émelie went on to do outstanding work in the field of energy, glimpsing ideas that 150 years later Albert Einstein would use as one of the keys that would unlock his theory of relativity. Voltaire seems to have had a problem with the idea that his lover was in many respects much more intelligent than he was, which was the main reason why they broke up.

All the while, the marquise continued to scandalise the male-dominated scientific establishment with her unconventional approach. She moved her bath into her living room so that she could bathe while debating physics, and had drinks and canapés served to the men who sat around her while the learned conversations went on.

In her early forties she became pregnant by a much younger poet, Jean François de Saint-Lambert. At that time, at her age, pregnancy was a death sentence. She bore a daughter, but neither she nor the child survived childbirth.

Despite her achievements, biographers were still much more interested in Voltaire than his sexy mistress sidekick. Even after her ideas entered the scientific mainstream the notion that a woman was behind them seemed so odd that people forgot who had originated them. Immanuel Kant, for example, said that counting Émilie du Châtelet as a great thinker was 'as preposterous as imagining a bearded woman'. It wasn't until the 1930s that better scholarship brought her some recognition.

THE DINOSAUR HUNTER

Another scientific name long since slipped into obscurity is that of the Transylvanian nobleman Franz, Baron von Nopcsa. Born to an aristocratic family in 1877 in what was then part of the Austro-Hungarian Empire, he stumbled across his lifelong obsession by chance. When he was about eighteen years old, his sister discovered some large bones on one of the family estates in Transylvania. Nopcsa was fascinated and took them to a geology professor in Vienna. So began the career of one of Europe's greatest fossil-hunters.

Some of his biggest discoveries were made in his own backyard. The local dinosaurs were smaller than similar species from other parts of the world, a fact Nopcsa attributed to dwarfism, the tendency for populations of large animals to become smaller in size when they are isolated on an island. Nopsca's studies on the geology of the Balkan region also resulted in a theory of plate tectonics, forty years ahead of its time. His pioneering techniques for fossil analysis and his prescient theories about dinosaur evolution and continental drift should have been enough to secure his place in science history, but his achievements were largely overshadowed by his personal and political eccentricities.

Nopcsa was privileged, arrogant and widely regarded as more than a little mad. Back in Transylvania he enjoyed the privileges of a baronial landlord as though he was playing a part in some fantasy royal operetta. When he travelled between his estates in his carriage, he insisted that peasants bow low to him as he passed by.

He allowed others to publish his scientific material – behaviour usually considered as academic suicide. Supremely self-confident and convinced of his intellectual superiority, his work veered from bouts of frenetic activity to sudden and total lethargy. Like the French scientist Buffon he seems to have been dazzled by his own brilliance. On a visit to Brussels, while in conversation with the already internationally famous palaeontologist Luis Dollo, he asked, 'Isn't it marvellous that I could have written such an excellent memoir while so young?'

Thanks to his immense wealth and influence at the court of the emperor of Austria-Hungary, Nopcsa enjoyed huge advantages over the average scholar of the day. He could travel freely through the empire on fossil-hunting trips and make regular visits to the great museums of Europe. During these escapes from court life he liked to shed his Viennese aristocratic finery and wear rough, native Balkan peasant dress. He would disappear into the Albanian mountains for months or even years at a time with his secretary and lover, a much younger man called Bajazid

Doda. There was also a couple of Albanian boyfriends who occasionally travelled with him.

Nopcsa was infatuated with Albania. He learned several dialects of the native language, amassed a huge library of books about the country, and used his influence to originate the discipline of Albanian studies; he even joined in the country's fight for independence from the Turks. His obsession with all things Albanian took a more bizarre turn when he offered himself up as a candidate for the vacant position of King of Albania.

The government of the newly independent state was looking ideally for 'an English Gentleman with an annual income of ten thousand pounds', on the basis that his connections and annual income would provide the necessary wherewithal to get Albania 'off the ground'. They offered the throne to the cricketer C. B. Fry, who declined reluctantly because he didn't have the necessary funds. After Fry refused, several other offers were made, including one to Lord Inchcape in 1921.* Nopcsa's campaign cited his aristocratic heritage and proposed an eccentric solution to Albania's financial problems – he would bring

---

* Lord Inchcape received the letter inviting him to accept 'the kingship of Albania', with the footnote: 'In case you turn it down entirely perhaps you would feel called upon to suggest the name of some wealthy Englishman or American with administrative power who would care to take up the cudgels on Albania's behalf.' Inchcape's response was not as helpful as the Albanians had hoped; he wrote back politely: 'I duly received your letter of the 29th ... it is a great compliment to be offered the Crown of Albania but it is not in my line. Yours sincerely, Inchcape.' He confessed later that he had absolutely no idea where Albania was.

the country an injection of cash by marrying an American millionairess. For the openly gay Nopcsa, the idea made sense: he already had a partner in his secretary Doda so it hardly mattered who he married.

When Albania turned down his generous offer and passed him over for a minor German noble, Nopcsa wasn't merely disappointed, he was furious. As it turned out they were probably doing him a favour, because the new King William of Albania was chased out of the country just six months later and Albania became a republic.

Sadly for Nopcsa, world events conspired to curtail his freewheeling lifestyle. In 1918 he found himself on the losing side in the Great War. The Romanian state seized his estates and his income and he had no choice but to settle in Vienna. Reluctant to give up his assets without a fight, he returned to one of his former estates but was attacked and beaten up by peasants wielding pitchforks. They left him for dead with a fractured skull, an injury that affected him for the rest of his life.

The swashbuckling dinosaur baron found the final years of his life difficult. To make ends meet he accepted a position with the Hungarian Geological Institute in Budapest, but the constraints of a day job didn't suit the proud nobleman and he quit his position so that he and Doda could go off on a three-thousand-mile motorcycle trip through Italy in search of fossils. To raise money to live on he had to sell most of his beloved fossil collection to the Natural History Museum in London.

By 1928 Nopsca's health was so frail that he addressed the audience at a palaeontological symposium in Belgium from a wheelchair. By 1933 he was completely broke and was forced to consider selling his precious collection of books and manuscripts so that he could pay his maid's wages.

Nopsca's career came to a sad, violent end on 25 April that year. He served Doda a drug-laced cup of tea, then shot his sleeping lover twice through the head with a pistol, then turned the gun on himself. The nobleman had prepared his exit carefully. As well as a sealed will addressed to a Viennese lawyer, he left a number of farewell messages including a letter to the police. It read: 'The motive for my suicide is a nervous breakdown. The reason that I shot my long-time friend and secretary, Mr Bayazid Elmaz Doda, in his sleep without his suspecting at all, is that I did not wish to leave him behind sick, in misery and without a penny, because he would have suffered too much. I wish to be cremated.'

11

Abominably Rich

In Scotland, a mile north-west of the town of Golspie in the county of Sutherland, you can't miss the 100-foot statue looking down from the summit of 1,293-foot Ben Bhraggie. 'The Mannie', as it is known in those parts, was built in 1834 by public subscription. Remarkably, money for the statue came in from far and wide, but there were few local donations. The legend chiselled into the stone plinth recalls that it was erected by 'a mourning and grateful tenantry (to) a judicious, kind and liberal land-lord'. There's a grim irony in the wording, because the man it commemorates (in the eyes of some Scottish

347

nationalists, 'Scotland's own Stalin') forcibly evicted at least fifteen thousand crofters from his 1.3-million-acre estate. The monument is regularly vandalised and there was once a campaign to have it blown up and scattered over the hillside. Other people think that it stands as a very useful reminder of how a greedy and criminally insensitive aristocrat was responsible for one of the darkest episodes of Scottish history.

For a foreign visitor arriving in Britain for the first time two hundred years ago, the most striking thing would have been the staggering wealth inequality. Away from the glitzy world of the Mayfair gentlemen's clubs and the fashionable spas of Bath and Cheltenham, the economic reality of the country was disastrous. A succession of bad harvests was causing genuine hardship and millions of people were living in grinding poverty. As many as two out of every five families struggled to pay for their basic item of food: bread. For those lucky enough to find work, the average rural labourer's wage had fallen from around fifteen shillings a week to six shillings. The penal code was savage: men faced transportation for stealing a pheasant to feed their children.

At the other end of the scale, the wealth of the wealthiest was astonishing. The British aristocracy was the richest and most powerful body of people on the planet, with accumulated fortunes that were so huge that even in twenty-first-century terms they are impressive: when adjusted for inflation they are breathtaking. An elite of super-rich, titled families owned lands in several counties and private art collections that could rival almost any in the world, living on a scale comparable with that of any Arab prince or Russian oligarch today. When the Earl of Yarborough died in 1875 his stock of cigars alone sold for enough to pay labourers on his estate for the next eighteen years. For most of these super-rich aristocrats the economic realities of life for their employees was beyond their comprehension. Lord Bessborough, for example, cut down on the number of gardeners at his country home because he was appalled to find that there were twelve of them each earning half a guinea a week: at the time he was paying off his wife's gambling debts of £32,700. The 1st Earl of Londesborough, who had his servants lay a mile of red carpet from his villa to the sea whenever he and his family visited the seaside at Scarborough, gave his employees chequebooks so they wouldn't hassle him with requests for money.

The 6th Duke of Devonshire was one of a handful of super-rich aristocrats who could enjoy an annual six-figure income; at the time anyone earning just five thousand pounds a year could consider himself very wealthy.* When he was still in his early teens a concerned family auditor commented to his father, 'he (your son) appears to be disposed to spend a great deal of money'. 'So much the better,' came the reply. 'He will have a great deal of money to spend.' Indeed he did. Although the high-living fifth duke, not to mention his gambling-addicted wife Georgiana and various mistresses, had put a massive dent in the family fortunes, the sixth duke still inherited four country houses and three London palaces supported by a huge income from land in Ireland and eight English counties. He had so many houses he complained that he couldn't find

---

* In 1825 a married man earning five thousand pounds a year could afford to maintain a household of about twenty-four servants.

the time to visit them all. In addition to his various magnificent mansions he owned large swathes of the West End of London and had considerable mining interests in Derbyshire and Yorkshire Not that he ever got his shoes dirty by visiting them: when he expressed curiosity about the workings of his Grassington lead mine he had a full-scale model of it made and delivered to his home instead. He was delighted with the results, remarking that it was 'the best piece of mechanical imitation I ever saw, entirely absolving me from any necessity of going to look at my subterranean property in the bowels of the earth'.

Not even the Devonshire fortune, however, came anywhere near that of the richest of the landed rich, the 1st Duke of Sutherland. For most of his adult life he enjoyed an annual income of around three hundred thousand pounds – several times that of his nearest aristocratic rivals, the Dukes of Devonshire and Bedford, who were considered extremely rich with fifty thousand pounds a year apiece. The precise value of his estate at death is unknown but it is estimated that he was easily worth seven million pounds and possibly as much as ten million pounds (at the lower figure, his wealth would have been around £21.4 billion in today's money), a fortune surpassing even that of the banker Nathan Rothschild. This made him not just the richest member of the aristocracy and the richest man in Europe, but one of the richest men who had ever lived.

The Sutherlands were probably the ultimate example of how great wealth and social status could be achieved by marrying the daughters of multi-millionaires. They weren't the first aristocratic family to marry their way to status and riches, but they did it with bewildering speed and then lost it almost as quickly to bad investments and family strife.

Their rise began with a Yorkshireman, Sir Thomas Gower, who succeeded to his baronetcy and his estate in Sittenham in 1630. He married Frances Leveson, heiress of Sir John Leveson, making him the owner of two large estates, Lilleshall in Shropshire and Trentham in Staffordshire. Their son William Leveson-Gower married another heiress, Lady Jane Granville, daughter of the Earl of Bath. Their son John did even better, marrying a daughter of the 1st Duke of Rutland.

With each passing generation the Gowers married well, conveniently adding to their steadily accumulating fortune, climbing the aristocratic ladder, rung by rung. They were already one of the richest families in England, but the one member who truly gilded the lily was John Gower's son Granville Leveson-Gower. He married three times, each wife the daughter of very wealthy men. The second, Lady Louisa Egerton, was the eldest daughter of the immensely rich Duke of Bridgewater. As a reward for political services Granville was also created 1st Marquess of Stafford. By the end of the eighteenth century the Leveson-Gowers had a string of titles, immense wealth and several magnificent houses, but their eldest son George went one better by landing the biggest catch of them all, the hand in marriage of Elizabeth, Countess of Sutherland, thereby uniting two of the biggest aristocratic fortunes in Britain.

The 'leviathan of wealth'

The Countess Elizabeth's family had a bloodthirsty history, but according to tradition it began with a man who fought cats. The Earls of Sutherland were supposedly descended from a Norse invader who landed at the coast of Sutherland and was set upon by several wild moggies. After a long and fierce battle he killed them all, surviving to found the Sutherland dynasty. The current Countess of Sutherland still celebrates this slayer of small mammals with a wild cat on her coat of arms and the motto *'Sans Peur'* – 'Fearless'.

The circumstances of the accession of Elizabeth, 19th Countess of Sutherland, were truly tragic. In 1766 her father, the eighteenth earl, while playing with his infant daughter Catherine at Dunrobin Castle, accidentally dropped her on her head, causing a fatal injury. The parents were devastated and sent their youngest daughter Elizabeth to stay with her grandmother while they went away to grieve at Bath. During their short break, both parents contracted 'putrid fever' (typhus) and died within a fortnight of each other. Elizabeth at this time was barely twelve months old.

It was the first time in more than five hundred years that an Earl of Sutherland had died without a male heir. There followed five years of dispute over the succession, as two distant male cousins challenged Elizabeth's right to inherit, but the infant countess eventually secured her position in 1771 when the House of Lords decided in her favour. It was an inheritance worth fighting for, because Sutherland estates comprised almost a million acres of windswept highlands at the northernmost tip of Scotland.

As well as being noted for her considerable wealth the young Elizabeth was widely regarded as a great beauty. Among her many famous admirers were the writer Sir Walter Scott and the prime minister William Pitt. The

Duke of Wellington, who knew an attractive woman when he saw one, described her as the 'great ornament' of Pitt's society. With Britain's most eligible bachelors to choose from, in 1785, when Elizabeth was twenty, she married George Leveson-Gower, the 2nd Marquess of Stafford.

Her new husband was a rather timid man with very little charisma. In his youth he had been frail and sickly and in his thirties he was afflicted by gout and poor eyesight. He seems to have suffered from an almost total absence of personality. Most people thought him extremely boring and even his grandson described him as 'dull'. His idea of relaxation was poking around in ponds looking for weeds, or examining all the cobwebs around his house for insects. There were just a couple of things that were really memorable about him. The first was his large, beaky nose, which stood out from his long, solemn face like a ship's prow. The other was his gob-smacking, spectacular wealth.

The marquess's beautiful new wife Elizabeth enjoyed flaunting her beauty, money and status and was the subject of a great deal of attention and gossip. Her dull husband, meanwhile, was under strict orders from his physician to avoid sexual intercourse for the sake of his lordship's failing eyesight. During this extended period of abstinence Elizabeth became pregnant with their second son Francis. It was widely speculated that the father was in fact her husband's brother-in-law Lord Carlisle.

Lord Stafford was elected to the Commons as MP for the old family seats of Newcastle-under-Lyme and Staffordshire. At the age of thirty-two, with no diplomatic experience, he was appointed British ambassador to France on the basis that he spoke French fluently. It was

1790 and he had a close view of the Revolution – a little too close in fact, when he and his wife were briefly arrested and detained by the Revolutionary tribunal at Abbeville. The experience must have been terrifying but it didn't seem to have put him off being liberal, relatively speaking, in his politics.

In 1803, in addition to the enormous landholdings he acquired in Scotland through his wife, he inherited from his father estates in Yorkshire, Staffordshire, Wolverhampton and Shropshire. In that same year he also inherited the entire fortune of his maternal uncle Francis Egerton, the childless last Duke of Bridgewater. The eccentric duke had been a sharp investor in the temporary art market created by the French Revolution, mostly put up for auction in the 1798 fire sale that followed the guillotining of their then owner, the Duc d'Orléans. He left his nephew the finest private art collection in the country at that time, plus an even greater sum of cash. No wonder the diarist Charles Greville described George Leveson-Gower as 'a leviathan of wealth'.

The statesman Benjamin Disraeli noted that the Sutherlands had made their fortune solely from 'a talent for absorbing heiresses', but the family's luck wasn't just confined to advantageous marriages. In 1720 one of Lord Stafford's forebears, Lord Gower, was one of the select circle of men who perpetrated the South Sea Bubble affair. Where others lost fortunes, Gower was one of the biggest winners. He sold out before the bubble burst and pocketed sixty-four thousand pounds, a profit of 300 per cent on his original investment.

Then there was the coal. As landowners, the Sutherlands were able to exploit the mineral resources on their estates through extensive mining. They also benefited from the boom in canal enterprise and railway construction from the 1760s through to the 1920s. By 1826 Lord Stafford was both the biggest canal owner and the biggest railway owner in Great Britain. The family even built their own railway with their own train to run to their Highland estates (the third duke, a railway fanatic, drove it himself).

The Sutherlands owned more houses than they knew what to do with – never less than six and at one point as many as eleven. While living mainly in London, they maintained huge country seats at Lilleshall and Trentham. In the summer the family retired to Dunrobin Castle in Sutherland where they spent their time shooting grouse, stalking deer and fishing salmon. In 1803 they inherited Bridgewater House in London and along with it one of the largest private art collections in Europe. They also built Gower House in Whitehall, now gone, but long regarded as one of the most beautiful houses in London.

The jewel in the crown was Stafford House (now called Lancaster House) in St James's, the biggest and most expensive of London's private homes. Made of Bath stone and spread over three floors, it housed a fraction of the family's art collection, including works by Hogarth, Raphael, Rubens, Reynolds, Tintoretto and Van Dyck, and was manned by a full-time staff of fifty-four indoor servants. The magnificence of Stafford House was such that when Queen Victoria visited it she pointedly remarked to her host, 'I have come from my house to your palace'. Fellow aristocrats also found the family's wealth unsettling. Lady Granville, sister of the immensely wealthy 6th Duke of Devonshire, described the Sutherlands as 'abominably rich'. This was her account of dinner with Lady Stafford in Trentham in 1810:

> The dinner for us two was soup, fish, fricassee of chicken, cutlets, venison, veal, hare, vegetables of all kinds, tart, melon, pineapple, grapes, peaches, nectarines, with wine in proportion. Six servants to wait upon us, whom we did not dare dispense with, a gentleman-in-waiting, and a fat old housekeeper hovering round the door to listen, I suppose, if we should chance to express a wish. Before this sumptuous repast was well digested, about four hours later, the doors opened, and in was pushed a supper of the same proportion, in itself enough to have fed me for a week. I did not know whether to laugh or to cry.

With great wealth came great power. While living a life of almost unrivalled grandeur, the Sutherlands also exercised complete control over thousands of people on their huge landed estates. Their abuse of this power made them, according to one historian, 'the most hated family in Europe'.

THE CLEARANCES

Neither Lord Stafford nor his wife made much of an effort to ingratiate themselves with the locals on their vast Scottish estate. Raised in London, Elizabeth was English in everything but her birth certificate. She spoke no Gaelic and allegedly hated Scottish customs and manners. She didn't even visit her Highland inheritance until she was seventeen. As for her husband, he was content to busy himself by buying art and improving his various estates in the south. It was not until 1812 that he turned his attention to Sutherland.

The Highland economy in the early nineteenth century was in terrible shape. The living standard for most people was never far above famine level. It was also one of the remotest parts of the British Isles, isolated, rugged and barren without a single road in the whole county and only one bridge. The people of Sutherland, Lord Stafford's advisers told him, were lazy and backward, happy to dig for potatoes and live off money sent home from sons who had migrated. One of the estate managers William Young described them as 'savages'. It would be much more profitable for the estate, Lord Stafford's advisers told him, to get rid of his tenants and turn the land over to large-scale sheep farming. The tenants would have to go, whether they wanted to or not.

Forced evictions were a fact of life in all rural communities throughout the British Isles. Across the countryside, landlords and their agents employed the threat of expulsion to terrorise tenants into voting as they were instructed, or to enforce higher rents, or better farming methods, or to deal with people whose only crime was their poverty and their inability to pay the rent.

One of the most pitiless evictors among the Victorian landlords was the villainous, mentally unstable William Clements, 3rd Earl of Leitrim, who inherited ninety thousand acres of land spread across the Irish counties of Leitrim, Donegal, Galway and Kildare in 1854. He terrorised the occupants of his estate. He once ordered the massacre of his tenants' goats after they had chewed his recently planted saplings, and when some other tenants mistakenly ploughed up some pasture, he forced them to replace it by hand, sod by sod. Although white-whiskered and in his seventies, he was alleged to have raped several Catholic servant girls, forcing them to have sex with him under threat of eviction of their families from his land. The allegations were never proven but it all helped feed the image of him in popular imagination as a monstrous, ruthless tyrant. Over a period of twenty years he survived a number of assassination attempts. His luck ran out in 1878 when he was shot and bludgeoned to death in an ambush on a north Donegal roadside. At the time of his death he was in the process of throwing out another eighty tenants.

In 1811 Lord Stafford's commissioners, factors, law agents and ground officers set about emptying the Sutherland glens to make way for sheep. Even the Church got in on the act: the local preacher threatened the highlanders with hellfire if they resisted. In many cases those evicted had held land under the family for upwards of two hundred years. No compensation was paid for lost homes or personal possessions destroyed. Many people starved and froze to death where their homes had been. Families who had spent generations rearing goats and growing crops were told to resettle on the coast and fish for a living. Many of the displaced were coerced into emigrating, often in the guise of philanthropic relief. Occasionally the evicting officers were secretly working with emigration agencies that had contracted the people to depart on waiting ships.

Where the evictions met opposition there were pitched battles, with injuries incurred on both sides. In some of the most infamous cases, houses were demolished or set ablaze to prevent their reoccupation by the evicted tenantry. A local, Donald MacLeod, reported seeing 250 homes ablaze in a single district; the fires burned for six days.

In 1814 one of Lord Stafford's more ruthless agents, Patrick Sellar, was tasked with removing hundreds of people to create his own massive sheep farm. Sellar was a thug and the evictions carried out by him were, according to one historian, 'of the order of brutality expected of a Norse raid a thousand years year earlier'. He was accused of many acts of cruelty, but one took place in June 1814 in Strathnaver that earned him international notoriety.

Most of the menfolk were away in the hills searching for and retrieving lost cattle when Sellar arrived with his men to target a house belonging to a tinker called William Chisholm. In the house was Chisholm's mother-in-law Margaret MacKay, a bedridden woman in her nineties. When the occupants complained that she was too old to be removed, Sellar replied, 'Damn her, the old witch, she has lived too long. Let her burn.' The house was torched and she died within the week from her injuries.

In April 1816 Sellar was sent for trial on charges of arson and murder. The jury, reminded by the judge Lord Pitmilly that Chisholm was probably a squatter and a sheep-stealer, took just fifteen minutes to return a verdict of 'not guilty'. Despite widespread condemnation, Sellar was allowed to keep his job and the Sutherland Clearances continued apace, although now he was more careful not to burn houses until after the tenants had vacated the premises. His work would be remembered in Sutherland as 'Bliadhna an Losgidh' – 'the Year of the Burnings'.

Lord Stafford was unmoved by the bad press. He acknowledged that some hardships had been experienced, but shrugged it off as the inescapable cost of progress. His wife, the countess, who had supplied much of the energy and initiative for the Clearances, was even less sympathetic about the suffering of her tenants. She asked her chief agent, James Loch, 'to encourage Sellar in trouncing these people who wish to destroy our system . . . I do hope the aggressors will be scourged.' After a brief tour of the area during which she had seen some of her starving tenants, she observed, 'Scotch [*sic*] people are of happier constitution and do not fatten like the larger breed of animals.'

Despite the vast amount of money and effort poured into his clearance policy Lord Stafford personally gained nothing from it. His investment never made a return. After 1820 the price of wool fell drastically and sheep farming was a failure. His diversification into other industries, especially fishing, also made a loss.

Lord Stafford's apologists point out that he was not a clever man and was only going along with the best economic advice given him. Others say that he was essentially weak and easily dominated by his considerably more ruthless wife. Whether or not either of these excuses absolve him in some small measure for the human suffering he caused is very debatable.

In 1833 Lord Stafford was created the 1st Duke of Sutherland for his services to politics. He lived to enjoy his new rank for just a few months, dying from the effects of a stroke aged seventy-five. At the time of his death, the Sutherland estates amounted to about one-and-a-half million acres – equal to about three times the size of the country of Bahrain. Charles Greville observed, 'I do believe he was the richest man who ever died.'

360

In 1825 the first duke gave his eldest son, George Granville, the estate of Lilleshall as a wedding present. He was expected to learn how to live off its income and scrape by on just twenty-five thousand pounds a year. As a rule of thumb, at that time an affluent family could get along very nicely on a thousand pounds a year – the equivalent today of around £120,000.

George Granville was forty-seven when he succeeded to the dukedom. He was a very sensitive and retiring character and eventually became stone deaf, which made him seem even more withdrawn. In 1814, during a trip to Berlin he fell madly in love with the very married Queen Louise, wife of King Fredrick William III of Prussia. This hopeless, unrequited passion endured for several years and he was so smitten that he fell dangerously ill on hearing of her death.

A bachelor until the age of thirty-seven, he suddenly emerged from his long sulk over Queen Louise and married seventeen-year-old Harriett, daughter of the 6th Earl of Carlisle. She went on to serve as Queen Victoria's Mistress of the Robes for twenty-five years and became her close friend and confidante. Harriett enjoyed huge social influence, a measure of which was seen in 1859 when the unemployed silk weavers of Spitalfields pleaded with her to accept a roll of magenta silk to have it made into a dress. She did, and within a few weeks the Spitalfields looms were working day and night to keep up with demand for copies of her dress.

The second duke took more interest in the welfare of his tenants than his parents had done (although it could hardly have been less). In 1947 he was confronted with the effects of the potato famine in Sutherland and was so moved that he promised that he and his family wouldn't eat potatoes again until the crisis was over. He had a sharp reminder of how deeply unpopular his family were that same year when he tried to raise two hundred men from his estates for the 93rd Highland regiment to fight the Russians in the Crimean War. There wasn't a single volunteer; one old man told the duke to his face that he was more unpopular than the Czar: 'If he [the Czar]took possession of the Sutherland estates we could not expect worse treatment at his hands than we have experienced at the hands of your family for the last fifty years.'

The story of the Sutherland family fortune from 1833 and the death of the first duke was one of decline. In every year that followed, their income fell. Their outgoings, however, did not and the Sutherlands continued to spend, spend, spend. The second duke continued to buy new properties, meanwhile altering and rebuilding their existing houses at fantastic expense. Trentham Hall near Stoke-on-Trent was dramatically altered when the architect Sir Charles Barry was hired to produce a much grander statement of the duke's wealth. Barry was employed again in 1849 when the duke added to his family's growing collection of palatial houses by acquiring Cliveden House in Buckinghamshire: this was the stately home Julian Fellowes originally had in mind as the family seat of the Granthams in TV's *Downton Abbey*. Shortly after the duke bought it, Cliveden was almost completely destroyed by fire and had to be rebuilt.

The second duke had two sons, of which the youngest, Lord Ronald Gower, was one of the few openly gay aristocrats in the Victorian period that wasn't driven into exile. It was generally known that he lived with a man called

Frank Hird,* whom he had adopted as his son. Lord Gower was a friend of Oscar Wilde and the basis of the character Lord Henry Wotton in *The Picture of Dorian Gray*.

Their eldest son, who succeeded as the 3rd Duke of Sutherland, was an altogether queerer fish. George Granville William Sutherland-Leveson-Gower, 3rd Duke of Sutherland, was a conspicuous oddity. He sported a fantastic topiary of facial hair and generally wore a mismatch of tartan and tweed and massive hobnailed boots, a look Lady Florence Paget described as 'a little unwashed and rough'. He chainsmoked cigarettes, cheerfully flaunting the convention that posh people didn't light up in public places. He had an enthusiasm for innovation and all things technical, which took him off in all sorts of unexpected directions. He was on board Brunel's *Great Eastern* when one of the boilers exploded, badly burning and scalding many sailors. He was one of the original backers of the Suez Canal scheme and a good friend of the Italian patriot Giuseppe Garibaldi, who enjoyed the duke's hospitality at Stafford House as well as on board one of the duke's three private yachts.

The 3rd Duke of Sutherland was also a pioneer motorist and owner of Thomas Rickett's steam car, the first car manufactured for commercial sale in 1858. He was vice-president of the Aeronautical Society of Great Britain. He also dug for gold, although why he thought he needed more is anyone's guess. One of his more useful ventures was a coalmine sunk near his Trentham estate, which he named after his daughter, Florence.

* Leading to Wilde's witticism, 'Frank may be seen, but not Hird.'

Mostly he was mad about steam engines. He built his own private steam railway in Sutherland and often drove it himself. Friends invited to accompany him on the footplate were given an upholstered seat in front of the coalbunker. Unlike his two ducal predecessors he showed no interest in politics. One newspaper reported euphemistically, 'The Duke of Sutherland makes up for his silence in the arena of public life by a good deal of practical wisdom exhibited in other directions.' *Punch* was less generous about his abilities, noting: 'He is clearly the wrong man in the wrong place on any platform except that of a steam engine.'

The duke had a child-like fascination for fire engines. He liked to dress up as a fireman and attend fires in London in his own private fire engine. He had a contact in the Chandos Street Fire Brigade who tipped him off whenever there was a blaze. When news of a fire came through, no matter what he was doing or what social function he was attending, the duke would drop everything and rush to the fire. When the Alhambra music hall caught fire in 1882, the duke and his friend the Prince of Wales were on the roof with hoses when part of it fell in, killing two firemen.

He was a member of the prince's gang of wealthy hangers-on, the Marlborough House set. Entertaining 'Bertie' was a fearfully expensive project. There were hosts prepared to economise for a whole year, or get into debt, just to put him up for a weekend. The duke was among the few who could afford to indulge him at length. In 1873 he also entertained the Shah of Persia, who took his fellow guest the Prince of Wales aside and remarked that their host and his estate were 'too grand for a subject', before advising quietly, 'You'll have to have his head off when you come to the throne.' The duke was thought to be one of

Bertie's more raffish acquaintances; Queen Victoria observed tartly, 'He does not live as a duke ought.' In fact, the story of the 3rd Duke of Sutherland's private life makes for a diverting journey down one of the stranger byways in aristocratic history, because there were widespread suspicions that he was a murderer, or at least an accomplice to one.

AN ACCIDENT OF A MELANCHOLY NATURE

The third duke's wife, Anne, was an intensely religious woman who spent much of her time composing hymns. The last ten years of her marriage were desperately unhappy. By the early 1880s her husband was increasingly absent, spending anything up to five months of every year abroad, usually on his steam yacht *Sans Peur* with a married woman described as his 'travelling companion'.

The woman in question was Mary Caroline Blair, born in 1848 and one of seven children of the Rev Richard Michell, Principal of Magdelen Hall, Oxford. Her eldest brother Edward was legal adviser to the King of Siam, while another, Richard, was a High Court judge. Mary Caroline, however, was unquestionably the most ambitious of the Michell siblings. She was regarded as a beauty, although photographs of her make this hard to credit. They show a voluptuous but less than ravishing dark-haired lady with a manly jawline staring down the camera with a look reminiscent of the young Manchester United midfielder Roy Keane.

In 1872, aged twenty-four, she married her cousin, thirty-seven-year-old Arthur Kindersley Blair. He was a former officer in the 71st Highland Light Infantry and had served during the Crimean War at the siege and fall of Sebastopol and in India where his regiment was active in quelling the Indian Mutiny. He left his regiment in 1861 and, by 1872, had taken up a position as a general land and business agent for the 3rd Duke of Sutherland.

The duke was twenty years older than Mrs Blair. When they met, his hair had already turned white and he had taken on the appearance of a down-at-heel department store Santa Claus. It's probably fair to say that her attraction to him was largely based on his ownership of 1.3 million acres of land and eleven homes. By 1883 their relationship had deepened to the point where the duke and Mrs Blair were openly flaunting Victorian convention and being seen together often and in public.

In October that year Mrs Blair's cuckolded husband, Arthur, was staying with her at Bohespic Lodge near Pitlochry where the couple and their daughter were apparently spending a rare family holiday together. One afternoon he went grouse-shooting alone. Sometime around 5.50 p.m. as he was returning he slipped and his gun went off, shooting him directly through his heart and left lung. He was barely a hundred yards from a nearby farmhouse and half a mile from his home. According to the police report, the gunfire alerted Mrs Blair, who rushed to the scene and found her husband dead with the gun beside his body. A local doctor travelled five miles to pronounce Arthur Blair dead. There were no witnesses. A second doctor, who carried out the post-mortem, concluded his report with two words: 'Supposed accident'.

The local police concurred and there was no further investigation. Mrs Blair was allowed to forgo questioning because she was too distraught to be interviewed, although the grieving widow was sufficiently recovered to immediately accompany her ducal lover on a long yachting trip to the Far East. The local newspaper took no interest in the event at all, apart from a brief paragraph obliquely noting that there had been 'an accident of a melancholy nature'.

The local rumour mill, however, went into overdrive. Arthur Blair was well known and liked in the area and there were many questions unanswered. How did a soldier with extensive experience of handling firearms manage to shoot himself by accident? Why was his long-estranged wife so conveniently close at hand to discover his body? How did she locate the body so quickly with only the sound of echoing gunfire to guide her? And how exactly was she able to arrive on the scene ahead of the tenants of the farm who were much better placed to get there first?

It was widely speculated that Mrs Blair had asked her husband for a divorce, and when he refused, she shot him in anger. Others suspected it was the duke himself who shot him. Another theory had it that Blair had taken his own life, driven to despair by his wife's infidelity with his employer. The duke, it was speculated, covered up the suicide to prevent the scandal that would inevitably ensue.

According to the official version Blair was alone on the moor, but the idea that the duke had something to do with it gained so much currency that subsequent various press reports were openly placing him at the scene. The *Glasgow Herald* reported that Blair was 'accidentally shot by the Duke' and the *Evening Times* asserted: 'Mr. Blair was killed by the Duke accidentally while they were out hunting.'

If the shooting was an accident, it was a very convenient one indeed for the duke and his mistress, and someone or other went to great lengths to make sure that the circumstances went unexamined. Arthur Blair was buried almost five hundred miles from where he fell, in London's Paddington cemetery. The affair between his wife and the Duke of Sutherland meanwhile continued as though he had never existed.

At the time of the shooting the duke was already estranged from his wife, who was now living in miserable solitude at one of their many homes, a white-walled villa in Torquay which she had renamed Sutherland Lodge, or occupying two rooms in Stafford House, lying around on a sofa under a red silk eiderdown, surrounded by dozens of parrots and mynah birds. Her friend Lady Paget described her circumstances as 'wretched'. Despite everything, however, it seems that the duchess had still not completely given up on the possibility of reconciliation with her husband. Her hopes would soon be dashed in the most humiliating manner possible.

In 1887 the duke was planning yet another trip abroad when he was struck down with a respiratory illness and confined to his bed at Trentham Hall. His doctors thought that he would die soon and sent for his family. The duchess arrived with her children in tow only to find that Mrs Blair was already at his bedside. There followed an almighty scene during which the wife and the mistress screamed at each other across the duke's bed, each demanding that the other should leave. The duke decided to back his mistress and so the duchess retreated. From that day on the children would never forget or forgive their father for choosing the greedy, scheming Mrs Blair over their mother.

In November 1888 the duke set off on another luxury voyage on his yacht with his girlfriend in tow. The duchess found the yacht's passenger list with the name of her husband's mistress on it. The pain of this discovery was too much to bear. She took to her bed and just under two weeks later died from a sudden and unexplained illness. It was rumoured that she had taken poison.

The duke was in America when he heard about his wife's death. When asked for instructions as to what should be done with her body he replied sharply, 'Bury it.' He issued a short statement later, explaining that he wouldn't be returning home for his wife's funeral. All that mattered to him was that he was now free to marry his mistress.

According to Victorian convention widows and widowers should not remarry until at least twelve months after a spouse's death. The duke waited just three months before marrying Mrs Blair in Florida, where the couple had built themselves a forty-acre ranch. Neither of the duke's two sons or his daughter attended the ceremony, appalled by their father's callous treatment of their mother and full of hatred for his new wife. This hatred deepened when the newly-weds returned from honeymoon and, within a couple of hours of her arrival at Stafford House, their stepmother took charge of her predecessor's wardrobe and began wearing her clothes and underwear.

The Jailbird Duchess

In 1888 a newspaper article listed the richest men in the world. The 3rd Duke of Sutherland was ranked tenth, with a fortune estimated at six million pounds and an annual income of three hundred thousand pounds. In today's terms he was worth £2.5 billion with annual earnings of £126 million in an age when, by today's standards, the rate of income tax was also incredibly low. With a fortune this big at stake it was almost inevitable that a squabble over inheritance would occur sooner or later, and when it came it was the nastiest estate dispute of the century.

The former Mrs Blair was now immersed in a world of luxury and excess beyond the reach of the average duchess, let alone the average woman in Victorian Britain. Yet any dreams that she may have entertained of becoming a grand society hostess, as previous Duchesses of Sutherland had been, were soon forgotten. Her husband had given deep offence by failing to attend the funeral of his former wife, the queen's personal friend, and had remarried far too quickly. The duke and his new duchess were shunned by polite society.

The dispute between the duke and his children meanwhile continued to fester. In 1891, the duke's twenty-five-year-old daughter Lady Alexandra died. It was an opportunity for the family to come together but the duke and his son squabbled over who should pay her medical bills. The friction between the two warring parties came to a head in 1892 when the duke printed a written account, privately published, detailing all of the spats and petty arguments that had occurred between himself and his eldest son, titled 'Record of Events about Quarrel between Themselves and Lord Stafford'. It was a bizarre and tactless piece of self-justification with the duchess's hand in every page. There was no doubt that this was her attempt to pit the duke against his own children by exacerbating an already incendiary situation.

In September 1892, the third duke died suddenly at Trentham of a perforated ulcer in the stomach, aged sixty-four, leaving behind a sizeable mess to go with his immense riches. After his second marriage to his long-term mistress in 1888, the duke had changed his will ten times. Even as he lay dying, a telegram went out summoning his solicitor to make one more amendment, giving the duchess, on his death, an immediate payment of fifty thousand pounds in cash.

When the will was published it caused a sensation. The old duke had left everything to his widow. For his children, apart from the odd family heirloom, there was nothing at all. Lord Stafford, now the 4th Duke of Sutherland in name only, was left completely beholden to and dependent upon a stepmother he despised.

In March 1893 the fourth duke challenged his father's will. The court ordered the immediate seizure of all documents at Stafford House so that they could be examined to see if the late duke's true intentions were being correctly interpreted. At first the dowager duchess flatly refused to comply, insisting that the documents were of a 'personal and highly confidential nature'. Reluctantly she gave way and the papers were removed to a solicitors' office in Whitehall, neutral ground where all parties could inspect them at length.

The two sides and their respective legal teams faced each other across a wide oak table, scrutinising each document as it was produced. At one point the duchess accused the fourth duke of tampering with the paperwork. Then, to all-round astonishment, she picked up a bundle of documents, read one of them, then calmly walked over to the fireplace and tossed it into the open fire. When the duke's counsel remonstrated with her, she replied: 'That document was a letter to my husband before I was married. I shall do as I like.'

Six days later, the duchess was tried for contempt. She

asserted that the destroyed document contained nothing of importance relating to the will; it was only a letter from the late duke relating to an 'unpleasant incident' between a steward on his yacht and a maid. The judge sentenced her to six weeks in prison plus a fine of £250. After sentencing, she walked out of court and jumped into a cab. All of the newspaper reporters hanging around outside assumed it was taking her directly to Holloway prison. It was only later that everyone realised that she had simply gone home.

The next day her doctor made excuses on her behalf; she was suffering from 'severe nervous depression and the shock resulting from the mental strain which she had endured'. He produced a medical certificate confirming that she was unfit for prison. The duchess's contempt for the legal system, however, had not gone completely unnoticed and moves were already in hand to arrest her. After some discussion it was decided that she could stay at home for now and present herself at Holloway at 6 p.m. the following day. The press was unsympathetic. The *Daily Mail* reported that she had done a 'contemptuous as well as contemptible thing'. The *Daily Chronicle* noted that she 'deserved to be horsewhipped'.

The next day, two hours and forty minutes late, Duchess Blair, as the press now called her, arrived at the prison gates and was taken to her 'cell', possibly the most comfortable ever afforded to a Holloway inmate. It was 25 feet long by 15 feet wide and, according to one newspaper report, 'bore as much resemblance to an ordinary prison cell as a cotter's kitchen does to a ducal drawing-room'. Fitted out by the furniture dealers Maples, it was attended daily by a maid, who served the duchess food delivered by

Harrods, which she ate off her own plates. She was allowed to receive friends and read newspapers and books. She was also exempted from the routine menial work expected of all prisoners – oakum-picking and the tread-wheel. The most difficult part of her imprisonment was the daily 6 a.m. alarm call. Barely two weeks had passed before her doctors were petitioning for her release on health grounds, pointing out that since arriving at Holloway she had lost weight. The Home Secretary Herbert Asquith dismissed the appeal and she was made to complete the rest of her six weeks of luxury confinement. As soon as the dowager duchess's embarrassing spell in prison was out of the way, the bitter row over the will resumed.

The Sutherland Will Case was widely expected be the most sensational and protracted legal wrangle of the century; in the event, however, there would be no titillating courtroom revelations. In 1894, in an out-of-court settlement, the new duke received back the estates in return for paying the dowager duchess a cash sum – as much as £750,000 (today worth around fifty million pounds) – plus an annuity of four thousand pounds. The duchess insisted on being paid in cash, so the Bank of England issued special one-thousand-pound banknotes at her behest.

The deal came as a huge disappointment to newspaper editors eagerly anticipating much mud-slinging on both sides. *The Spectator* noted, 'Society has been defrauded this week of a sensation.' Given the animosity between the dowager duchess and her late husband's children, there was a great deal of speculation as to how and why the deal came about. Perhaps both sides came to their senses, realising that a bitter fight to the death in the courts was in nobody's interests but the lawyers'. Or was there a skeleton in the Sutherland family cupboard that both sides wanted to be kept hidden?

The dowager duchess didn't leave the stage quietly. In 1896, aged forty-eight, she married Sir Albert Rollitt, a successful lawyer and steamship company owner. In his will, the third duke had left the Sutherland jewels for her 'use and enjoyment during her life'. After the settlement she was forced to return most of them, but was able to hang on to a string of pearls, rated by the *Illustrated London News* as 'one of the greatest jewels of the world'. She also amassed a large gem collection of her own, which she liked to show off in public, resisting her husband's advice to wear replicas as a precaution against theft.

In 1898 at the Gard du Nord railway station as the couple were about to return from a holiday in Paris, a thief snatched her jewel case containing more than forty pieces worth around twenty-five thousand pounds – nearly two million pounds in today's terms. It was quite easily the biggest jewel heist of the age. The culprit, a professional thief called Henry Thomas Sands,* also known as 'Harry the Valet', was apprehended six weeks later after a frantic manhunt across Paris and London, but only a small number of the gems were recovered. His trial, attended by the duchess herself, was eagerly followed by the world's press. The *New York Times* reported that Sands was 'one of the cleverest jewel thieves in Europe', but in truth he was no real-life Raffles. The arrest came about not because of fine detective work by Scotland Yard, as they claimed, but after Sands made the fundamentally stupid mistake of boasting

---

* This was the name on his birth certificate, but at the time of his arrest he was going by the name of William Johnson.

about his crime to try to impress a woman he was infatuated with. Then he embarked on an epic spending spree that was impossible for even the average London bobby to ignore. One evening he offered to pay for his whisky in a Shoreditch pub with five hundred pounds in gold.

In 1906 the dowager duchess chose to spend some of the windfall from her will settlement by building Carbisdale Castle in Scotland, stocking it with the finest works of art she could muster. Forbidden to build anywhere on the Sutherland estate, she positioned it just outside their lands on a prominent hillside. The castle was designed around a tower with clocks on three sides only: the missing face, strategically pointing towards Sutherland lands, was said to show that she didn't wish to give the duke the time of day. It was known locally as Castle Spite.

Meanwhile, the once mighty Sutherlands had to do what the rest of the British aristocracy did in the early twentieth century. Caught in a grim three-pronged pincer movement of low land prices, agricultural decline and massive death duties, they drew in their horns. The torpedo that really hit them below the waterline was the will settlement. It had taken generations of advantageous marriages to make the Sutherland fortune but it took just one marriage to bring the family to their knees. A large chunk of their capital had been lost in the painful court battle, a huge blow to their finances from which they never recovered.

The fourth duke had to cash in his ancestral chips to survive. Between 1899 and 1901 he sold 120,000 acres of land. Next to go were two of the family houses. Trentham Hall, with no one willing to take it on, was bulldozed and the contents sold at auction for five hundred pounds. Stafford House, the great London palace of the Sutherlands, was sold for sixty thousand pounds. Some of the proceeds were used to buy land in Canada, where the duke was planning on building a new permanent home while offering the rest of the land to tenants from the Sutherland estates on favourable terms. There were few applicants to take advantage of his largesse. The capital required was far more than most working-class people could afford, nor was the irony lost on those with longer memories. The aristocrat whose great-grandfather had burned the poor Highlanders cottages about their ears and evicted them without remorse, was now offering a 'settlement' in a far-off country to people whose forefathers had escaped the Sutherland Clearances; it was adding insult to injury. The fourth duke's Canadian adventure was cut short when he died at Dunrobin Castle, aged sixty-one.

His son oversaw the biggest break-up of the once mighty Sutherland estate. Pressed by existing debts of nearly two hundred thousand pounds and with fresh death duties to pay, the fifth duke embarked on more massive land sales. It was only because his forefathers had chosen to spend some of their money wisely on amassing one of the greatest art collections of England that the family's fortune wasn't completely obliterated.*

* Relatively speaking, the Sutherland fortune is still impressive. At the time of writing, Francis Egerton, 7th Duke of Sutherland is worth an estimated £580 million according to *The Times* Rich List 2016, thanks largely to accumulation of artworks including Raphaels, Titians, Tintorettos and Poussins.

12

Eglinton's Folly

The saying 'more money than sense' may have found its apotheosis in Archibald Montgomerie, 13th Earl of Eglinton.

In the early nineteenth century, continental Europe and parts of the USA got carried away with a strange new craze for medievalism and all things Gothic. In Britain, interest in the Middle Ages became something of a national obsession. The standard-bearer for the movement was the author Sir Walter Scott, writer of popular romances such as *Ivanhoe*. To Scott and other like-minded Romantics, the medieval past was not only a source of picturesque tales,

377

but also stood as a model of gentlemanly behaviour – the 'golden age of chivalry'.

Of course Scott's idea of chivalry was very far from the real thing. In its original form, chivalry was a code of conduct designed to protect aristocratic families from the people beneath them. It was an expression of aristocratic solidarity – class war, if you will. This is how the thirteenth-century Spanish knight Ramon Lull described the chivalric code in his book *The Book of Knighthood and Chivalry*.

> After protecting God and the King a knight's next duties are to go hunting, give lavish feasts and fight in tournaments. After that he must ensure that he terrorises the peasantry . . . for because of the dread that the common people have of the knights, they labour and cultivate the earth, for fear lest they be destroyed.

Not much gallantry or romance in that.*

Nevertheless, Scott's fake version of 'Merrie England' was hugely popular and in the 1800s everyone was mad for a bit of fake Arthurian chivalry, which was fantastic news for the author because the Victorian literary marketplace was saturated with his writings right up until the 1890s.

There was also a Gothic revival in architecture, which received an official seal of approval with the choice of Charles Barry's Gothic plan for the new Houses of Parliament. Meanwhile, the aristocracy followed suit and lavished vast amounts of their wealth on rebuilding and

---

* Nor was Scott's history particularly strong on the First Crusade, when knights chivalrously ate babies and massacred the entire population of Jerusalem.

altering their houses in the new Gothic style, with turrets and moats, and stuffed their halls with genuine and fake medieval arms and armour, the fashionable collectibles of the day.

One nobleman went a lot further. Among the new imitation Gothic piles was Eglinton Castle in Ayrshire, home of the Scottish Earls of Eglinton. The family title was created for Lord Hugh Montgomerie by James IV as a reward for fighting on his side at the Battle of Sauchieburn in 1488. The Eglintons had their share of eccentrics. Lady Susanna Eglinton, third wife of the ninth earl, was considered to be the most famous aristocratic beauty of the eighteenth century. Her looks caused quite a stir. It was said that when she first rode out in Edinburgh she took the city by storm; rich suitors offered her their titles and fortunes, amateur poets vied with one another in composing amorous sonnets in praise of her eyebrows, and young bloods fought each other before breakfast or shot themselves at twilight, victims of the jealousy or despair she apparently inspired. The bewitching countess rode proudly by, heedless of the havoc she was causing.

Widowed at the age of forty, she lived for another fifty-one years and retained her good looks into her eighties, which she attributed to washing her face daily in sow's milk. In her later years she preferred the company of rodents to that of men. She took all her meals accompanied by rats, which she summoned at mealtimes by tapping on the oak panelling. Her son, the 10th Earl of Eglinton, was shot dead during a scuffle with a customs and excise officer: his murderer hanged himself, thereby cheating the hangman of his day's wages. His brother and successor, Archibald, the eleventh earl, died childless, so the title, and the family seat Eglinton Castle, passed to a kinsman, Hugh Montgomerie.

The castle was originally an eighteenth-century Georgian mansion but the twelfth earl had it knocked down and replaced with a massive Neo-Gothic fantasy castle, in the popular style of the day, complete with castellations, turrets and a moat. Today it stands in ruins, but in 1839 it was one of the most spectacular stately homes in Scotland, according to a contemporary description, 'uniting in a great degree the notions of feudal grandeur with the more elegant refinements of good taste'. The twelfth earl's fascination for all things feudal was inherited by his son, with disastrous consequences for the family finances.

In June 1838 the new young Queen Victoria was due to be crowned in Westminster Abbey, having acceded to the throne just over a year earlier when her uncle William IV died of pneumonia. The British public, swept along by *Ivanhoe*-mania, were looking forward to the coronation ceremony in the abbey, which was to be followed by a magnificent state, medieval-style banquet in Westminster Hall.

During the festivities there were several antiquated feudal customs to observe. For example, the Archbishop of Canterbury was to present the queen with a mess of dilligrout, a watery porridge containing plums (a big favourite of William the Conqueror, apparently); meanwhile the Duke of Athol was to gift the queen a pair of falcons.* Fortunately not all of the ancient coronation

---

* The 12th Duke of St Albans was considerably put out at the queen's 1953 coronation when, as Hereditary Grand Falconer, he was refused his permission to exercise his hereditary right to

customs were still observed: at her coronation in 1559 Queen Elizabeth I had a cat burned in a wicker basket to symbolise the releasing of demons.

Another old ritual that was still maintained, however, was at the centrepiece of Victoria's coronation. An actual knight in shining armour, the Queen's Champion, would ride into Westminster Hall on his horse, fling his gauntlet to the ground and challenge everyone present to deny his sovereign's right to the throne. Assuming no one among the assembled guests took him up on his offer, the Champion then had to back his horse away from the royal table, reversing all the way down the hall to the entrance – not an easy thing to do, especially in full armour.

It didn't always go to plan. In 1685, at the coronation of James II, the gauntlet had been flung with so much enthusiasm that the Champion had followed it to the floor and lay there on his back in heavy armour like a stranded beetle, causing the king to laugh out loud. Four years later, at the coronation of William and Mary, when the Champion threw down the glove, an unidentified old woman picked it up and ran off with it. At the coronation banquet for George IV, the horse ridden by the king's Champion was hired from a circus and when greeted with applause, it went into its full routine of tricks.*

---

attend with a live falcon on his arm. Palace officials suggested he turn up with a stuffed bird instead, but the duke was having none of it and boycotted the ceremony.

* Coronation feasts were often riotous, disorganised affairs. After King George I's coronation, London newspapers carried an advertisement pleading for the return of stolen royal silverware including 'dishes, trencher plates, knives, forks, spoons and salts'.

Sadly, no one at Victoria's coronation got to pass judgement on the Champion's gauntlet flinging or horse-reversing skills. In 1838, the country was in the grip of a recession. Poor harvests resulted in heavy grain imports, pushing up the price of food. The British economy was a shambles, poverty was rampant and many workers were starving. The Whig government, remembering the public outrage caused by the huge expense of the previous coronation banquet of 1821, decided that perhaps it wasn't a good time to be laying on such an ostentatious display of self-indulgence after all.

The prime minister, Lord Melbourne, announced that, for economic reasons, anachronistic medieval ceremonies were now cancelled. There would be a coronation banquet, but at the relatively modest cost of seventy thousand pounds, not the £240,000 expended by George IV. And there would definitely be no Queen's Champion.

Although there was some popular support for the decision, the ruling classes were incensed. There were angry exchanges in the House of Lords and a Tory petition demanding that the full traditional ceremony with all its medieval frippery be reinstated. Lord Melbourne, however, stood his ground and Victoria was crowned minus some of the usual trappings. The British aristocracy were livid; they called it the queen's 'Penny Coronation'.

One person who felt especially cheated was the twenty-seven-year-old Archibald Montgomerie, 13th Earl of Eglinton. He was a famous patron of the turf (his jockeys rode in tartan) and of the champagne industry – by some accounts he drank nothing else. It was his proud boast that his capacity for bubbly was second to none. He was bragging about this at the Jockey's Club in Newmarket one day when Colonel Peel, brother of Sir Robert, offered to put him to the test and introduced him to his brother-in-law Sir David Baird, who proceeded to drink Eglinton under the table in a magnum-for-magnum contest. It continued until the earl, deathly pale, conceded defeat and staggered off to bed; Baird meanwhile celebrated his win by opening another bottle then calmly played a game of billiards.

Between backing horses and drinking champagne Eglinton also found time to serve as Lord Lieutenant of Ireland, twice. He is only remembered at all, however, for the most extravagant Gothic folly of the age.

Eglinton was born at the height of the Gothic Romantic movement and steeped in the lore of chivalry and jousting. In fact, the Eglinton family had some form when it came to jousting. Their kinsman Gabriel, Comte de Montgomery, had earned considerable notoriety after accidentally killing the King of France during a freak jousting accident in 1559. A shattered lance somehow found a chink in the king's visor and managed to pierce the royal head just beside the eye.

Like many of his class Eglinton was appalled by the penny-pinching Whigs' decision to redact the queen's coronation, stripping it of its medieval splendour. He was particularly irked because his own stepfather, as Knight Marshal of the Royal Household, was to have had the job of leading the Champion's horse up Westminster Hall.

One of Eglinton's friends suggested, probably as a joke, that he should stick it to the government by laying on his own medieval joust. A rumour quickly spread that Lord Eglinton was going to hold a tournament at his country estate in Scotland. When someone asked him if the rumour was true, Eglinton had a rush of blood to the head; he replied, 'Yes,' he was going to lay on a full-scale medieval joust, with knights, armour, lances – the lot. He would teach those skinflint plebs the Whigs that the age of chivalry was far from dead.

Some of Eglinton's more sober friends pointed out to him that an actual medieval tournament would be a rather difficult and expensive project to pull off. The combatants would have to be kitted out with full suits of armour, lances, costumes and the like; the cost of equipping even one knight would be astronomical. But Eglinton was coal-rich, spoilt and impulsive and used to getting his own way. All doubts about the wisdom and practicalities of staging the event were simply waved aside.

KNIGHT FEVER

The date for Eglinton's Gothic extravaganza was set for Wednesday 28 August 1839. It was to be held at his Scottish estate and would feature a magnificent chivalric entertainment, complete with chain-mailed jousters on caparisoned horses, a court of noblewomen attending the Queen of Beauty (Georgiana Seymour, Duchess of Somerset) plus all the pageantry and combat you could ask for in a proper medieval entertainment. Eglinton invited 2,690 VIP guests, including the future Napoleon III of France and the playwright Richard Sheridan, and catered for an additional 1,500 members of the public. Invited guests would also be treated to a medieval banquet, dining on roast peacocks, boars' heads, barons of beef and bowls of dilligrout, following by dancing late into the evening to the sound of lutes and harpsichords. Eglinton also appealed to the public to arrive in suitable period fancy dress, to which many enthusiastically complied. Whigs and other radicals were not welcome.

In the event an estimated one hundred thousand made the trek to Eglinton's corner of Scotland to see what all the fuss was about. Transporting the spectators to the venue required the use of two special trains and every cart and carriage within a twenty-mile radius, providing the biggest traffic jam yet seen in Scotland. The thirty-mile road from Ayr to Glasgow was so clogged with carriages that many of the attendees abandoned their transport and continued on foot.

Initially, 150 prospective knights had expressed an interest in taking part in the tournament, but most backed out when they realised the cost and the difficulties of laying their hands on an actual, fully functioning suit of armour. Samuel Pratt, a dealer in medieval armour at No. 47 Bond Street, London, supplied the bulk of the kit, but it is unclear how many of the suits were genuine. Some of the armour used was loaned from the Tower of London, but no one anticipated that changes in diet and health since the late Middle Ages had increased average stature, and most of the suits were too small.

The figure was whittled down to around forty knights, who turned up for a full dress rehearsal and pledged to give it a go. On the day, however, only fourteen knights, including Eglinton, turned up to take part. Among them was the Earl of Craven, who brought his own priceless suit of Milanese armour inlaid with gold and worn by his ancestor at the Battle of Crécy.

Eglinton's decision to use only lightweight lances after being threatened with prosecution if anyone was killed in the tournament was perhaps an early sign that not everything would turn out as planned. The event was supposed to open at noon with a great parade of knights and their entourages, but there were no marshals to control it and it ended up in a knightly gridlock. By the time the parade was ready it was more than three hours late.

The day began fine and sunny, but Eglinton had not accounted for the fact that the tournament's location was near coastal mountainous terrain and prone to frequent, torrential rainfall. Just as the parade got under way, the skies opened and it started to pour.

Eglinton had chosen to stage the tournament on a low-lying meadow next to a river. The jousting area, which was only just above the river level during the summer, quickly flooded. As *The Times* reported, 'The lists in the park of Eglinton Castle at this time exhibit the appearance of a pond.' Nevertheless, the tournament went ahead.

The sight of nineteenth-century gentlemen trying to overcome the difficulties of moving around in several inches of mud while wearing ill-fitting, full-scale body armour was not as thrilling as Eglinton had hoped. As it turned out, no amount of reading *Ivanhoe* can compensate for actual jousting experience, of which the participants had none, and the knights' efforts only produced roars of laughter as the horses skidded and squelched through the mud. Many of the lightweight lances, weakened by rain, simply fell apart.

The highlight of the spectacle pitted the 'Scotch and Irish Knights', including Eglinton and the Marquess of Waterford, against the 'English Knights', including Viscount Alford, who appeared in the guise of the Knight of the Black Lion. Whether because of some personal animosity or from frustration with the weather, it was widely reported that the battle between Alford and the madcap Waterford was genuinely violent; they 'struck each other oftener than the rules permitted' and had to be pulled apart.

Very few spectators could tell who any of the knights were, unless they had some practical knowledge of heraldry and could read the quarterings on their shields, and only then with the aid of a telescope, although one source managed to identify the Marquess of Londonderry, who 'was completely drenched', giving him 'a most grotesque appearance'. Thanks to the large number of raised umbrellas, many in the crowd were unable to see anything at all.

Meanwhile, the makeshift roof that was supposed to shelter the galleries gave way and everyone got soaked. There was also an unfunny jester, who cracked some feeble jokes then went off in a huff. The soggy revels were finally abandoned when the mud-splattered, miserable belle of the ball, the Queen of Beauty, scampered off to find somewhere dry to sit. Embarrassingly, Eglinton also had to inform his VIP guests that the pavilion in which the great banquet was to be held hadn't withstood the rain either. His blue-blooded cast and audience, their medieval hairdos sodden and lank, retreated into a marquee that leaked water at every crevice.

Waterlogged and chilled to the bone, the spectators began to drift away, which for most was easier said than done. The rain had flooded the Lugton Water, which ran around three sides of the jousting field, and none of the carriages was able to cross it. Stranded and without transportation, thousands of disappointed spectators were forced into chaotic retreat, slogging homeward on foot through morasses of mud.

On the plus side no one was actually killed, nor indeed

did anyone get hurt, apart from a minor injury to the wrist sustained by one of the knights, the Hon. Mr Jeringham.

The press had a field day of its own. In that year of severe depression it was just what the nation needed – a spot of comic relief in the form of the aristocracy expensively making fools of themselves. Critical opinion was unanimously harsh. The tournament was variously described in the press as a specimen of 'medieval mania', 'a fiasco', 'the greatest failure of the century' and, possibly a little too harshly, 'the most magnificent abortion that has been witnessed for two centuries'. Eglinton, the Victorian 'wally with the brolly', was ridiculed mercilessly up and down the country as 'the knight under the umbrella'. The young Queen Victoria noted in her diary, drily, 'It had turned out to be the greatest absurdity.' For Eglinton it had been a personal disaster costing him a painful forty thousand pounds, burdening his family with debt from which it never recovered.*

Later, Eglinton developed in interest in golf, which in 1861 took him to a tournament in St Andrews, where he suffered a fatal stroke. A couple of years before he died, he wrote up his life story. Of the unhappy events of 1939, he simply wrote with disingenuous understatement: 'I gave a tournament at Eglinton.'

They really don't make people like the 13th Earl of Eglinton any more, which, despite the way they have entertained us with their adventures over the years, is probably just as well.

---

* In 1925 the contents of Eglinton Castle were sold at auction and the roof was removed. What remained was used by the army as target practice.

388

Select Bibliography

DIRTY, ROTTEN RICH SCOUNDRELS

Ashe, Geoffrey (2005), *Hell-Fire Clubs: Sex, Rakes and Libertines in Eighteenth-century Europe.*

Gray, Francine (1999), *At Home with the Marquis de Sade: A Life.*

Hopkins, Graham (2002), *Constant Delights: Rakes, Rogues and Scandal in Restoration England.*

Linnane, Fergus (2010), *The Lives of the English Rakes.*

Scriven, Marcus (2010), *Splendour and Squalor: The Disgrace and Disintegration of Three Aristocratic Dynasties.*

Sharpe, James (2014), *Crime in Early Modern England 1550–1750.*

Tolstoy, Nikolai (1978), *The Half-mad Lord: Thomas Pitt, 2nd Baron Camelford, 1775–1804.*

PLAYING DEEP

Atherton, Mike (2007), *Gambling: A Story of Triumph and Disaster*.

Cannadine, David (2005), *The Decline and Fall of the British Aristocracy*.

White, T. H. (1993), *The Age of Scandal*.

Ziegler, Philip and Seward, Desmond (1991), *Brooks's: A Social History*.

LORDS OF THE BIZARRE

Donaldson, William (2002), *Brewer's Rogues, Villains and Eccentrics*.

Freeman-Keel, Tom (2003), *The Disappearing Duke: The Improbable Tale of an Eccentric English Family*.

Girouard, Mark (1978), *Life in the English Country House: A Social and Architectural History*.

John, Duke of Bedford (1960), *A Silver-plated Spoon*.

Sitwell, Edith (1971), *English Eccentrics*.

PRIDE AND PREJUDICE

James, Lawrence (2009), *Aristocrats: Power, Grace, and Decadence – Britain's Ruling Classes from 1066 to the Present*.

Lieven, Dominic (1992), *The Aristocracy in Europe, 1815–1914*.

Master, Brian (1975), *The Dukes: The Origins, Ennoblement and History of 26 Families*.

Smith, Virginia (2007), *Clean: A History of Personal Hygiene and Purity*.

THERE'S NOWT SO HARD AS TOFFS

Baldick, Robert (1970), *The Duel: A History of Duelling*.

Hopton, Richard (2007), *Pistols at Dawn: A History of Duelling*.

Kiernan, V. G. (1988), *The Duel in European History: Honour and the Reign of Aristocracy.*

Norris, John (2009), *Pistols at Dawn: A History of Duelling.*

SEX AND SNOBBERY

Douglas-Home, Jamie (2006), *Stately Passions: The Scandals of Britain's Great Houses.*

Foulkes, Nick (2004), *Scandalous Society: Passion and Celebrity in the Nineteenth Century.*

Murray, Venetia (1998), *High Society: Social History of the Regency Period, 1788–1830.*

Murray, Venetia (2000), *Elegant Madness: A Social History.*

Rubenhold, Hallie (2015), *The Scandalous Lady W.*

Wallace, Carol (1989), *To Marry An English Lord.*

Worsley, Lucy (2011), *Courtiers: The Secret History of the Georgian Court.*

SPORTING GRANDEES

Foulkes, Nicholas (2010), *Gentlemen and Blackguards: Gambling Mania and the Plot to Steal the Derby of 1844.*

Mason, Tony (1989), *Sport in Britain: A Social History.*

Norridge, Julian (2008), *Can We Have Our Balls Back, Please? How the British Invented Sport.*

Stratmann, Linda (2014), *The Marquess of Queensberry: Wilde's Nemesis.*

Sutherland, Douglas (2015), *The Yellow Earl: Almost an Emperor, Not Quite a Gentleman.*

OUT FOR BLOOD

Beaufort, Duke of (1981), *Duke of Beaufort: Memoirs.*

Blackwood, Caroline (1987), *In the Pink.*

Griffin, Emma (2008), *Blood Sport: Hunting in Britain Since 1066.*

Pagnamenta, Peter (2012), *Prairie Fever: How British Aristocrats Staked a Claim to the American West.*

OFFICERS AND GENTLEMEN

Corvi, Steven and Becket, Ian (2009), *Victoria's Generals.*
David, Saul (1997), *The Homicidal Earl: The Life of Lord Cardigan.*
Regan, Geoffrey (2012), *Great Military Blunders.*

THE GENTLEMEN AMATEURS

Bryson, Bill (2010), *Seeing Further: The Story of Science and the Royal Society.*
Gribbin, John (2003), *Science: A History 1543–2001.*
Gribbin, John and Mary (2003), *FitzRoy: The Remarkable Story of Darwin's Captain and the Invention of the Weather Forecast.*

ABOMINABLY RICH

Hamilton, Duncan (2011), *The Unreliable Life of Harry the Valet: The Great Victorian Jewel Thief.*
Lees-Milne, James (1991), *The Bachelor Duke: A Life of William Spencer Cavendish, 6th Duke of Devonshire, 1790–1858.*
Prebble, John (1967), *The Highland Clearances.*
Richards, Eric (1973), *Leviathan of Wealth: Sutherland Fortune in the Industrial Revolution.*
Sutherland, Duke of (1957), *Looking Back.*
Tindley, Annie (2010), *The Sutherland Estate 1850–1920.*

EGLINTON'S FOLLY

Anstruther, Ian (1986), *The Knight and the Umbrella.*

Index

Use of 'fn' after a page reference indicates a footnote

Index